Latinx Writing Los Angeles

LATINX WRITING LOS ANGELES

Nonfiction Dispatches
from a Decolonial Rebellion

Edited by Ignacio López-Calvo and Victor Valle

University of Nebraska Press | Lincoln & London

Acknowledgments for the use of copyrighted
material appear on pages 215–17, which
constitute an extension of the copyright page.

Publication of this volume was assisted by the
Virginia Faulkner Fund, established in memory
of Virginia Faulkner, editor in chief of the
University of Nebraska Press.

Library of Congress Cataloging-in-Publication Data
Names: López-Calvo, Ignacio, editor. |
Valle, Victor M., editor.
Title: Latinx writing Los Angeles: nonfiction
dispatches from a decolonial rebellion / edited
by Ignacio López-Calvo and Victor Valle.
Description: Lincoln: University of Nebraska
Press, 2018. | Includes bibliographical references.
Identifiers: LCCN 2017026966
ISBN 9781496202413 (cloth: alk. paper)
ISBN 9781496214577 (paper: alk. paper)
ISBN 9781496206152 (epub)
ISBN 9781496206169 (mobi)
ISBN 9781496206176 (pdf)
Subjects: LCSH: American literature—Hispanic
American authors. | American literature—California—
Los Angeles. | Hispanic Americans—Literary collections.
| Hispanic Americans—Intellectual life.
Classification: LCC PS508.H57 L45 2018 |
DDC 810.8/0868—dc23 LC record available
at https://lccn.loc.gov/2017026966

Set in Whitman by Mikala R. Kolander.
Designed by L. Auten.

To Lucía and Elena Rodrigo López; to Mary, for finding Anaïs in Mexico, and to Ali, for helping us to read the book of a city

Contents

Acknowledgments

We would like to thank Martín Camps, Rafael Chabrán, Stephanie Fetta, Antonio Morillo, Alicia Ramos-Jordán, Robert Rudder, Marco Valesi, and Francisco Vásquez for their valuable support and critical contributions, as well as Toby Miller for his critical genealogy of the U.S. English major in *Blow Up the Humanities* and Rita González for curating the *Phantom Sightings: Art after the Chicano Movement* exhibit that introduced us to Julio Cesar Morales. We also want to thank the Huntington Library; the pair of translation grants we received from the University of California, Merced's Center for the Humanities; the invaluable opportunity Harvard University's Radcliffe Institute for Advanced Study gave Victor to begin researching and writing this project; and the Fulbright Foundation Fellowship program for the time it gave him to scour Mexico City's bookstores and libraries.

LA's Latina/o Phantom Nonfiction and the Technologies of Literary Secrecy

VICTOR VALLE

What a comparativism based on equivalence attempts to undermine is the possessiveness, the exclusiveness, the isolationist expansionism of mere nationalism.

—GAYATRI CHAKRAVORTY SPIVAK

I am still haunted by a scene in the film *Chinatown*, the one in which private eye J. J. Gittes returns to find the Mexican peasant boy he had spied on in a previous scene speaking to city water engineer Hollis Mulwray in the middle of the Big Tujunga Wash. Gittes, who has followed Mulwray to the boy because he is tailing the engineer, needs to know what the boy told him. The ensuing dialogue between detective and boy reveals clues that will undermine his theory of Mulwray's alleged crime. He is not an adulterer; the real mystery is about water—when and why the Department of Water and Power secretly releases it from its reservoir when the city is supposed to be in the middle of a drought.

Well, that at least is the question the film wants us to ask. But there is something about the pair of riverbed scenes that remind me of the narratives that usually frame the representation of LA's peripheral spaces. That elusive quality suggests itself in the way the camera in that first scene frames the surrounding landscape in which Gittes tracks Mulwray's arrival in the Big Tujunga Wash and which encourages me to take in so much more than the detective's gaze. Although the camera asks us to stand with Gittes on the bridge and look down through his field glasses to Mulwray's car as it rumbles to a stop in the rocky wash, my eyes scan the familiar background: the dry river bottom carved into the alluvial field and San Gabriel Mountain silhouettes that ring the horizon's limits in shades of coppery haze. Like other native Angelenos, my memories of these interior valleys tell me that though the scene's daylight is fading, the riverbed rocks are releasing the summer heat they soaked up during the day.

Because of what that landscape means to me, the boy enacts a specific alchemy of meanings in Robert Towne's 1974 noir classic. In that desolate space, the hand-sewn shirt of peasant manta the boy dons and the old gray, swaybacked mare he straddles suggest the memory of an exhausted rancho era, a memory that passes through the frame like an apparition. The cryptic dialogue of the second riverbed scene confirms that sense of strangeness.

"Howdy," Gittes begins, evoking the Old West. "You were riding out here the other day, weren't you?"

No answer, just the somber gaze of the boy's deep brown eyes.

"Do you speak English? *¿Habla inglés?*" Gittes presses.

"*Sí,*" the unnamed boy answers, coloring the scene's strangeness with irony; he understands him perfectly well but chooses to answer in Spanish to underscore this oracle's mysterious reticence. The trajectory of the rider's path is quite clear, however.

He emerges from the northern edge of the boulder-strewn wash. The sense of desolation we get from watching him traverse it tells us that he comes from that parched landscape beyond the camera's frame. That scene, and the preceding city council meeting in which the drought emergency is debated, confront us with a well-developed California chronotope—the desert that threatens to swallow the city.[1] In that thematic, the boy's silence, which expresses the desert's power to silently overwhelm urban civilization, establishes a metaphorical equivalency between boy and menacing wilderness. Observed there, he is the native whose haunting memories of defeat judge the city on behalf of the wilderness. The rocky wash the mare cautiously negotiates suggests another phantom; a time when there was water, enough to cover its boulders with moss. Now a chalky color, they would paint your palms white if you touched them.

The filmgoer who accepts these tacit equivalencies also understands that the unnamed boy without need of human shelter belongs to, and thus speaks for, that wasteland. He haunts the suburban scrublands the way the Latina/o body lingers at the fringes of LA's popular and literary imagination. He is the film's ghost of a disappeared world that is not entirely dead or alive. *Chinatown* thus illustrates the paradox of a haunting body uprooted from its places, which conveys two postcolonial premonitions. The first occurs during the boy's interrogation; the second occurs when Gittes follows Mulwray to the El Macondo Apartments.

Peering down from a rooftop into a faux-Spanish courtyard, the detective catches the engineer with a girl young enough to be his daughter. She primly models a new dress for him as they chat in Spanish, until Gittes dislodges a roof tile that falls into the patio and shatters their conversation. It is, for those who understand it, nothing more than a casual father-daughter moment. But Gittes, who does not understand Spanish, reads the scene as tawdry, an older man's awkward prelude to sexual intimacy with an underage mistress. Because he must stay in character, Gittes also misses the meaning encoded in the building's name. That postmodern irony is reserved for the viewer who remembers Gabriel García Márquez's magical realist classic, *One Hundred Years of Solitude*, a novel of incest foretold, set in Macondo, a mythic town somewhere in Latin America.

Sometimes, when the phantom materializes in the writing of Latina/o authors, it contemplates its impending cultural death. In 1877 Pastor de Celis, Mariano J. Varela, and S. A. Cardona, the editors of *La Crónica*, a Spanish-language newspaper published for its LA and San Francisco readers, eerily defied their transformation into phantoms with these words: "We still have a voice, tenacity and rights," they wrote, "we have not yet retired to the land of the dead," or at least not yet, their manifesto implied.[2] If the *Crónica's* editors now seem to invite us to imagine what it would feel like to defy their cultural interment, conceptual artist Harry Gamboa Jr. gave voice a century later to the body that talks back from that grave.

In a series of experimental emails posted between 1995 and 1997 and titled "Phantoms in Urban Exile," Gamboa Jr. explicitly connects these two ideas, phantom existence and cultural interment, in an essay-manifesto-confession that testifies to what it feels like to embody late-twentieth-century Chicana/o urban subjectivity: "I've heard rumors that the freeways in LA are the concrete ribbons of a package that will never be opened before exodus," he begins. "The asphalt coating of billions of square feet is the icing on the multiple social layers of a dysfunctional environment." Further on he says, "I am crawling under the oppressive smog and heat until my bones are bleached white near the anonymous necropolis of stranded motorists," to reinforce and complicate the preceding burial allusions.[3] The "rumors" we hear suggest muffled East-side voices filtering up through asphalt to disrupt the seeming solidity and smoothness of LA's urban transportation network but also the body's peril in a specific location. It is the city's Eastside, scarred by crisscrossed freeways, which has been sacrificed to the region's transportation needs. We have a few options with which to imagine the mythic connotations of "exodus" here. It may be the future urban development that will once and for all uproot Chicana/os from their remaining urban places, or it is the apocalyptic end-time of LA's urban experiment. In the meantime, as we wait for the arrival of one of those futures, we hear faint voices, Chicana/os and other marginalized subjects, escape from under the entombing surface of late-twentieth-century car culture—a defining achievement of urban industrial modernity.[4]

Until very recently, however, LA's Latina/o phantoms had mostly appeared in the popular culture when depicted as mestiza hot tamales, servile gardeners and house maids, drug-peddling pachucos, trespassing "illegals," and the other essential demons of moral panic typically represented in their racialized urban haunts. Somehow that phantom always seemed to disappear from media visibility when it performed the humanizing intimacies of day-to-day living and the other expressive and intellectual practices that embodied its humanity. These cumulative hauntings have also shaped the city's literary life.

Many "influential writers," urban historian, architect, and poet Dolores Hayden wrote, "have been unable to perceive the importance of the city's nonwhite population, unable to recognize that people of color occupy any significant part of the urban landscape. Such writers may go downtown, but never or rarely to East LA or South Central. The focus of their landscape becomes houses, swimming pools, cars, and pop culture."[5] Literary representation of the city's postmodern morphology has typically obsessed over its built environment, the boundary configurations of its social geography, and media depictions that emphasize its culture of simulated spectacle. Consequently, fully realized literary representations of Latina/o subjectivity in their varied (not every Latina/o lives on the Eastside) urban places has been rare.

LA's continuing demographic, cultural, and economic transformation heighten the contrast between the hybridity of its lived culture and the narratives and images canonized in its literature. Today, according to the Pew Hispanic Center, Latina/os constitute more than 53 percent of the population of U.S. city regions, with nine of these metropolitan areas concentrated in the Southwest.[6] While the LA canon has constructed a monolingual literature circumscribed by a strict genre hierarchy and national borders, the city's transnational exchanges of immigrant bodies, commodities, capital, subjectivities, stories, and metaphors enact an alternate spatial order of actual and potential transgressions Saskia Sassen recently summarized in her theorization of the global city: "This type of city cannot be located simply in a scalar hierarchy that puts it beneath the national, regional and global. It is one of the spaces of the global, and it engages the global directly, often by-passing the national. Some cities may have had this capacity long before the current era; but today these conditions have been multiplied and amplified to the point that they can be read as contributing to a qualitatively different urban era."[7]

LA, a city of international commerce, manufacturing, and cultural production, is anything if not a global crossroads and has performed that role for some time. The sixteenth- and seventeenth-century *crónicas* (chronicles), *memorias* (memoirs), and *relaciones* (reports of individual colonizing feats) written on the way to and from this far-flung outpost between colliding empires prefigures our global moment. This writing also opened a domain for the nineteenth- and twentieth-century Latina/o nonfiction narratives to populate with new, hybrid subjectivities that defy the national script of immigrant assimilation U.S. literary anthologies still frame as "minority" literature. The LA canon's disappearance of its oldest literature of fact, however it defined its relation to the empirical, therefore bestowed a functional benefit for those who saw themselves as the inheritors of modernity. It prevented its twice-colonized subjects, the Latina/o phantoms in their midst, from troubling the pursuit of their private dreams or that fraction of them validated by a city's grand capitalist epic. This is the veil of secrecy our anthology will try to pierce with its exceptions to the canon's fabric of silences. But we cannot appreciate the tears they threaten without understanding the patterns they disrupt, without identifying the mechanisms by which the loom of a literary culture maintains the secrecy of Latina/o nonfiction, and why unraveling its disciplinary weave should precede this collection's texts.

Another Literary Loom

Nicolás Kanellos, in his 2011 landmark *Hispanic Immigrant Literature: El sueño del retorno*, has identified three major thematic tendencies in these nonfiction narratives: the political exile, most often male and a member of a dispossessed elite, preoccupied with return to the homeland, where he will seek justice and regain his former status; the Latina/o economic refugee with strong working-class identification who struggles to preserve her or his culture while fighting for human or labor rights; and the native who clearly embraces the United States as homeland yet struggles for recognition of civil rights, albeit as a member of the working class or as a landowner who struggles to regain lost land. Because these are mutable literary themes and not the expression of the writer's DNA, it was not uncommon for some *cronistas* to initially write from an exile's perspective and then invent a native voice later in life. "In some texts an immigrant may confront life in the grand U.S. Metropolis," Kanellos observes, "while in the next he may represent his culture as exiled, as in *El México de afuera* (Mexico abroad), that is, a Mexican colony existing outside of Mexico; and in another he may assume a native posture because, after all, as in the case of Adolfo Carrillo, he has lived in the United States for more than thirty years and become a voting citizen."[8] Other texts develop a native thematic, whether in the city or the countryside. In these works, Kanellos writes, "there is no question of return to a homeland; this is the homeland. This attitude is as true of the Californio narratives and Tejano autobiographies of the nineteenth century as it is of Nuyorican and Chicano literature today." The nineteenth-century writing life of Francisco Ramírez poignantly illustrates this theme. "Ramírez, born and educated in California and trilingual (he spoke French too), wrote as a native Californian while in Los Angeles but went into exile in northern Mexico, where he experienced the dislocation . . . of the political refugee."[9]

The LA canon's relatively recent discovery of a Latina/o urban literature would seem to have guaranteed the recognition of its native literary subjectivities. But for two recent modest exceptions, however, at least seven decades of LA anthologies and criticism have framed this literature as the work of exiles, immigrants, or a racial minority, anything but a subjectivity that represents its relation to place from a native perspective in a continuing transnational dialogue. Consequently, this canon, and the national literature that constructs it, continues to effectively minimize the transnational dynamic operating within Latina/o narratives when they situate themselves within third, or hybrid, places between nations. The canon's lingering reluctance to account for narratives that deliberately undermine or ignore the fixities of national borders thus ensures the invisibility of the serpentine routes through which Latina/o nonfiction writers invent their urban "native" identities. That failure to fully engage Latina/o creative nonfiction's radical cosmopolitanism, its ways of thinking and acting around, under, and beyond the nation-state's categories and spatial imaginary, of being at home in parallel homelands, also postpones the day when LA realizes its potential as a global literary city.

My line of criticism calls for some qualification, however. It is not directed against a recent generation of writers who happen to be from or write about LA, or its recent urban critics and historians, such as Mike Davis, who has scrupulously noted its history of Latina/o marginalization and class inequalities as well as their revitalization of the city's economy and culture in works such as *Magical Urbanism: Latinos Reinvent the U.S. City*. Nor is it concerned with the aesthetic merits of individual LA-related works or authors, their often-expressed criticism of the deficiencies of LA writing, the city's reputation as a refuge for minor genres, or the triviality of the anthology as a critical form. No, my inquiry focuses on the LA anthology precisely because it has been treated as a less-than-serious literary form. My emphasis on this question takes its cue from Walter Benjamin, who, in his critique of German tragic drama, argued that minor literary works constitute a more representative sampling of a literature's texts because they are the "ideal embodiments of the genre." In contrast to the literary masterpiece, which "will either establish the genre or abolish it" in a rare achievement of conceptual, stylistic, and formal synthesis, the minor work innocently gives up the discourses and social practices that disciplined its expression.[10] We can use Benjamin's judgment to isolate the elements that have constituted the LA canon's "ideal" iterations as a minor literature because its codes, discursive motifs, and social practices stand out more clearly in their relative lack of elaboration.

Hence my focus on the canon's exclusionary effects: I want to show how its literary technology, including the discourse of its urbanity, have reinforced the prevailing knowledge of LA's spaces and places. Taking the spatial turn to the text, however, not only requires that we look beyond LA's palm tree clichés and utopian descriptions of its multicultural geography. It asks us to examine those spatial metaphors and narratives through which a city's literature constructs its uniqueness in opposition to that which is external to it, the non-city of desert wilderness, so that its authors may plot LA's place in the national field.[11] The LA canon performs this function whenever it represents the antiurban as "nature," the savage as a wilderness denizen, and the Latina/o immigrant as alien Other; it does this whenever it plots a city's literature on the national field. My approach to the global city inside the text thus builds upon Benjamin Fraser's *Toward an Urban Cultural Studies: Henri Lefebvre and the Humanities* and the strategic opportunities for democratic interventions it identifies in the urban university humanities program. Fraser addresses the theoretical linkages between complex urban spaces and nonfiction literary forms when he observes the continuing "disconnect between how humanities scholars engage the urban and how social scientists view cultural products."[12] I try to bridge that divide by promoting the integration of critical urban studies with the humanities. My approach theorizes a research project that refuses to isolate the global city's built environment from its urban subjectivities. Its approach to urban literary cultural studies therefore stresses "the value of close readings of cultural texts, whether those are traditionally literary texts, filmic texts, graphic novels, popular music forms (albums, songs, etc.), visual representations of the city (photography, digital media, video games, etc.), or any other concrete form of urban social practice."[13]

A Colonial Prehistory

A crucial aspect of the LA canon's unacknowledged literary prehistory appears in the conquest and postconquest English-language memoirs and travelogues that represented the city as a discrete and identifiable domain of meaning. These works quickly populated their pages with phantoms—indigenous subjects represented as degraded or threatening others or romantic and nostalgic depictions of their exotic subjects. The production of this literary culture, which would play an important role in marketing Southern California as a sunny idyll that begged for suburban and industrial development, coincided with actual and symbolic assaults upon the Spanish-language *cronistas* and their editors. The marginalization of LA's oldest literary tradition began when Mexican civic leaders, editors, and writers like Francisco Ramírez were threatened with violence when they denounced the mid-nineteenth-century lynch war that targeted Mexicans and other Latin Americans. William D. Carrigan and Clive Webb have so far confirmed 547 lynching deaths throughout the Southwest between 1848 and 1928, though they suspect that the actual number, based on evidence of unconfirmed cases, is much higher.[14] The practice of ghost making later hounded others, such as the Flores Magón brothers, into jails, exile, and death in the 1920s. General Harrison Otis Gray's *Los Angeles Times* answered Magonista plots to overthrow the Díaz regime and their collaborations with the international anarchist cause with a red scare that set the stage for the Palmer Raids and Ricardo's Flores Magon's 1922 murder from beatings in Leavenworth Penitentiary. Meanwhile, contrary to period gender and racial stereotypes, several Latina anarchists in Los Angeles spoke out at rallies and wrote for the Magonista *Regeneración* or an anarchist tabloid such as *Pluma Roja* (Red Quill), written and edited by the Colombian Blanca de Moncaleano.[15] For the rest of that select number of men and women who continued to publish, there was the social and economic violence of writing in a second-class language and a déclassé genre for readers in newly created *colonias* of the dispossessed. For if language, racial, and class connotations signified by an author's name were not enough for the new Anglo majority to ignore Latina/o literature, then the commercial taint of daily journalism—and that period's pursuit of a politically disinterested, spiritual literary art—all but guaranteed its obscurity.

Only those forced to survive in LA's Latina/o literary culture would notice that other city (surely not the underground metropolis George Warren Shufelt populated with a race of Mayan lizard people) buried in plain sight.[16] Though deprived of the English-language media's authority and struggling to overcome the challenges of developing local literary institutions in a hostile environment, the Latina/o community, during a 150-year span beginning in 1850s, cocreated a popular Spanish-language journalism that constituted that community's predominant form of literary practice.[17] These imposed social conditions, circuits of media dissemination, and anticommunist hysteria no doubt restricted LA's *cronistas* to a particular social universe. That universe, its network of habits, attitudes, and daily routines of the literature's working-class audience, was quickly remade in the embrace of twentieth-century industrial capitalism. The literary culture that evolved from the social marginalization of Latina/o reading audiences would nevertheless indigenize its journalism—that is, encourage Latina/o journalists throughout the United States, Kanellos writes, to adopt the subjectivities of immigrant workers from their respective urban milieus: "The defense of workers and their families" defiantly proclaimed on newspaper mastheads "extended from the West to the East Coast and was common not only in Mexican communities but also among Cubans and Spaniards of Tampa and the Cubans and Puerto Ricans in the New York area."[18]

In Los Angeles that tiny fraction of Latina/o writers depended on the city's Latina/o working class until the 1960s, when the civil rights and antiwar movements coincided with improving employment opportunities in corporate media for a small number of Latina/o writers, such as Rubén Salazar, who joined the *Los Angeles Times* in 1959. The works compiled here show how the shadow of that urban working-class culture, its native places and subjectivities, would stubbornly reappear in the narratives, place memories, and language of Latina/o nonfiction, despite the profession's corporate rituals of journalistic "objectivity." The increasing availability of Spanish-language media, whether encoded as telenovelas, magic realist novels, or newspapers, thus offered countervailing narratives that reinforced the emergence of a community's distinct though varied literary sensibilities.

The 1960s and 1970s in Los Angeles also saw new and established Latina authors turn to literary journalism and other nonfiction forms, after first experimenting with poetry and the novel. The percentage of Latina/o writers who entered corporate media, however, would stagnate and then slowly decline in the late 1990s, as the industry's post-Fordist restructuring shrank media opportunities everywhere. Despite these circumstances, these writers, mostly journalists, continued to stage narratives of resistance against or within the translations of multicultural Otherness the corporate media expected of them whenever they expressed the Latina/o community's working-class values, traditions, and outlooks. The growing body of Latina/o reporting and feature writing on immigration-related issues illustrates the social identifications of that historical orientation in the spaces afforded them in the mainstream media.

Still, the increasing number of Latina/o writers who began to receive national recognition for their work since the 1980s,[19] and the literary scholarship that preceded and followed it, has done little to disturb the way the LA canon understands Latina/o literature, particularly its nonfiction. That paradoxical result had much to do with the context in which these increasing opportunities for Latina/o nonfiction writing occurred. Its local working-class and immigrant ethos had made the transition from a difficult regime defined by prolonged overt racial violence and the Cold War's ideological repression to a racially blind neoliberal present in which the state's disciplinary apparatus, with the compartmentalizing aid of the digital revolution, quietly normalizes the racialization of the growing Latina/o middle and working classes.[20]

Intriguingly, Latina/o literary nonfiction's entombed voices brought me to Jacques Derrida's theorization of literary "hauntology," or the regime of "truth" a society creates to remain in a permanent state of nonrecognition. And so today, despite the recent attention its authors and scholars have received, Latina/o nonfiction can still be interpreted as a haunted literature "that pushes," as Colin Davis writes, "at the boundaries of language and thought,"[21] waiting for the English literature programs that dominate literary instruction to create a space for its texts and criticism to fully exist, without qualification or translation. Meanwhile, as we wait for this transformation to occur, the other humanities mine the city's Latina/o nonfiction to narrate LA's cultural and social history or explore the alchemy of subaltern identity formation but rarely as a literary tradition with its own aesthetic ambitions. Despite recent investigations of individual creative nonfiction writers and the rapid increase of university courses taught on that subject, U.S. literary scholars still give scant critical (theorized) attention to the broad and varied field of English-language creative nonfiction now referred to as the "fourth genre."[22] This newcomer genre's relatively lower status, coming as it does after centuries of poetry, novel, and drama criticism, has the unintended effect of making the nonrecognition of Latina/o literary nonfiction nearly automatic. Critical works such as *Reading Autobiography: A Guide for Interpreting Life Narratives* by Sidonie Smith and Julia Watson have recently mapped life writing, including recent Latina/o autobiography and memoir, but not creative nonfiction. The greater critical recognition recently granted to life writing thus ensures a fracturing of critical focus, one that prevents creative nonfiction and life writing from becoming simultaneously visible within a single literary domain, even though their genres blur into each other on a shared spectrum.

Michel Foucault's theorization of discipline and governmentality suggests a way to transform Derrida's hauntology into a method for understanding how the technology and practices of literary secrecy operate. Nearing the end of his life, Foucault retheorized governmentality, a neologism Roland Barthes had coined to mean the "art" of governance, or the dispersed material and conceptual techniques of social, economic, and political administrative practice that would, through a long period of trial and error, produce that field of effects known as the modern nation-state.[23] Foucault's formulation of governmentality proposed a radical defamiliarization of the governing practices with which its subjects and administrators interpreted the unitary nation-state. Where the habits of practice and received knowledge persuaded others to ignore the rips in the discursive field called the national reality, he noticed the intricate weave of administrative technologies that constantly repair its "naturalness."

Beginning in the late medieval period, the governments of modern nation-states began to borrow and elaborate upon the techniques of disciplining the populace it sent to prisons, hospitals, factories, and the battlefield. In time the proliferation of techniques of governmental discipline not only produced internal contradictions that undermined older governmental functions; they revealed that the state did not possess, contrary to Orwell's "Big Brother," a coherent, essential core of truth. Rather, the nation-state effect stemmed from the weave of different and sometimes incompatible administrative techniques the populace perceived as the workings of a unitary rationality. Foucault would therefore frame governmentality as an "ensemble" of "institutions, procedures, analyses and . . . calculations and tactics that allow the exercise of this very specific albeit complex form of power" that identifies the population "as its target," political economy "as its principal form of knowledge," and the security apparatus "as its essential technical means."[24]

As John Marx recently wrote, many literary works are also strongly implicated in the state's preoccupation with measuring, defining, mapping, and disciplining the "population." "Fiction and verse," Marx argues, "shape a literary sort of governmental thought whenever they associate character with group, population with territory, and administration with defining what it means for a population to be secure, productive, or otherwise well off."[25] The same processes occur in literary criticism: "When literary criticism analyzes, affirms, and interprets accounts appearing in novels, poems, and plays, it supplements such aesthetic interventions and makes their formulations newly intelligible to and actionable within administrative institutions, particularly the university."[26] It is important to remember here that a society's administrative weave includes the techniques by which it constructs its definition of a racial or ethnic "majority" and minorities, or insider citizens and outsider aliens, and that the construction of a differential hierarchy often involves the deployment of literary techniques that render so-called minority populations explicitly visible in some circumstances and invisible in others.

Though often represented as a minor critical literature, the LA literary anthology also participates in reinforcing the existing governmental demographic definitions and their necessary silences. At the semiotic level, editorial selection implicitly assigns meanings to its texts by stressing specific framing interpretations at the expense of others while postulating generalizations about the city, its history, its population, and its spatial configuration. Together editorial selection and spatial framing elaborate a theory of the city and necessary constituent silences that circulate with other governmentalities. It is therefore impossible to extricate the canon from its enmeshments with the city's networks of power. Its critics and editors not only reaffirm the technologies marshaled to discipline subjectivities, genders, bodies, and territories that construct the city's populace and spaces; their repeated omissions reinforce the administrative policies that have cloaked the alien Other in secrecy.

However, because these administrative techniques are enacted by individuals, governmentality must also address the ways literary technologies discipline its practitioners. Three of Foucault's four categories of technology help explain how these disciplinary effects occur. They consist of the semiotic, or "technologies of sign systems," "'technologies of power,' [which] form subjects as a means of dominating individuals and encouraging them to define themselves in particular ways; and 'technologies of the self,'" which individuals apply to themselves "to make themselves autotelically happy."[27] Clearly, literary texts reiterate the discursive via the signifying practices of representation, but they also express the codes that regulate a profession's definitions and domains of legitimate literary performance.[28] As with other forms of discipline, a literary canon's socializing efficacy depends upon the intimacy of its effects, not its coercions. Foucault would argue that the dispersed technologies of bio-power and the technology of the self gradually cultivate tastes and habits of self-discipline its practitioners embody in their respective professions—the newspaper or magazine writer's cubicle, the book publisher's suite, or the professor's classroom. Social rewards—such as peer recognition, promotions that deliver increased salaries and/or administrative power—derived from performing these technologies not only shape the practitioner's subjectivity; they maintain the invisibility of the canon's disciplinary effects for those who administer and consume its texts.

My close reading of the LA canon's anthologies and critical texts identifies six literary technologies that reproduce the construction of a marginalized urban Latina/o populace and its places: spatial metaphors and narratives of an essential national, class, racial, or gender difference; mimetic metaphors and narratives that imagine the urban as a morphology of surfaces; spatial metaphors and narratives that define the urban in opposition to "nature" and local place memories; the recoding of high/low genre hierarchies of literary taste that maintain national, class, racial, and gender distinctions; strict English monolingualism that reinforces class, racial, gender, and national boundaries; and a division of labor and disciplinary practices of the self that normalizes the reproduction of these technologies.

Sequencing Literary Technologies

One of the earliest opportunities to see the workings of the canon's loom of literary technologies appeared in Franklin Walker's *A Literary History of Southern California* of 1950. Walker's attempt at a comprehensive review of the region's literary history has the great virtue of allowing us not only to see how he handled popular and literary themes already familiar to his readers but to identify the literary technologies that generated them. The "Gringo" authors he interpreted through "American" exceptionalism's national lens read the region's development as a conflict between Euro-American civilization and savage wilderness that must inevitably overcome California's geographic isolation and cultural backwardness. Walker's chronotope relies on Phil Townsend Hanna's 1931 *Libros Californianos, or Five Feet of California Books*, which turned a purported evolution of taste in popular music into his scheme for a historical periodization: "Weirdly barbaric melodies," Hanna (as quoted by Walker) contends, "gave way to plain chant; plain chant succumbed before the *alabado*; the *alabado* passed into 'Oh, Susanna'; 'Oh, Susanna' vanished before 'Old Black Joe'; and 'Old Black Joe' has been displaced by 'I Can't Give You Anything but Love, Baby'"[29] Hanna's strange arc of colonizing progress began with Native American savagery and culminated in that early-twentieth-century civilizing achievement known as "Old Black Joe." To Walker, Stephen Foster's praise of an old slave's loyalty to his master represented Southern California's "Middle Nordic Period," a time when Southern California's "essentially unpretentious middle-class soul was well attuned to such national folk melodies as 'Old Black Joe.'"[30] Walker did not need to tell his readers that this Nordic period stood for an essential Middle American white goodness or consciously acknowledge the implied violence of his ennobling musical analogy. Instead, he deployed a gentile tone to presume the inevitability of indigenous and Hispanic cultural death because he expected his mid-twentieth-century readers to uphold the naturalness of the region's white supremacist order. His racialized periodization, temporally anchored by a nostalgic recollection of slavery, cemented his marginalization by linking Mexican and Hispanic culture with another LA theme, the Hollywood simulacrum: "No one felt really at home with the fiestas and the Indian pageants. Good old-fashioned Christmas and the Fourth of July remained the favorite celebrations of the year. No textbooks featuring the activities of Spanish explorers and mission padres were able to compete seriously with McGuffey's readers and Harper's geography, and the excitement of rodeos and fandangos was superficial compared with the emotions aroused by a torchlight political procession or a good old circus parade."[31]

Walker's "No one" speaks for Southern California's Middle Western white majority. He believed their sobriety and wholesomeness no longer required the services of the early-twentieth-century Spanish fantasy heritage, which had been used to market real estate to California's new white majority, or Hollywood's phoniness. The new actuality he tried to articulate denied the Mexicans, who had survived their conquest, a chance to comment on the new white supremacist status quo based on homespun Middle American racist values. He also refused to recognize Latina/o contributions to the region's literary culture. Walker only acknowledged the Spanish chroniclers (Fathers Crespe, Font, and Serra) insofar as they supported his commentary about Southern California's real authors, the Anglo newcomers.[32] Similarly, he briefly acknowledged the newspapers Ramírez and Clemente Rojo published but not their pointed critiques of Yankee imperialism nor their contributions as editors and writers who defended Mexican civil rights against the Anglo lynch mob. The nonfiction writings of San Diego's María Amparo Ruiz de Burton and the Magonistas received no mention at all.

Meanwhile, the only presence California's natives can claim in Walker's cultural history was the one Richard Henry Dana and Mary Austin granted them. For Dana the Californio was a vain, feckless, and defeated Spanish don. The marginalization of Mary Austin's mestizo Mexican peon was not actually misery but the ennobling wisdom of those who accept what the desert gives them. Walker, stressing the artifice of Mexican culture, and, implicitly, their negligible literary contributions, thus leads his reader to a pair of conclusions. First, the Mexicans in his midst are not real Americans and, therefore, not equals endowed with complete legal, political, or cultural citizenship. Second, that first act of erasure allowed him to portray greater Los Angeles as an empty paradise in which the latest wave of white midwestern settler writers were building a truly honest literary culture without Hollywood or Hispanic affectations. Walker's verdicts, however, did not assert new ideas. He simply reinforced the naturalness of governmental and media narratives that had constructed Mexican foreignness and that mobilized anti-Mexican discrimination, mob violence, and mass deportations from the 1930s to the 1950s.

David Fine's introduction to his 1984 volume, *Los Angeles in Fiction: A Collection of Original Essays*, illustrates the durability of the canon's arsenal of literary technologies. Despite a thirty-four-year lapse since the publication of Walker's literary history, Fine's introduction, supported by the essays it theorized, reiterated the canon's major motifs even though the post–civil rights era in which it appeared now rejected Walker's white supremacist assumptions. Fine explicitly reaffirmed the city-of-outsiders motif when he noted that "any discussion of the Los Angeles novel must begin with the observation that it is chiefly the work of the outsider—if not the tourist, then the newcomer. With a few exceptions, largely contemporary ones, its shapers have been men and women born elsewhere who for a time lived and worked in Southern California, frequently as script writers." Fine's Hollywood reference implicitly smoothed the transition to the city-without-memory and city-against-nature motifs by alluding to the dream factory that manufactured the LA simulacrum. He argued in the next paragraph that the city's "first significant generation of Los Angeles writers—the generation that was to confer upon the city a modern fictional definition—did not appear until the 1930s."[33] The essays he compiled supported that assessment. All of them, including Raymund A. Paredes's essay, "Los Angeles from the Barrio: Oscar Zeta Acosta's *The Revolt of the Cockroach People*" (which we address in our second essay), ignore the possibility of a "modern" Latina/o literature, let alone fourth genre literary works predating Helen Hunt Jackson's 1884 novel of Southern California, *Ramona*. He then delved into post-1930s LA novel's way of imagining how the ocean, the desert, recurring chaparral fires, and the quake-prone earth conspire to destroy the city's precarious and fraudulent artificiality.[34] The city-against-nature motifs Fine aptly identified in his volume's essays thus reinforce LA's representation as the eastern city's ugly, anarchic opposite, a divergence from civilized urbanity spatialized by the city's placement on the national map's far western limit.

The canon's next installment came the following year. Bill Mohr's edited collection *"Poetry Loves Poetry": An Anthology of Los Angeles Poets* (1985) continued to deploy the literary technologies that had erased the city's Latina/o literary memory. In a bid to win critical recognition for the poets he selected, Mohr boosted the collection as the first to present "the work of Los Angeles poets in a national context."[35] That value-enhancing act, which tried to put the city's poets on the national literary map, also carried the echo of the military conquest that enabled its plotting. The spatial logic of one colonizing act was complemented by two others. At the level of language, Mohr identified Williams, Stevens, Eliot, and Pound as the "four outstanding poets in the first half of this century,"[36] a gesture that encouraged favorable comparison of the anthology's contributors with the four poets. This judgment, however, also accepted the way the curricula of the period tacitly universalized English-language poetry in a city that wrote in several languages. The essay's claim that its poets "were born elsewhere, ranging from Germany, Russia, China, England, Cuba, and Poland to San Francisco, Philadelphia, and Cleveland, as well as little towns in the Midwest,"[37] also recycled the city of exiles motif, even as it intimated its multicultural present. Direct engagement with that multicultural urbanity, a discourse developers promoted to redevelop the downtown skyline and market the city's hosting of the 1984 Olympic Games, might have left a small gap to introduce the complicating reality of racial inequality. But even an aggressive engagement with the city's military-styled policing of racialized communities and continuing de facto residential racial segregation would have not guaranteed a day of reckoning with LA's coloniality.

Touching this third rail of LA cultural politics would have been extraordinary for a non-Latina/o poet or critic at that time. But the erasure still deserves attention for what it reveals about the canon's literary technology. For Mohr's egalitarian embrace of the city's immigrant poets laboring in the shadows of the world media capital could still not overcome the structuring effect of framing the city's poetry as a late-twentieth-century story. Though selecting works written from 1980 to 1984 did not require ignoring what the archive of Chicana/o and Latin American literary criticism might say about the anthology's four Hispanic-surnamed authors or how postcolonial ghosts might haunt its fifty-eight other contributors, it certainly made it much easier.[38] This elision only seemed natural then or now because the hemisphere's legacy of European conquest has not yet acquired the purchase that English-language humanities bestow on the U.S. history of slavery to address the question of race.

The glib introduction Eve Babitz wrote for *Los Angeles Stories: Great Writers on the City* continued, in 1991, to recycle the exiled writer motif and the canon's technology of national framing. Babitz played up LA's not–East Coast attributes (sunshine, beaches, and flower-scented nights) as enviable positives: "It's not

New York—but that's the point," Babitz writes. "In fact, that it's not New York or anyplace else ruthless and cold and brutal is the happy ending. No east coast winter ever came. Here we just go on picnics," she concluded, a year before the LA riots delivered an apocalypse Nathanael West would have relished.[39] All the other works of fiction in this edition, except for an obligatory Oscar Z. Acosta excerpt from *The Revolt of the Cockroach People*, recycled well-worn media motifs in strict genre categories. LA was a city for hedonist readers and writers, an implied sensory hierarchy that precluded the possibility of serious intellectuals who are also hedonists. Then again, Babitz was only interested in prepping the reader to enjoy well-known works as fresh summer reading.

Less than a decade later, poet-editor's Paul Vangelisti's *L.A. Exile: A Guide to Los Angeles Writing, 1932–1998, written with Evan Calbi and published in 1999*, reiterated the city-without-memory and city-against-nature motifs. Vangelisti, who framed the landscape as ahistorical nature, foreclosed the possibility of a chronology that would allow for Latina/o historical memory: "Whether from other parts of the U.S. earlier in the century, or from Latin America and the Pacific Rim more recently, the settlement and growth of Los Angeles has never enhanced cultural stability. In this respect, the first half of the 1900s is certainly no different than the latter half, regardless of the languages the settlers brought here."[40] And although his literary magazine, *Invisible City*, and subsequent translation projects would recognize the importance of Latin American poetry, Vangelisti, at least in this anthology, seemed to have lost sight of something obvious: LA's Latina/o community. The city's antagonistic growth against its asserted "cultural stability" never succeeded in completely erasing one of its most important foci of continuity: what Mike Davis has referred to as the "radical conservatism of [East LA's] Chicano culture in music, dress and language—but most of all, loyalty to place. Chicanos are the only segment of the LA population that isn't lost."[41]

Vangelisti's anthology framed the nature-versus-city antagonism more starkly when he quoted Theodor Adorno, who wrote that the landscape "bears no traces of the human hand." Seen from a moving car, "the vanishing landscape," Adorno continued, "leaves no more traces behind than it bears upon itself."[42] Vangelisti did not factor in what Adorno did or did not know of the eighteenth- and nineteenth-century cattle grazing, which produced the golden hillsides the theorist scanned from a moving car, or the massive water and flood control projects that reengineered LA's "natural" landscape. Instead, he used Adorno's interpretation of the automobile to reinforce the idea of an ephemeral city surrounded by the desert's indifferent and alienating no-where-ness. To Adorno, the canon's quintessential exiled outsider, it is the modern automobile's speed that prevents the city's denizens from making sense of or giving meaning to an alienating landscape.[43] Interpreting that speed effect as a universal of the LA urban experience, however, assumed that place making depends on fixity, on holding space, an idea that those of East LA's low-riding culture defy whenever they turn their tricked-out *ranflas* into moving place makers.

The next decade's LA anthologies did not substantially disrupt the phantom-making machinery. In 2000 David M. Fine reaffirmed the LA canon's dominant territorial metaphor in *Imagining Los Angeles: A City in Fiction*. For Fine the city derived its "essential literary identity" from "the decades since the 1930s—in the hard-boiled fictions and tough guy detective stories, Hollywood novels, and apocalyptic fictions—as the place resting dangerously on the edge of the continent, the place that forces one to look back to sources and origins."[44] His claim makes sense if you accept its implicit assumptions. The darkly hued Mexican half-castes, the recently Christened Indians, the Paiute-speaking Tongva villagers nearly eradicated by the mission system, and the Asians who arrived soon after never appeared on the city's list of founding families. The precarious edge to which he referred instead established the western national limit and all the colonizing events that produced it.

The following year David L. Ulin's introduction to his 2001 anthology, *Another City: Writing from Los Angeles*, reiterated the city-without-memory and urban morphology motifs and a belated and potentially promising recognition: "We are in the presence of a whole new generation of writers, for whom Los Angeles is neither escape route nor meal ticket, but, in the most fundamental sense, home."[45] He acknowledged the difference between the Los Angeles of literary exiles "who arrived grudgingly, lamenting lost histories, lost landscapes" and a recent generation of homegrown or at least settled authors who harbored no desires of returning. His inclusion of Luis Alfaro's "How Minnie Ripperton Saved My Life," a nonfiction reminiscence about how the author's embrace of a South Central's African American culture helped him accept himself as a gay Latino, illustrated one of the rewards of this modest shift, even as it reinforced the theme of recent Latina/o immigrant arrival. But instead of pausing to ask if Alfaro's piece suggested a line of inquiry that might detect cracks in the canon's edifice, Ulin slid back into LA's well-established city-without-memory motif that precluded the possibility of an autochthonous Latina/o urban literary culture that preceded the collection's only Latino nonfiction contribution.

The next passages from his introduction show how his framing turned the city's spaces into a field of flattened surfaces. He quoted Joan Didion to explain why the city's literary culture has failed to produce a work, like the great early-twentieth-century New York novels, that makes sense of the city's sprawling size and profound fragmentation in a unifying narrative: "What she means is narrative in the grand sense, a collective mythology under whose influences all our individual experiences may, in some strange way, cohere."[46] But Southern California and LA proper, contrary to Ulin's assessment, had indeed inspired grand totalizing narratives. These, however, were often coded like Didion's—in works of creative nonfiction or cultural criticism, not novels or poetry. Mike Davis's *City of Quartz* represents one of those totalizing works, a devastating one that established a critical frame for LA's postmodern theorization. Several decades earlier, Carey McWilliams gave us *North from Mexico*, whose first chapter, "The Fantasy Heritage," a collage of "Spanish" California's narrative motifs, constructed a metanarrative of the Mexican population's cultural dispossession and thus an avant la lettre work of Chicana/o cultural studies.

Ulin was not prepared, however, to acknowledge how limiting genre preferences, when joined with the city's spatial clichés, reduced its memory to a flattened present. The combined effect of these literary technologies is hard to detect because they are veiled by a subtle conflation detectable in Ulin's next sentence about Didion: "She's right about that; when it comes to LA, even to think about an all-encompassing narrative is to miss the point of the place, which sprawls and tumbles shapeless like a vast amoebic mass. . . . No, it only makes sense that LA writing reflect the city's scattered energy: diffuse, defined by its own lack of definition, not the product of some homogenous aesthetic but of smaller, individual voices raised above the din."[47]

These passages, and another in which Ulin referred to LA's "literary cacoph-ony," assume an equivalency between the city's complex, seeming formless-ness, and the impossibility of hearing, and therefore formulating, a totalizing narrative. No wonder editors, who remained daunted by an urban complexity that defied their assumptions, resorted to this aural metaphor, "cacophony," to complain about the "din" they could not hear. His word choices appeared to register defensive anticipation of the criticism the volume might invite and his frustration of arriving at an interpretive framework that reconciled his canonic practice with the city's increasingly vocal diversity.

Ulin, however, cannot accept all the blame for being frustrated by the city's seemingly amoebic built environments and scattered voices. Many important works of the LA school of urban studies that predated his anthology also suc-cumbed to their own surface-obsessed readings of the city. Even so, a small handful of literary and scholarly works had already begun to read surface as symptom—the concluding social and material embodiments of serial cre-ative destructions in a post-Fordist city at the crossroads of world trade. They noticed the rationalities of competing forms of late-twentieth-century capital accumulation and their enabling neoliberal governmental technologies and how both structured the weave of the urban matrix that coalesced and enacted the processes of place making in a city of growing inequalities.

The following year, in 2002, Ulin published *Writing Los Angeles: A Literary Anthology*, a collection that reiterated the city-without-memory, city-against nature, and surface morphology motifs. The *Los Angeles Times* book review editor addressed the first of these themes by noting that the city's literature was "chiefly the work of the outsider—if not the tourist, then the newcomer." He reinforced his judgment by deeming the three local Latino authors he anthologized as late-twentieth-century developments and not a continuation of an eighteenth- or nineteenth-century literary practice.[48] He introduced the "urban" versus "elemental" motif a few paragraphs later, when he observed: "The story of Los Angeles has always been, on the most basic level, the story of the interaction between civilization and nature. Mary Austin's early essay, 'The Land,' delineates in unblinking detail just how unforgiving is the desert ecosystem on which the city was superimposed."[49] Here again, Ulin accepted the naturalness of the nature-civilization dichotomy that underpinned the idea of the urban in so much late-twentieth-century urban studies scholarship. Nor did he notice how "nature's" metaphysical cage prevented him from recognizing the ecological, economic, and cultural metabolism that constructed the city's urbanity and built environments. The city's superimposition on the desert appeared too recent to grant it any historical standing. His story of the city therefore denied the possibility of a literary chronology in which Mexicans predate the grand westward gesture that put the city at the continent's edge, a spatial orientation reflected in the anthology's contributors—only four of seventy-seven were by Latino authors.

Ulin complicated the meaning of his limited nonfiction sample by including a passage from Octavio Paz's "The Pachuco and Other Extremes." That first chapter of the Mexican Nobel laureate's 1950 meditation on the Mexican national psyche, *The Labyrinth of Solitude*, relied on his recollections of a brief visit to LA in 1944. Crucially, the poet's return to the city of his childhood came a year after U.S. servicemen, egged on by local newspapers and government, terrorized the city's Mexican American population during the Zoot Suit Riots.[50] In the essay Paz attempted to triangulate the universals of Mexican national character by plotting the "Pachuco" archetype as one of its extreme exceptions.[51]

Not surprisingly, his attempt to isolate the universal traits of Mexican national identity required that he ignore the riot's contextual details. Admitting these contingencies would have interfered with a style of psychoanalytic narrative he borrowed from his Mexican predecessors, Julio Guerrero, Samuel Ramos, Emilio Uranga, and Jorge Carrion.[52] Like other nineteenth- and early-twentieth-century classical ethnographers, Paz and his Mexican contemporaries equated the individual's personality with a national cultural ego they had conveniently frozen in a savage prehistoric past. His identity construct of the Pachuco achieved that effect by subtracting the trauma the riot inflicted on LA's Mexican community. That excision allowed Paz to put the Pachuco on the psychiatrist's couch to hear his patient confess a profound sense of inferiority but not the obvious causes of the patient's distress. Diagnosis: "The *pachuco* does not want to become a Mexican again; at the same time he does not want to blend into the life of North America. His whole being is sheer negative impulse, a tangle of contradictions, an enigma." His idea of the Pachuco archetype hungered for Anglo punishment, which he believed symbolized the Mexican psyche's failure to evolve a healthy national identity. Not surprisingly, the poet's famous observation that LA's spaces are haunted by traces of a Mexican culture that "floats, never quite existing, never quite vanishing," reinforced, by attributing to it a quality of essential cultural sameness, one of the necessary tropes of Mexican national authenticity.[53]

But one wonders how Ulin could introduce Paz's essay two years into the twenty-first century without noting the essay's fall from grace. Not only had the ideas he borrowed from cultural anthropology, area studies, and psychoanalysis come under increasing derision after the 1960s, but Chicana/o scholars had, by the time of the anthology's publication, exposed the racist media hysteria that had invented the violent gangster upon which the poet's image of Chicana/o delinquency depended. Meanwhile, younger Mexican scholars questioned Paz's narrative of unique national character as nothing more than a method for disciplining Mexico's intelligentsia and thwarting the nation's democratic impulses.[54] The Chicana/o critiques of his essay eventually led Paz to apologize for his characterization of LA's Chicana/os but not for his ideas about Mexican national character. None of these cross-border debates, however, register in Ulin's introduction, a silence that, in reiterating the hoary plausibility of Mexican American pathology, revived the canon's essentializing metaphysics.

That year, 2002, Lionel Rolfe published an expanded edition of his 1981 study, *Literary L.A.*, which added one essay on the Chicano author Oscar Zeta Acosta because his beat-influenced writing, *The Autobiography of a Brown Buffalo*, appeared to mesh with his theory of LA bohemian writing.[55] But the revised edition, which ignored works of Latina/o nonfiction and Chicana/o literary criticism that did not fit or contradicted Rolfe's narrow bohemian genealogy, failed to create a critical framework with which to challenge the city-without-history and city-against-nature motifs that continued to disappear Latina/o nonfiction.

The first direct, though timid, questioning of the canon's genre technology emerged in 2003. In *The Misread City: New Literary Los Angeles* Scott Timberg and Dana Gioia's collection of critical and literary works announce their decision not to propose another totalization of the city's literary legacy. Their initial instincts seemed sound, gesturing, as they did, toward the possibility of a postcolonial reply to the canon's critics: "When Southern California's literary life has been discussed, it has too often been by outsiders. Some of them get it; most don't. Los Angeles may dictate the new electronic culture to the rest of the world, but in literature it remains half colonized." Part of the blame for that result, Timberg and Gioia argued, had been the city's failure to develop "a serious critical milieu."[56] Unfortunately, the vagueness of their assertion closed off the kind of inquiry that would explain why such a milieu had failed to develop. They sidestepped the questioning of that milieu's social relations of cultural production and the literary technologies that constructed the canon's menagerie of phantoms the moment they assumed that the failure was entirely localized. They then move from one missed opportunity to another promising critical notion, namely, that their "goal was not to be definitive or timeless but rather, to be culturally useful—informed, thoughtful, and contemporary. We hope the book functions like a good museum show. We have included pieces with which we disagree because they seemed strong and provocative."[57] Despite the failure to recognize their curatorial choices as a tacit commitment to the existing literary technologies, the intention of welcoming debate remained commendable, as it suggested the possibility of a critique of the canon's previous theorizations. Unfortunately, a failure to realize that intention prevented them from following through on their critique of the West Coast–versus–East Coast spatial dichotomy, and discovering how different urban literary cultures nevertheless reproduced the normative technologies of national literary secrecy.

The volume's editors instead retreated to triteness. It "is not necessarily a bad thing," they argued, "that Los Angeles literary life differs from that of New York or London," an argument that reiterated the city's essential uniqueness.[58] What is it about the LA "thing," an entity imagined here as a kind of container—aside from its proximity to powerful media industries and distance from eastern intellectual circles its editors bemoan—that revealed something intrinsic about its literary culture? Blaming another industry and the externality of not being New York evaded the effort of attempting a comprehensive interpretation of the processes that have constituted LA's literary culture.

And yet, despite these deficiencies, *The Misread City*'s articles indirectly acknowledged LA's experience of globalization. Ulin's article "Like Any Paradise" also made a tentative approach to this theme: "In some sense, such developments are a sign that LA is becoming more cosmopolitan; we live in a complex society, and it's only fitting for the city to reflect that idea." And then, a page later: "To a certain extent, there's an element of the postmodern sensibility in this, the late-twentieth-century concept that all ideas and structures are fair game."[59] His timid recognition of what literary critics had been arguing two decades earlier revealed another tear in the canonic fabric. The welcome introduction of two critical articles, one about John Rechy, the other by Ixta Maya Murray, appeared to confirm new sources of external pressure, except that these authors were recognized novelists, not the excluded nonfiction experimenters of genre hybridization who had already critiqued that "cosmopolitanism."

Not surprisingly, even the canon's editors who chafed at its exclusions still reproduced its orthodoxies. For example, although *Latinos in Lotusland: An Anthology of Contemporary Southern California Literature* (2008), edited by Daniel Olivas, did the important work of breaking the silence by introducing the first Latina/o short stories and novel excerpts, it still overlooked important aspects of LA's Chicana/o narrative production since the 1960s, particularly its genre-blurring experiments written after the 1970s by conceptual artists Harry Gamboa Jr. and Guillermo Gómez-Peña's in his 1990s LA period. It postponed, in other words, the task of questioning the canon's practice of publishing the "best" or "classic" examples of orthodox genres.

The Cambridge Companion to the Literature of Los Angeles (2010), edited by Kevin R. McNamara, by contrast, represented the first critical collection to introduce an essay that explicitly discusses the works of California's nineteenth-century Mexican writers. The problem with "The Literature of the Californios" by Rosaura Sánchez and Beatrice Pita, however, was not the essay but its setting. Its analysis of the discourses of Californio nonfiction introduced non-Latina/o readers to what they should have learned from Latina/o scholars a few decades earlier. But because the greatest share of LA's Latina/o literary production has consisted of *crónicas* and other nonfiction forms, the collection's editor should have also commissioned a second critical essay on the aesthetics of LA's Latina/o nonfiction,[60] or the ways these authors performed the codes, discourses, and genres of nonfiction writing to generate distinct literary styles or personas. James Kyung-Jin Lee's "Pacific Rim City: Asian American and Latino Literature" by contrast, which solely concerned itself with fiction, did something comparable to that when he established important equivalencies between a newer generation of Latina/o fiction writers and their Asian American counterparts, a recognition that prefigured studies of LA as a crossroads of global literary dialogue. The overall impression of the *Companion*'s essays, however, showed that they avoided critical engagement with its Latina/o creative nonfiction by reinforcing the canon's high/low genre dichotomies. These silences resonate when contrasted to J. Scott Bryson's essay in the collection, "Surf, Sagebrush, and Cement Rivers: Reimagining Nature in Los Angeles," and the way it framed Joan Didion's, John McPhee's, Mike Davis's, and D. J. Waldie's literary nonfiction as explicitly literary works. Bryson's essay concluded with another important shift when he discussed Jenny Price's "Thirteen Ways of Seeing Nature in L.A.," an essay that posed a radically new challenge for LA's writers: "What we need in L.A., as elsewhere is a foundational literature that imagines nature not as the opposite of the city but as the basic stuff of modern everyday life."[61] Price recognized the seamless ways the urbanizing adaptations that transform our surroundings also fostered the conditions that generate new adaptations. These effects, which then spark new human adaptions to the prior urban condition, fuel further environmental transformations, a reinforcement loop that resituates the human and nonhuman dialectic in an all-embracing metabolic ecology.

Bill Mohr returns to the critical scene in *Hold-Outs: The Los Angeles Poetry Renaissance, 1949–1992*, a 2011 study in which he argued for the originality of LA's postwar poetry. For Mohr the city would generate a scene of its own for local outlaws and their small presses, a "there" that coalesced in pre-gentrified Venice Beach, until reaching its ultimate expression in the poetry and publishing collective known as the Beyond Baroque Foundation. That nonprofit collective (the one in which he happened to play a formative role) generated the city's literary field when it featured and published that scene's most important poets: Leland Hickman, Wanda Coleman, and Charles Bukowski. His portrayal of the Venice Beach and Beyond Baroque poets as the best expression of the city's postwar poetry, which he reinforced with extensive quotations of the Venice Beach, Beyond Baroque, and Long Beach Stand Up poets, also generated its necessary phantoms.

They gather like ghosts at the margins of Mohr's condensed summaries of the 1980s "multicultural" poets when he granted a limited visibility to Latino writers (their works summarized in all but two pages) but not their words.[62] Depriving their works of their interpretative codes separated the poet's utterances, grounded in LA's lived urban material and historic contexts, from their signs and their linkages to that other global literary system encoded in Spanish and its hybrids. The disembodiment that stripped the texts of their discursive and aesthetic frameworks of intelligibility reinforced the naturalness of his preferences. While it is easy to speculate about Mohr's desire to feather his literary legacy, questioning his motives would miss the way the following passage overlaid the city's literary field onto the national territory: "Many poets in Los Angeles believed that appearing in *Bachy* [a poetry journal] was as commendable as having a poem in *Epoch* or *Paris Review*. . . . If a poet such as Kate Braverman appeared in the *Paris Review* and *Bachy*, as well as *Momentum* [Mohr's journal], the local consensus was that these were all equally commendable feats. If this equivalency were to be perceived elsewhere in the country as West Coast arrogance, we regarded such a reaction as proof that the East Coast was in no mood to grant Los Angeles poets a seat at the table of equals."[63] Apart from its questionable suppositions, it is hard to ignore the way his defensive bicoastalism confirms the nation as a bounded field.[64] He reinforced that national spatiality when he suppressed similarities between cities to simulate the drama of literary combat between metropolitan giants; the same goes for his boosterish calculations of literary rank. He reinscribed the field's national boundaries when he pleaded for LA's special place in "American" literature, a parochialism both coasts have enforced with their adherence to a flattening monolingualism.

The next contributions to the canon, one anthology and two critical studies about LA poetry, began to incrementally address, some more directly than others, the literary technologies that disappear LA's Latina/o nonfiction while still upholding the canon's genre hierarchy and English-language monolingualism that maintain its phantom status, especially within humanities curricula and pedagogy.[65] Little wonder that Latina/o nonfiction authors and literary scholars who directly engage the global and transnational in avant-garde explorations of urban spatiality and subjectivity remain in a kind of limbo, relegated to the margins of the cultural turn but still beyond the scope of mainstream humanistic inquiry.

Gloria H. Anzaldúa, in her seminal essay "Border Arte: *Nepantla, el Lugar de la Frontera*," explores this condition of displacement (and the threat its expression poses) when she turned to Mesoamerican cosmology's "Nepantla," or concept of an in-between place, to theorize borderlands spaces. The radical quality of her challenge, which took the form of a critical review of the Denver Museum of Natural History's exhibition of *Aztec: The World of Moctezuma*, exceeded the conventions of the mainstream art review's reliance on polemic argument and mimetic representations of exhibit artifacts. Instead, her *crónica*-like juxtaposition of bilingual code-switching, memoir, art history, and aesthetic philosophy strove to expressively and critically perform mestiza cultural theory's Nepantla places: "I think of the borderlands as Jorge Luis Borges's Aleph, the one spot on earth which contains all other places within it. All people in it, whether natives or immigrants, colored or white, queers or heterosexuals, from this side of the border or del otro lado are personas del lugar, local people—all of whom relate to the border and to the nepantla states in different ways."[66] Her performance of mestiza/o identity, and resulting subversion of the national's normative binaries of race, gender, sexuality, and class, suggest another way of spatializing urban subjectivity. They not only invite us to experience the fragmented embodiments of socially constructed urban subjectivity; they open the place-making imaginaries that "las personas del lugar" invent to heal their memories of "la herida," or the colonial wound from which they were uprooted. The global city's flâneurs, Harry Gamboa Jr. and Guillermo Gómez-Peña, would take the next step and make the urban dimensions of Anzaldúa's place thinking explicit. Their experiments in genre violation set off a dialectics of urban spaces and places that dramatically performs and critiques their hybridized embodiments of urban subjectivity. Like Anzaldúa, they transpose their lived experiences of urban spatiality into a formal dialectic that subverts the technologies of literary secrecy that MFA Creative Writing programs still enforce.

Pulitzer Prize–winning novelist and essayist Junot Díaz, whose writing demonstrates an encyclopedic grasp of Latina/o literature's postcolonial

Caliban challenge to the national field, recently focused on the entrenched "whiteness" of his MFA writing experiences to reflect upon the totality of these exclusionary effects: "Simply put: I was a person of color in a workshop that was not interested, philosophically or pedagogically, in trying to account for my racialized ontology. I was a person of color in a workshop whose theory of reality did not include my most fundamental experiences as a person of color—that did not in other words include *me*. . . . My workshop's whiteness more or less barred my reality, my voice, from its conversations. It ensured that I was not witnessed in class, not by the faculty or by the majority of my peers. It was an act of silencing, of erasure, of negation—of violence."[67]

Locally, a review of Southern California's premiere MFA programs reveals a comparable result, despite the region's majority Latina/o presence and pronouncements extolling the virtues of its multicultural diversity. Creative Writing course descriptions, teaching positions, guest lecturers, texts and journals, for example, would betray a particularly weak showing for Latina/o writers, texts and instructors and near-complete exclusion of U.S. Latina/o literary nonfiction and Latin American *crónica*, two interwoven forms that should be read together to understand their transnationalism and literary genealogies.

This anthology has therefore selected works for the threats they pose to the LA canon and other city literatures. Instead of attempting to replace one canonic totalization for another, it proposes a critical practice for disrupting literary secrecy by identifying the techniques that construct the national literary field. Identifying and understanding the national metaphors that disappear the global city's "majority minority" literature, including nonfiction, also suggest opportunities for concrete intervention. First, disrupting a national literature from the heart of the neoliberal metropolis would pave the way, as Walter D. Mignolo argues, for "delinking" Latina/o literature from the coloniality of the Western humanist "universals" that implicitly marginalize it. Or, as Mignolo argues from a transnational perspective, "if in Europe and the United States languages and literatures in the past three hundred years have been defined in tandem with national ideologies, the future requires the participation of all those languages and (sub) continents (Asia, Africa, Latin America) that have been left out or that have occupied a secondary role in cultures of scholarship of the modern North Atlantic world."[68] English and Creative Writing programs,

especially those in which Latina/o and other immigrant students now constitute pluralities or majorities, are the ideal places for launching this dialogue.
In the California State University (CSU) system, to cite one example, students
of color comprised 62 percent of the California State University system's 2015
enrollment; Latinos accounted for 37 percent of CSU enrollment.[69] But the
agenda for such a dialogue cannot be decided in advance; rather, its decolonizing objectives must emerge from its participants, the phantoms, as they
discover their voices and bodies and commonalities in that borderlands space
of the "colonial wound" that lies beyond humanism's present universalizing
framework.[70] Second, disrupting the technology of national literature in the
classroom can reinforce ongoing citizen efforts in the streets to challenge
what the city is to its customary interpreters: the developer, the architect,
the geographer, and the urban planner. Arming the formerly silenced and
invisible others to fight for their "right to the city," as Henri Lefebvre enjoined,
could thus open truly transnational democratic spaces for hearing Nepantla's
phantoms in the public square. In such a global city, English departments and
planning commission meetings would become laboratories for translating
and interpreting hidden literatures—not just Spanish but Mandarin, Hmong,
Zapotec—back to its citizen-readers.

Donald Trump's unrelenting campaign to racialize the Hispanic immigrant, above all Mexicans, as inherently criminal predators now provides the
humanities a unique opportunity to examine the literary technologies that
structure its marginalization of Latina/o nonfiction. Fortunately, California's
political establishment, from the governor on down to the cities, counties, and
public universities that have vowed to enact a comprehensive plan to protect
the targets of Trump's pogrom, suggest the scale at which the humanities
may imagine this strategic opportunity. For the breadth of laws and policies
that progressive supermajorities are prepared to enact to defend the nation's
largest population of undocumented immigrants are indeed impressive given
recent history. In 1994 a majority of Californians approved Proposition 184, an
initiative that tried to turn governmental apparatus into a prod to expel the
undocumented. From 1930 to 1934 state and local governments, newspapers,
railroads, and business councils in the southwestern states, led by California,
coordinated a moral panic that amounted to an illegal deportation of as many

as one million Mexicans, more than 70 percent of whom were citizens or legal residents.

Now contrast these sorry episodes to its unprecedented turnabout. An array of municipal and county governments, led by its largest cities, Los Angeles and San Francisco, as well as its public and private universities, have passed a variety of sanctuary laws and policies that prevent local police from serving as arms of the immigration police. In June 2017 the California state legislature allocated forty-five million dollars to pay for the legal defenses of all detained immigrants and approved oversight restrictions that attempt to prevent federal authorities from operating immigrant detention facilities in the state.[71] Enforcement of these counter-governmentalities are backed by the economic power of the world's sixth-largest economy and a 4.1 percent rate of job growth in 2015, twice the national average, while building a six billion–dollar budget surplus by the end of 2017.[72] California's resolve not only sets the ethical and legal bar for other progressive cities and states to emulate; it establishes a standard with which the humanities must measure their commitments to the undocumented. Let us make no mistake, this conflict of wills and laws will hasten, not delay, the process through which U.S. global cities invent new definitions of citizenship and the cultural commons upon which so much of their allure and wealth depend. The boldness of California's protective responses should challenge U.S. universities, so many of them in or near global cities, to question a "progressive" neoliberal status quo that would allow the humanities to proclaim support for "diversity" without decolonizing their relations to Latina/o immigrant students, labor, and literature.

Decolonizing Latina/o Nonfiction in LA's Writing

IGNACIO LÓPEZ-CALVO AND VICTOR VALLE

In 1995 Raymund A. Paredes, a career UCLA English professor who would eventually assume a position of prominence within the Texas education policy apparatus,[1] delivered an appraisal of Oscar Zeta Acosta's *The Revolt of the Cockroach People* (1973) in which he contrasted the novel's accomplishments to its nineteenth- and twentieth-century Latina/o literary predecessors. In building his comparison, however, he effectively stranded the nineteenth-century *crónicas* on a temporal island. The Los Angeles Mexican American writing, he pointed out, "dates from the 1850s, when *El Clamor Público* and other local Spanish-language newspapers began to publish poems and fictional sketches, some of which treated aspects of Los Angeles life. But these works are of limited interest, and the fact remains that extended fictional works about Los Angeles by Mexican American authors did not appear until the 1970s."[2] Clearly, Paredes, in finding *El Clamor*'s poetry wanting, betrayed a perceptual blindness that resulted from his early privileging of the published Chicana/o poetry and the *corrido*'s oral lyric forms.[3] It did not occur to Paredes to consider the possibility that the masterful defenses of Mexican civil rights Francisco Ramírez wrote and published in Spanish could be interpreted as literary performances that arguably surpassed Acosta's command of English. Thus, whether he intended it or not, his broad brush also ignored the blistering and eloquent critiques of U.S. imperialism and monopoly capitalism that a handful of Mexican anarchists had penned and published in early-twentieth-century Los Angeles. Paredes's bias in favor of the fictional text recruited the seemingly invisible high/low genre dichotomies that have helped to maintain Latina/o nonfiction's literary exile.

Despite the multifaceted techniques that disguise these disappearing effects, the threats and challenges nonfiction Latina/o texts have posed to the technology of literary secrecy are not so hard to grasp. The authors of this extremely varied literature have, at different times, recorded and denounced the progressive racialization and subalternization of Latina/os that have restricted or denied their claims to U.S. citizenship. At other times these writers, most notably early-twentieth-century anarchist authors, have challenged the imposition of national borders as nothing more than corporate capital's method for securing cheaper labor. Starting in the 1970s, Latina and Chicana feminist and gay nonfiction authors would launch a new series of literary interventions. Their celebrations and defenses of gay sexuality and non-binary gender identities would eventually lead to an explicit critique of the categories of gender, racial, class, and national difference that had marginalized their writing within and without the Latina/o community. Their critiques cut in multiple directions—against the socially constructed categories of the nation-state that had relegated them, as children of or members of the working class, to the status of second-class or noncitizens and against the 1960s male Chicano cultural nationalism that recycled colonial era and Mexican nationalist narratives of gender and gay difference to maintain a "heterosexist monopoly" on Chicana/o identity.[4] In the 1970s veteran Chicana/o writer-activists echoed the critical intentions of Latina nonfiction authors who challenged that monopoly of meaning with writing experiments that transgressed the boundaries of the essay, memoir, cultural theory, and poetry. Formed in that period of radical Left politics that spanned the Mexican Revolution to the mass labor mobilizations of the 1930s, these supportive though critical participant-observers noted that the early Chicana/o movement's emphasis upon a minority identity politics would eventually exhaust its generation's youthful energy and require a critique adequate to the emergence of Latina/o working-class urban majorities.[5] Meanwhile, a new generation of Chicana/o artist cadres such as Asco experimented with a variety of expressive forms, including subversive interpretations of nonfiction narrative, which explored and validated the spectrum of nonconforming Latina/o subjectivities, from gay to transgender and more, increasingly performed in the city's cosmopolitan spaces. Prior to, during, and after this literary avant-garde's emergence, Latina/o authors established themselves as professional journalists who launched a national dialogue on what it meant to be Latina, Latino, or Latinx in a global city. All these tendencies—the critique of racial, gender, sexual, class, and national boundaries and the embodied performances of these identities—eventually displaced Chicana/o cultural nationalism and opened a space for a dialogue focused on the intersections of transnationalism, globalization, and cultural hybridity in the neoliberal city.

The texts included in this collection can therefore be read as a geology of a contested urban present that, in challenging the uncritical, untheorized, or disjointed descriptions that kept this literature's rarely understood matrix of texts in the shadows, now requires a fresh reading of the literature's historical and literary precursors. Its focus on the urban emphasizes the meanings and functions of literary spatial and temporal domains, beginning with the seventeenth-century Spanish *crónicas de conquista* and *cartas de relación*, written during the conquest of the North American Southwest en route to California. The anthology's critical trajectory also requires challenging the assumption that this literature appeared ready-made and that its texts must be triangulated in relation to the "mainstream" nonfiction literatures of "objectivity" that had dominated U.S. English-language journalism and not the much older Hispanophone literatures that have periodically crystallized in U.S. Latina/o nonfiction. Indeed, we find many of the predecessors of U.S. Latina/o nonfiction informed by, or in critical dialogue with, the *crónicas de conquista* and *cartas de relación* written by colonial explorers who tried to present their adventures as fruitful investments for the Spanish crown or other potential sponsors. Using all the available rhetorical devices, including hyperbole, they depicted the so-called New World as a perfect opportunity for conquering new souls for the Catholic Church and collecting gold, silver, and spices for the empire but also questioned these purposes.

In North America, Álvar Núñez Cabeza de Vaca's (c. 1488–c. 1558) *Naufragios* (*The Shipwrecked Men*),[6] a Spanish-language *crónica* of his incredible trek through today's southeastern and southwestern United States (1542), illustrates this critical tendency by inconveniently documenting his expedition's failed *toma de posesión* (land takeover) and the astounding scale of an unintended genocide he witnessed on his decade-long trek from today's

Florida to what was then northern New Spain. Despite the subjectivity that characterizes the genre, Cabeza de Vaca's *crónica* declares the veracity of the facts he is relating in what is now considered the first historical narration, not to mention survival story / travelogue, written about the United States. Like U.S. Latina/o authors who today write nonfiction to assert truth claims that remind the reader of the text's objective moorings, his chronicle's persuasiveness relied upon mimetic correspondence to an external material world. The naming and narration with which Cabeza de Vaca symbolically laid claim to the land he "discovered" also relied upon the genre's implicit truth claims to apologize for the Pánfilo de Narváez expedition's 1527 shipwreck in what is now Tampa, Florida.

Likewise, the Franciscan Friar Junípero Serra (1713–84), who founded nine Franciscan missions in California between 1769 and 1782, and Father Juan Crespi, who chronicled these expeditions from today's San Diego to San Francisco, recruited the form to convince their royal and religious sponsors in Guadalajara, Mexico City, and Madrid of the project's success. The awe-inspiring or terrifying sense of scale of the Cabeza de Vaca adventure and Serra's epic of foundation will surface again in the larger-than-life scales of the early-twentieth-century anarchist *cronistas* and memoirs of the Mexican Revolution. The anarchists' deadly confrontation with monopoly capitalism occurs within a transatlantic and thus transnational spatial scale, while a boy soldier's recollections of revolution is staged in the vastness of the Chihuahuan wilderness, in which he struggled to survive the horrors of combat, thirst, and starvation.

To recognize the mimetic practices of Latina/o literature's colonial legacy does not, however, preclude the possibility that its river of nonfiction texts also carries entire cities of spectral voices in its current. For in adopting European literacy, the literature also questioned and subverted the West's dominant representational paradigm. The Hispanic literary archive is not, in this sense, that different from the hemisphere's English-language literature: both have marginalized testimonies of the hemisphere's indigenous as well as African and Asian diasporic nonfiction writers; both have deployed the Derridian "re-mark," those literary gestures that remind the reader they are reading a "true" story,[7] to subvert colonizing regimes of truth. We refer here to the European chroniclers of genocide, such as Bartolomé de Las Casas, who documented the eradication of the Caribbean's Taino and Carib populations, the native authors who wrote the *Historia de Tlatelolco desde los tiempos más remotos* in Nahuatl on or about 1528 in the Latin alphabet, and the anonymous seventeenth-century scribe who chronicled a strike of Nahua-speaking bakers that prevented a consortium of Spaniards from monopolizing its production in New Spain's Puebla de Los Angeles.[8] These inconvenient voices would make themselves audible again in the twentieth century, when Chicano memoirist Alejandro Murguía challenged Father Junípero Serra's now officially beatified image as a benevolent civilizer with his memories of a patronizing mission system that precipitated the near-collapse of California's native populations. These voices of negation have not only turned nonfiction's mimetic authority against the capitalist colonizing epic in the Americas; they have also invoked the fragmented, though persistent, echoes of pre-Hispanic writing systems and literary forms whenever their radically different ideas about writing, chronology, and representation found their ways into the Hispanic archive. Whether encoded in the circa 1540 Cuauhtinchan Map No. 2's narrative imaging of a native lineage's claim to local political authority, commodity tribute registers, migration myths, and indigenous chronicles of the Spanish conquest, Mesoamericans fused their hybrid methods of writing-painting, based in a preference for the paintbrush that blurred these European distinctions, with European alphabetic writing to question colonial authority and assert their ways of knowing and thinking.[9] The sixteenth-century writing instruments that Friars Bernardino de Sahagún and Diego Durán taught to their Nahua scribes in their efforts to effect more efficient conversions also preserved questioning pre-Hispanic ghosts. Hernando Ruiz de Alarcón's 1629 treatise against so-called Nahua sorcery inadvertently documented the exquisite poetry of Mesoamerican shamanic incantation.

That older poetics reappeared in Anzaldúa's nonfiction narrative *Borderlands / La Frontera* (1987), when she imagined the pre-Hispanic shaman's underworld journey as a ritual for inhabiting the trance states in which she experiences her death and rebirth into a bodily awareness of her "New Mestiza" identity.[10] Subsequent feminist theorizations of embodiment allow us to understand how her literary performance of the trance drew directly from the Mesoamerican cosmology's understanding of the human body as a ritual event (and not an object) made flesh by the convergence of cosmic and accidental forces.[11] Here the performance of space making strives to evoke an atmosphere in which we gain awareness of it from sensory experience. The conceptual space Anzaldúa invents for her literary performances, Walter Mignolo argues, thus represents a major theoretical achievement because it opens the positionality of an in-between space "from where to think rather than a hybrid space to talk about, a hybrid thinking-space of Spanish / Latin American and Amerindian legacies as the condition of possibility for Spanish / Latin American and Amerindian postcolonial theories."[12]

Latina/o authors would follow through with Anzaldúa's movement toward an aesthetics of performance and embodiment by writing nonfiction narratives that explore alternative possibilities of being and acting in a neoliberal globalized world. For example, anthology contributors Harry Gamboa Jr. and Guillermo Gómez-Peña reinvent the nineteenth-century flâneur in their performances of postmodern Chicano sensibility. Whereas the nineteenth-century flâneur chronicled urban fashion, parlor manners, and café society with a bourgeoisie dandy's condescending gaze, Gómez-Peña invents the persona of the "border brujo" who chronicles the juxtapositions, ironies, and radical hybridity of the deterritorialized global metropolis to subvert the hegemony of mimetic narrative from below and create an ambience for performing his subjective truths. Both these writer-performers also make their interpretive frameworks explicit, a major faux pas for conventional literary journalism or the novel, which ask their readers to deduce the author's ideas from the interplay of narrative and characters. Instead, they unsettle the naturalness of mimetic narration with rapid fluctuations between personal essay, memoir, conceptual performance, and manifesto. Finally, the subjective turn associated with memoir, autobiography, and the diary, which have long insinuated themselves in the *crónica* and U.S. literary journalism, particularly after the 1960s, when Anaïs Nin's journaling and the New Journalism (Truman Capote, Norman Mailer, Gay Talese, Joan Didion, Hunter S. Thompson, and Tom Wolfe) asserted their subjective truths, round out late-twentieth- and twenty-first-century Latina/o creative nonfiction's contributing forms and stylistic influences. Charting the spectral voices flowing through LA's Latina/o nonfiction literature, however, had lacked an epistemology of its borderlands spaces.

Among the critics who have attempted it is José David Saldívar, whose 1991 essay collection, *The Dialectics of Our America: Genealogy, Cultural Critique, and Literary History*, established three principles for a critical genealogy of Latina/o nonfiction. First, he challenged the additive logic of the neoliberal multiculturalist agenda by arguing that simply adding texts of racialized and gendered Others to the national literary canon would not be enough to reform the "American" exceptionalism that colonized and domesticated their meanings. Instead, the discourse of "America" itself, he argued, would have to be questioned before the so-called minority (therefore peripheral) literatures could become fully visible, audible, and legible. Second, Saldívar's revisionist reframing turned to José Martí's landmark anti-imperialist *crónica*-manifesto "Nuestra América" ("Our America"), published in 1891, for its reimagining of cosmopolitan decolonial spaces. Taking Anzaldúa's lead, Saldívar identified the borderlands as the name of that imaginary and actual place from which its texts could become audible and legible.

From these two principles, Saldívar proposed a third. Using Martí's "Nuestra América" as his model, Saldívar dissolved genre hierarchies to argue that the tools of literary criticism used to interpret the novel, poetry, or drama could be applied to Latina/o nonfiction. Taking this extra step opened a new critical space for interpreting Latina/o literary nonfiction, including its stance toward the United States and Latin America as well as its affirmations of what the U.S. and Latin American literatures have in common. In his own words, "The greatest shortcoming of the work being done on the American canon is not its lack of theoretical rigor, but its parochial vision. Literary historians (even the newer ones) and critics working on the reconstruction of American literary history characteristically know little in depth about the history, symbologies, cultures, and discourses of the Americas. One value of focusing on comparative cultural studies is that it permits us to escape from the provincial, limiting tacit assumptions that result from perpetual immersion in studying a single culture or literature."[13]

Thus, in the tradition of Latin American postcolonial and decolonial criticism, our anthology seeks to expand on Saldívar's project by focusing upon LA's Latina/o *crónica* and literary nonfiction as the most intense expression of an urban cosmopolitanism. It further assumes that the global city, the place where Othered people go to escape the economic-environmental disaster zones of neoliberal capitalism, embodies the arena in which they experiment in new humanizing identity projects by continuing to discover their differences as radical post-national commonalities.

The 2011 publication of Nicolás Kanellos's *Hispanic Immigrant Literature: El sueño del retorno* and his preceding decade of archive construction offered the other inspiration for our project. Our anthology focuses on the *crónica* and other nonfiction because these genres have always represented the largest source of Latina/o literary production, as evidenced by Latina/o documentary history in the United States holdings at the *Recovering the U.S. Hispanic Literary Heritage Project*. This project, directed by Kanellos, focuses on finding, preserving, and disseminating U.S. Hispanic culture from colonial times until 1960. It has compiled, microfilmed, and digitized thousands of original books, pamphlets, manuscripts, archival items, photographs, and personal papers produced by Latina/os in the United States. Significantly, among its holdings is a microfilm collection of approximately fourteen hundred historical newspapers published from 1801 through the 1960s (listed in Kanellos's *Hispanic Periodicals in the United States: A Brief History and Comprehensive Bibliography* [2000]), which gives us an idea of the scale of U.S. Latina/o nonfiction writing. The importance of these periodicals must not be underestimated since, as Kallenos explains, "almost all Hispanic immigrant newspapers announced their service in protection of the community in their mastheads and in editorials, and some of them followed up on this commitment by leading campaigns to desegregate schools, movie houses, and other facilities and to construct alternative institutions for the Hispanic community's use." Moreover, as he reminds us, "newspapers were the primary publishers of creative literature and had the most direct impact on the transmigrants owing to their immediacy and pervasiveness in the communities."[14]

To the cultural production of U.S. Latina/os, we add that of Latin Americans who write from the United States as exiles or critical visitors. Viviane Mahieux, in her study "The Chronicle," included in the 2012 *Oxford Bibliographies in Latin American Studies*, lists several important authors. As could be expected, one of the most celebrated is the Cuban José Martí, whose New York writings were not collected until 2003 in *En los Estados Unidos: Periodismo de*

1881–1892 (In the United States: Journalism from 1881–1892). As Mahieux explains, during the 1920s the Mexican José Juan Tablada also lived in New York, where he wrote his column "Nueva York de día y de noche" (New York during the Day and at Night) for the Mexico City daily *El Universal*. These writings would later be collected in *La babilonia de hierro, crónicas neoyorkinas* (The Iron Babylon, New York Chronicles [2000]). During the 1940s, she adds, the lesser-known Chilean Rosamel del Valle also wrote about New York for a Latin American audience. Fifty of her *crónicas* were collected in *Crónicas de New York* (Chronicles of New York [2002]). And this time from San Francisco, the Mexican Nobel Prize laureate Octavio Paz would write *crónicas* about the 1945 peace conference included in *Crónica trunca de días excepcionales* (Truncated Chronicle of Exceptional Days [2007]). In addition, Mahieux lists Alma Guillermoprieto's *Looking for History: Dispatches from Latin America* (2001), which collects her *crónicas* about different Latin American countries and public figures originally published in the *New Yorker* and the *New York Review of Books*. She also cites Diego Fonseca and Aileen El-Kadi's collection *Sam no es mi tío: Veinticuatro crónicas migrantes y un sueño americano* (Sam Is Not My Uncle: Twenty-Four Migrant Chronicles and An American Dream [2012]), with *crónicas* by the Peruvian American Daniel Alarcón, the Mexican Yuri Herrera, and the Mexican American Ilan Stavans in which they reflect about their experience in the United States. This anthology proposes, therefore, a significant redefinition of U.S. Latina/o literary history and another model for English, Spanish, and Latina/o studies. Along with *crónicas*, it assembles a selection of the life-writing genres of memoir and (auto)biography, as well as of epistolary writing, manifestos, testimonials, political propaganda, and other nonfiction genres, to suggest the arc of Latina/o thought from assimilationism to cultural nationalism and from Mexican nationalist to pan-Latina/o or transnational approaches.

Still, despite these achievements, Kanellos concludes that the marginalizing omissions that have disappeared the foundational "literature written in Spanish on American shores condemn that language and its speakers to perpetual foreignness and estrangement from the American nation."[15] To our knowledge, there are no book-length studies of the U.S. or LA *crónica* equivalent to Latin America's *Contemporary Mexican Chronicle: Theoretical Perspectives on the Liminal Genre* (2002), edited by Ignacio Corona and Beth E. Jörgensen, Esperança Bielsa's *Latin American Urban Crónica: Between Literature and Mass Culture* (2006), or Viviane Mahieux's *Urban Chroniclers in Modern Latin America: The Shared Intimacy of Everyday Life* (2011).[16] One reason for this dearth of criticism is that, as Kanellos points out, some American critics assume that first-generation immigrants do not write literature simply because they may not write it in English: "In their introduction the two editors [Katherine B. Payant and Toby Rose, in their edited collection *The Immigrant Experience in North American Literature: Carving out a Niche*] actually articulate their justification for studying second- and third-generation writers with roots in the Third World: 'This reflects the fact that first-generation, non-English speakers of any nationality seldom produce much literature.'" It is precisely this ignorance of an entire corpus of literature that led us to write this book.[17] Kanellos proves the opposite to be true, at least in the case of Latinas/os in the United States, with the large amounts of documents, books, and periodicals gathered by the *Recovering the U.S. Hispanic Literary Heritage Project*, many of them exhibiting the unbroken link with the pan-Hispanic imaginary. Our anthology shares his conceptual approach by taking for granted that U.S. Latina/o literature continued to draw themes, styles, and narrative forms for the same Hispanic tradition that preceded the U.S. annexation of Mexican territories. It is, therefore, not a recently born literature, as Kanellos correctly affirms. Likewise, it would be a mistake to conceive of Chicana/o, Nuyorican, and Cuban American literatures as segregated from one another: "These literatures are all intimately connected to trans-migrant culture and its literary expression; they must be seen on the continuum of transnationalism."[18]

Regarding our selection criteria, it is important to note that we have focused on works that have either never appeared in print; have not been recognized as literary; have not been recognized as pertaining to Latina/o literature; or have not been recognized as expressive of Latina/o literary forms or urban subjectivity. The selection of texts also responds to our goal of providing an inventory of different nonfiction forms, including both early and twentieth-century *crónica*, *testimonio*, memoir, letters, and examples of performance-inspired experiments in genre hybridity. Our selection's rationale also expresses our desire: to test the idea of an "urban humanities" of social intervention and institutional change; to open a new line of literary inquiry; to stretch the limits of what can be considered U.S. Latina/o nonfiction; and to include works we consider representative of their own subgenre and period. Each of these criteria, therefore, serves an overall critical purpose. While the selected texts are variegated in both chronology and subgenre, together they suggest the extent to which an entire corpus of Spanish- and English-language works has been ignored by critics of Los Angeles cultural production. Rather than suggest an act of canonic substitution, we have therefore envisioned this anthology as a collection of exceptions that attempts to disrupt the national literary field, an essential step in reimagining the humanities in the global city.

That critical-imaginative effort, however, requires a comprehensive view of a field, including a critical orientation that conceptualizes the complex fabric of LA's Latina/o nonfiction. But literary recovery cannot proceed without also addressing the uneven development of nonfiction literary criticism and the daunting variety of texts and subgenres that constitute the Latina/o nonfiction archive. For us simply acknowledging the complexity of this challenge was not enough. We had to tentatively imagine its totality to appreciate its complexity—the fabric of English- and Spanish-language literatures that have contributed to the weave of U.S. Latina/o nonfiction and its numerous hybrids—and to identify the disjunctions resulting from the uneven development of nonfiction literary criticism. As we hope to have shown, the greater levels of U.S. Latina/o and Latin American scholarship on literary nonfiction have not been matched by fourth genre criticism in the United States. Its U.S. scholarship continues to fracture its focus on individual works and subgenres—long form nonfiction narrative, personal essay, life writing, and biography. Meanwhile, English and Creative Nonfiction programs continue to teach the genre's fine points but not explore its comprehensive criticism. Latina/o literary nonfiction, however, pays a higher price for this uneven, fractured critical focus, regardless of the canon editor's or scholar's intentions.

We found evidence of these ruptures in Julian Murphet's *Literature and Race in Los Angeles*, and his interpretation of Luis J. Rodríguez's 1989 collection *Poems across the Pavement*. Murphet's 2001 study recognized the ways Rodríguez's poems mobilized a Chicana/o urban subjectivity deeply rooted in class struggle and its unique claims upon its places (Watts, East LA, and the LA

River) to challenge the canon's city-without-history motif. Indeed, Murphet challenged the canon when he used Rodríguez's poetry to question its recent postmodernist obsessions with surface morphology and simulacra, which reinforce representations of LA's multicultural illegibility and cacophony. "It will be recalled," Murphet wrote, recycling a Chicana/o idiom,

> that between 1822 and 1848, Mexico had possession over the entire region of Califas, before the Mexican-American war (and a few million dollars) handed the territory to the American victor. Since 1848, the anomalous position of Mexican-Americans, or Chicanos, in Southern California society has greatly helped to define its character and culture. At once "native," since they preceded the gringo settlers by many years, and outside the dominant bloc due to prevailing ethnic and linguistic chauvinism, Chicanos have never ceased to immigrate (legally and otherwise) to land that was once their own, but which now seeks violently to exclude and marginalize them.[19]

Unfortunately, because he built his argument upon the 1970s Chicana/o literary criticism referenced at the start of this essay, his analysis slid back into a presentism that overemphasized the 1960s Chicana/o poetry at the expense of LA Latina/o nonfiction. Closely echoing Paredes, Murphet implausibly argued that "it was not until the 1960s that Chicano literature emerged as such, having until that time lived a fugitive and anonymous existence in other forms."[20] Reliance on outdated Chicana/o literary criticism led him to ignore the older, richer archive of Latina/o nonfiction and recent criticism that have explored that literature's transnational networks and challenged the mostly male, Chicana/o cultural nationalism that pretended to provide ready-made identities for the increasing Mexican and Central American immigration that radicalized the city's labor struggles and politics.[21]

Again, the very scale of our undertaking, in attempting to address this critical and archival imbalance, points to an unfinished project, one that asks for reconsiderations of one-dimensional or simplistic theoretical approaches. It could not be otherwise. Many elements of our enterprise need to be tested before the weave of its literary domains can become fully visible. We therefore hope that this anthology will inspire others to test, correct, and improve upon our efforts to interpret the spatial imaginaries, place-making narratives, and transnational networks of Latina/o literary nonfiction in other U.S. global cities, such as New York, Chicago, and Miami. A deepened understanding of Latina/o nonfiction contributions would also inspire authors and scholars of other, non-English phantom literatures to construct other urban literary observatories. Furthermore, the accumulating visibility of formerly phantom literatures should eventually create constituencies for challenging the discursive service that the humanities still provide to the U.S. empire whenever they revalidate its myth of national exceptionalism and its latest fetish, the neoliberal governmentalities that fuel the financial crises and wars that drive new immigrants from the global South to the cities of the developed North. As the latest media images constantly remind us, by appealing to and exaggerating our fears, the global city's attraction to immigrants will continue because it continues to organize and administer a neoliberal economy that makes the hinterlands uninhabitable wastelands of despair.

Selections

Selection 1

Nonfiction writing in Los Angeles has its roots in the chronicles of European explorers, conquistadors, and friars who colonized the territories that are today part of the southwestern United States and the Mexican northwestern border states, including Baja California. In the fascinating collection of Jesuit chronicles about the settlement of Baja California, *Crónicas jesuíticas de la antigua California* (2000), edited by Ignacio del Río, we find an insider's survey of Jesuit activities in the peninsula from 1697 through 1767, when Charles III of Spain expelled the Company of Jesus, as well as of the indigenous hunter-gatherer groups that populated the area. The chronicles reveal the Jesuits' motivation to evangelize Baja California and to incorporate indigenous groups into a mission system that would transform them into peasant subjects. The text's representations of Baja California (the one that the Spaniards conquered first) give us the spatial imaginary of Jesuit evangelization. After all, until the nineteenth century Spaniards would talk about the Californias, Alta and Baja, as a single geographic unit. As Ignacio del Río explains, some of the texts, including the one from 1721 by the Italian padre IGNACIO MARÍA NÁPOLI selected in our anthology, are *cartas de relación* (letters or dispatches with a personal account of the conquest or exploration) explaining the first contacts with local indigenous groups. Other *crónicas* focus on the conversion of the Indians, a particular mission, an ethnographic view of an indigenous group, indigenous rebellions, or historiographic accounts. In the Jesuit *crónica* included here, we find the European priests' astonishment upon their encounter with a completely different culture. At the outset, once their initial mutual distrust is overcome, they are shocked to find out that one of the tribes, whose men and women are almost completely naked, has a woman as their ruler. When this indigenous group meets the Europeans, to the priests' disbelief, the men invite them to sleep with their wives. According to the chronicler, the Spaniards politely refused the offer. The chronicler also finds, in this strange (to him) custom, a reason for the presence of children with European features: he knows of the presence of English sailors in the area. Napoli, in a Spanish language influenced by his native Italian that nevertheless shares the Spanish habit of using culinary metaphors to construct native savagery, also describes Indian eating habits with disgust: they like to eat lice, lizards, mice, snakes, and other things the Europeans find repulsive. In the end, when an epidemic decimates the local population, the indigenous groups blame the Italian padre.

"With the Amicable People of Ensenada de Palmas"

Excerpt from *Breve relación de la nueva entrada al sur, en la copiosa gentilidad de la nación de los coras . . . , por el padre*

IGNACIO MARÍA NÁPOLI, S.J.
TRANSLATED BY IGNACIO LÓPEZ-CALVO

I did not stop entrusting the success [of the enterprise] to the Holy Virgin; under her powerful patronage, I hoped for the victory over the considerable delays that the Devil was plotting, and in case of having to return, I wished to first see some Indians so that I could give them something of what I brought through land and appreciate their temperament and talent. And while I was walking by myself by the beach, somewhat pensive, I met some naked Indians that came running toward me. One of them, very tall and fat, was the main shaman among them, all painted in black, and he looked like a devil. In his head he had some tales of deer skin and several feathers; his yelling was so horrendous and loud as the sky, singing and making unwanted gestures. This one had a very large mustache.

I, not knowing what to do . . . , commended myself to the Lord. I showed them a lot of love, telling them a few things in their language, which I had learned from the Indians of San José, who are of the same nation. I gave them knives that I had, and bringing them with me, they came to my tent, where I gave them boiled corn, I covered them with a sackcloth, I gave them hats and blankets, and then the screams ended.

They slept there with us, and seeing that we gave them things, they said that we were good and that they wanted to call more of their people, who were down there, but before they wanted us to hide the beasts, which scared them very much, and especially a dog, which made them shake.

They left in the morning to bring their people; they began to come in groups of thirty, and what surprised me the most was that they came without arches and arrows, and each one of them had several gifts in their hands to give me.

I, as they were coming, showed them love, made them sit down, put trinkets on their necks. I gave them hats, quite a bit of sackcloth, blankets, knives, and other little things that they appreciate. In not much time, we saw quite a number of people gathering, perhaps about five hundred men. And what confirmed that there had to be a much larger amount of people was that there were no elderly people, women, or children; therefore, keeping in mind the proportion, we guessed that there would be more than a thousand people.

I could not figure out what religion they have because they do not have the hair and ears cut, like the other people in the Californias. And since the interpreter was not there, it is hard for me to understand them; but I hope to get by with the little I know, asking them about the names of things, which I know how to ask in their language, and writing it down, and this way, so far, I have written almost a hundred of the most useful words.

What we saw is that they are a very docile and kind people. All men are naked; women . . . dress more honestly than others from California because they have some kind of underskirt made of palm. They eat seeds from the country, dragon fruit, a lot of fish, and a kind of fruit that is very good and tasty, which they call plum, which even though it is wild, it is very tasty and fresh, and it has the same shape and taste as apricots, and I cannot tell the difference between them. And this type is very useful since from the seed they harvest, and it is better than almonds or pine nuts. But since they do not have this fruit all year around, the poor souls, during the winter they eat again the same seeds that they ate during the summer, without realizing how disgusting this is. What I found disgusting was to see them eating lice, vipers, snakes, mice, and all kinds of filthy animals, such as lizards, roots of herbs, and even fish bones.

The biggest docility that we saw in them was that even though Father Jaime had brought some Guaycur Indians with him, his children, who are their mortal enemies, these Guaycurs, having come strongly armed with their bows and arrows, were well treated and taken care of by the Coras, his enemies, who came with no weapons and with a lot of trust in us.

For several nights the poor souls would offer their women to us, thinking [that gesture], as they guess in their kindness, to be an act of hospitality and lavishness. They would offer their women to us, who came a little later with some children, but still not being as many as the men, who were many. And when I told (to the person they considered their chief), in their language, that priests do not have or want women, they were very shocked. I cannot express the gratitude and love that they showed us, and especially to me, which is abundant among these gentile barbarians.

They gave me several deer leathers, which are big; they put several plumages on my head, weaved with little strings and painted in several colors; they gave me several trays made of palm, well made and in different colors, and many mallets made of palm beads, like thin and polished rosaries, putting them from my neck, which is the nicest thing they wear in their celebrations. Three times a day they all brought me the best food they could find of their fruits and agave.

I have never seen people as tall as these ones; their body was well proportioned, fat, and very white and red, and particularly the children looked like Englishmen or Flemish, being so white and red. I guess that some, the ones that look so different from the other ones, must be offspring of Englishmen because they have been in that cape, and they have waited for the Manila Galleon, which is where it stops; and since these poor souls offer their women as a courtesy, it is not such a wild guess among such heretic people.

Every day I give all these people a large pot of maize stew [pozole], which is the best gift they can receive and the only way to conquer them.

During the fifth day after our arrival, and even being distracted with the Indians, we did not stop being concerned about seeing the canoes empty of people; but the Saint Virgin prevented the Devil from triumphing all the way because the Indians, to whom I had asked to wait for said canoes with food and clothing for them, began to inform us, through gestures and signs and with some words I understood, that the canoes had arrived to the lagoons farther down five days earlier. The consolation we had was great, and then we tried to send an Indian with a piece of paper, in which we warned said canoes that we were in the upper side.

But it was not easy to find one who wanted to go because they were very scared of the paper, believing that it was some sort of spell or involved spirit; but through gifts, the bravest of them ended up going, but from time to time he would throw the piece of paper on the floor to exorcise it.

God decided that before the Indian arrived at the canoes, they themselves came to look for us and found us at the tent, where we were comfortable. Day after day a larger number of new people from those Indians would arrive, with whom I shared everything we had brought by sea at the time (it made us laugh very much).

An Indian woman appeared, dressed in very good and colorful deer leather, accompanied by several other Indian women, who were her entourage, like damsels. She came yelling horribly, singing, and with admirable power and command, such that later she handed over the command to the Indian with a mustache, and he, like everyone else, obeyed her as if she were a queen. And they later explained to us that this lady is the governor, the queen of this entire people.

And it is not a new thing because Father Jaime saw the first thing when he went to that cove thirteen years ago, that a woman was the one who governed; she was especially indulged as a queen, and she also reciprocated with some leathers and rosary mallets, trays and many fruits, which her maids were carrying. Then said queen ordered all those people to go find food, and then they brought such a large amount that we did not know where to put it.

It kept raining every day at the time, and even when we were half-covered by the sail, the floor was still humid and wet. The big novelty for the Indians was seeing the horses; and they called them *yappú*, which means "large deer." They shook in fear when they saw the boxes of dust, books, and paper, and when they saw us take them out, they would beg us, half-crying, to put them away and hide them.

We then began to carefully explore the land with the people, who also came in the canoes, although not as much as I wanted because the beasts we had were few and tired. We saw very beautiful and large palm groves, many reedbeds and many freshwater lagoons just by the ocean beach in said cove, very beautiful, with several *bateques* and water wells with no salt, which one could drink anywhere. We then sent two soldiers with beasts to said place of San Bernardo, to bring the supplies we had left behind. In the meantime we explored together with the captain other spots in that cove, less than a league from this mission. . . . It's all a path by a creek, and we found, in the foothills of those mountains, very good lands and without flooding, with a great river of running water, which is larger than, and as good as, the ones we have found so far in all the lands of California. But to bring the water out one needs some strength, and it is not as easy as the previously mentioned ones . . . farther up, but far from the mission.

The following day we went farther down, toward the south, near the tip of that cove, where there were more large lagoons and palm groves, very big, with spacious plains, many reedbeds and important water supplies, which move inside toward the hills; where it rains a lot every day, but the waters do not always reach the beach, where we were. We found several places that were very good for settling said mission. It is true that it would have been better to have found it in the said place of San Bernardo or in the plains of Santa Rosalía; but because they were uninhabited lands and the Indians were far, it was necessary to set foot where they live, to manage to convert them, while I was with them.

The following day we went to explore two leagues farther down, and I liked the place very much because of the very beautiful view of both the land with the width of the sea and because it has a very high mound where we can build the house. But after thinking about it and pondering, I thought it would be better to stay where we were since the first day because I would have gone farther from the mission of La Paz, the only place whence I can hope for help to find supplies until I can grow food.

Having, then, made that decision, we went to explore the mound, which is quite high, and, even like a mountain, it has a nice view, and it will become a good plain.

The infernal enemy, very upset, set another trap: he put mistrust in the heads of these Indians who saw us exploring this land, without our being able to explain why we were doing it, and they also saw that with us there were

Guaycur Indians, their enemies, with whom they have had several battles and deaths, which they celebrated in their face, and they imagined that we sent people to call the Guaycur Indians, when we sent people back to pick up the supplies left behind in San Bernardo, so that their enemies would come to kill them all, which is the only and worst harm that they receive from one another, even though they are from the same nation and language. And since these were without bows and arrows, off guard with women and children, they determined to return, and they began to leave, fleeing scared.

Much was then my pain, seeing the Devil triumph, since I was about to baptize them, at least those thirty-three who were together. And to that end, every afternoon I gathered those little children, giving them food to tame them and see if the number of them was growing, as I hoped, together with the others who were missing. I had sent people to call them promising knives to whomever brought them so that on September 8, on the festivity of the birth of Our Lady, I could baptize them all together.

I went rapidly by the beach to stop them and began, as I could, to explain to them, lavishing them and giving them several gifts, that I had not sent people to call their enemies, the Guaycures or the Aripes, but to bring the food left behind to give it to them. The Virgin wanted them to come back with me, and since it was night, they made their fire, and I went to bed, leaving them calm. But since I observed that they were alert all night with their bows and arrows that they had brought from their village, we did not stop either to post soldier sentinels, to prevent something from happening to us.

I went to rest more consoled, after seeing that I had managed to make them stay, determined to not wait any longer for their baptism the following morning; but as soon as we woke up, we found out that during the night they had all left, and there was not even a boy left.

We became very suspicious upon seeing how much they mistrusted us, and we stopped celebrating Mass for some time, not knowing what could have happened to us; but I did not lose hope, and I commended myself to the advocate of the sinners, who is also mother of the conversion of the souls, and we saw the prodigy because on the same day in which is the Novena for her birth, we saw the women come with a few men, who were carrying several boys and girls on their backs, coming very fast to offer them for sacred baptism.

The following day, other men began to come, and with them came the Indian woman who was their governor, who, once she was close to us, began to scream horribly and to sing with an infernal voice several songs and spell, in the place where we had come, where their Guaycur enemies are, screaming horribly so that their enemies would not come to kill them. And they did the same thing every night, even more than during the day, and in the end their leaders, singing their songs all night like a litany, to which the chorus responded, did not allow us to close our eyes for several nights.

Once our people came, we began to prepare the hill and to cut palms in order to build a house soon, but we only could leave it roofed, waiting for our return, when we could build the adobe walls. We left several things in it, such as a pot and another tool, because of the difficulties we were now going through, not having enough beasts or boats ready to transport them again.

For two days we did not see their chief with the big mustache who always helped us. We did not know . . . what to think; we thought that he might have gone down to call other Indians, so that they come. I was praying . . . among the others who were not far from us, and I went with the captain to their village, on foot, to see if the Indian with the big mustache would appear. And once I arrived there, I found him lying down on the floor, sick and half-crying. And on top of him was an old Indian, who is the shaman, who stroked him and yelled, singing songs, scaring death, and he hit his navel and all his body, which only this was enough to kill him.

I then had all the people around him go away, and the nurse, and checking the ill man, I realized that he only had a cold, with a little fever. I gave him some tortillas to eat, and it was necessary to cover him with a cloth, of which God had given us, from the chill of the night. He became comforted, and the next morning he got up and came to us, a little better, which was the same day in which we returned again to La Paz.

Several of them had begun to get a cold, and they always tend to guess that we brought the illness because one of their principles is that there is no death or natural illness and that all is because of a spell. And while I was in La Paz, where an epidemic had begun among the Indians, the interpreter told me that they said my arriving there had brought the disease because I am a witch doctor, and the sign is that I have a long beard.

Before leaving said Ensenada de Palmas, I told the Indians to take care of the house we had started and the utensils that were inside it, and they, with signs and gestures, promised me to watch over it. I told them that I was leaving but I would return to live with them and that I would bring food to give it to them and that I would return in a few days.

Selection 2

Moving on to nineteenth-century Los Angeles, one of the first leading Latina/o voices in Los Angeles journalism was the teenager FRANCISCO P. RAMÍREZ (1837–1908). At the early age of fourteen, he began to work for the journal the *Los Angeles Star*, which had a Spanish-language section titled "La Estrella de Los Angeles." In 1854 Ramírez became the editor of this section, and in June 1855, at age seventeen, he founded and became the editor of the four-page *El Clamor Público* (The Public Outcry), the first Spanish-language weekly newspaper in Los Angeles and the third newspaper published in the city in any language. A tireless civil rights activist and outspoken community organizer, his liberal editorials in *El Clamor Público* condemned slavery and advocated for racial equality, the rights of minorities, and the education of women. He protested the discrimination and lynching of Hispanics in the United States and chronicled their odyssey into the disempowered status of second-class citizens. Until the weekly journal was closed down on December 31, 1859, the idealistic Ramírez encouraged Hispanics to abandon Californio ranchero conservatism and embrace the democratic franchise. He advised his readership on how to vote in presidential elections, usually recommending the Republican Party. The Republican Party had been founded in 1854 by antislavery activists, ex-Whigs, modernists, and ex-Free-Soilers.

Paul Bryan Gray's 2012 work *A Clamor for Equality: Emergence and Exile of Californio Activist Francisco P. Ramírez*, points out that Ramírez alienated most people around him, including Anglos who, sympathizing with slavery in the South, frowned upon his calls for racial equality for Mexicans, blacks, Chinese, Indigenous Californians, and Mexicans. Gray adds that Ramírez's principles, sympathetic to nineteenth-century Mexican radical liberalism, were also at odds with the conservative attitudes of Los Angeles's Mexican community and with the political apathy of most Los Angeles Mexicans (20). Regarding his political trajectory, Ramírez went from a moderate tone that supported the U.S. Constitution's ideals and promoted cooperation between Mexicans and Anglos to a more radical one that protested slavery and racial inequality. Ramírez went through other changes in his political views. According to Gray, in 1869 Ramírez became an attorney in Los Angeles but eventually had to flee in disgrace to Mexico for his involvement in promoting a fraudulent certificate of deposit. In 1908 he died in exile in Ensenada in complete anonymity, and unremembered in Los Angeles. Nothing was left of his days as a public figure, a lawyer, and a socially conscious young editor of *La Estrella de Los Ángeles*, *El Clamor Público*, *La Estrella de Occidente*, and *El Nuevo Mundo*, between the ages of eighteen to twenty-three (251).

In the selected *crónica*, "Folleto notable" (Notable Leaflet), published in *El Clamor Público* on March 19, 1859, Ramírez calls for an alliance between the Catholic Latin nations of the New and the Old World, and more specifically for a Franco-Spanish alliance, to put an end to the United States's annexationism and imperialism. Ramírez demonstrates his awareness of foreign affairs and the foreign press in his unyielding opposition to U.S. foreign policy. In his view the clash between Latin American nations and the United States not only suggests Comtian positivisms' progression from barbarism to civilization but also the racial-religious war that began in Europe during the Reformation. Like José Martí, Ramírez prophetically warns against the United States's insatiable thirst for territorial conquest and the importance of Cuba in its designs. The only way to save civilization, he assures his readers, is the alliance of the "Latin races." This selection also suggests much about his relationship to his French neighbor and mentor, Jean-Louis Vignes, his desperate alignment with French designs in the Americas, and probably the reason Ramírez attained an impressive command of literary French in three *El Clamor Público* issues he published to attract the city's French readers.

The Public Outcry. Noteworthy Pamphlet

FRANCISCO P. RAMÍREZ

TRANSLATED BY ROBERT RUDDER

In France a pamphlet has just been published that has attracted a great deal of attention. Its title is: Letter to His Majesty, Emperor Napoleon III, concerning the French influence in America and the Message of Mr. Buchanan. In publishing this letter, the *Courier des Etats Unis* says the following: It would be very difficult to make a precise judgment of this work. In spite of its having many inaccuracies, there is no hiding the fact that it holds, in a violent explosion, the sentiment of European opinion with regard to the politics of the United States as have been manifested by marauding expeditions, the Ostend Manifesto, and the latest Message of Mr. Buchanan. It also contains a vehement expression of moral censure against the Union in which there is nothing fictitious or personal. Since the country's press has been so preoccupied with this piece of writing, we hope there may be found in it a healthy sense of the need to vindicate the reputation of the United States, which at present is most in jeopardy in the eyes of the world.

The Latin Alliance

At the same time that, under the mask of progress, religious rebellions began to place Catholic unity in jeopardy, Catholicism made the world complete by revealing the existence of America; the great Isabel gave Christopher Columbus the means to carry out a mission that was given by God Himself, and the discovery of a new Continent, by mocking all the calculations of science and human reasoning, manifested the superiority of revelation over them. The Latin races that civilized the ancient world also civilized the new one, conquering it for the Faith and for unity, in the same way that they had conquered its rulers, and gaining in the virgin territories of America the land they had lost in Europe. Nevertheless, their adversaries were not long in following them to that new field of battle, and it is likely that in it will occur the struggle that force our times to resolve, once and for all, the great questions of race and unity that were posed by civilization and its adversaries.

America is divided naturally into two large parts that are joined by an isthmus whose possession will necessarily tempt the side that wishes to absorb the other at any cost. Not far from this isthmus, and like an observatory that Europe maintains in the most important Gulf in the New World, rises a fertile island that nothing has yet been able to strip from the power of the sons of those who discovered and civilized it. The conquest of the isthmus is the death of politics of Latin Europe; the invasion of the island is the death of religion. The isthmus becomes the road for new conquests as legitimate as that of the isthmus itself: the island is the arsenal of the fleet that would be created to come to overthrow Catholicism in Europe itself. And this is no exaggeration. Mr. Soulé, in person, confessed such projects, without concealing them from the Court in Madrid, and before he left Europe he made a pact with all the declared enemies of the Latin race. The desire of the United States to possess Mexico and Cuba has the objective not only of enlarging its territory and satisfying its interests; it is also obeying an idea diametrically opposed to what normally informs France. It is because they want no other civilization than that which they claim to have; it is because they are committed to all the men who are condemned by European societies. If the democratic republic triumphs in the New World, all kingdoms, all empires in the universe, will turn against it, and it will therefore be useful and legitimate to destroy them by force or by cunning. The United States is the foolhardy Reformer that, not having been able to triumph over Latin civilization with the assistance of Coligny, crossed the seas to return with force and fight against that civilization.

One of the great misfortunes of our times is that statesmen find it impossible to rise above political, commercial, industrial, or financial matters and judge the unlimited consequences that the triumph of the United States and the Monroe Doctrine can bring about in the future. For that reason, it is most urgent to have an alliance between the Latin races of the Old and the

New Worlds. . . . It would have been dangerous yesterday to counsel those statesmen to rise to such heights, because it would have been easy to accuse them of having let themselves be dragged along by chimeras that were more illusory than fearsome; because the threats were muffled, the dangers were not in sight, the invasions were disguised. But today it is impossible to have doubts: The threats are shouted aloud, the invasions are extolled, the dangers are certain. There is no fear of being treated like Cassandra when we prophesy that the object of the next attack will be civilization.

And what could increase that danger is the conviction that the threats being put forth by the president of the United States in his latest message only deserve to be scorned and that a disdainful smile is the best they deserve. In these times of ignorance, in which only the great minds can see the dangers the masses are unable to glimpse, the middle classes, who have become skeptical, think they can overcome everything with sarcasm, without recalling that the decadent Romans, while sitting around their tables loaded down with food and wines, laughed at the barbarians until the very moment when those barbarians burst into the hall and smashed the goblets of the orgy against their own lips. In such cases, a smile is not a sign of strength but of cowardice; disdain is the fear of seeing yourself compelled to fight. Adversaries like pirates and their sponsors are never deceived; they launch their ships and bring one to tears even before the smile can disappear.

Even supposing that it would be foolish to ask our degenerate times to consider something besides material interests, whose measures are so small when they are not subject to interests of another sort, Mr. Buchanan's message deserves no less than an energetic reply from Europe. Because the day that shared relations between America and the rest of the world disappear, the material interests of Europe will be severely compromised. Our commerce, our industry, will be ruled instead of imposing rules, and the discovery of the New World will have the unimaginable consequence of bringing on the death of the old one.

Notice, on the other hand, how quickly the level of audacity of the adversaries of civilization has risen as the level of our convictions has fallen. There is talk of the unity of atheism while we scarcely dare speak of the unity of faith. Mr. Buchanan talks about the right of peoples to be free of all guardianship, when we hardly dare to declare that those people who have a common belief are of one voice. Catholic sovereigns, upheld by God and their subjects, make use of obliqueness to reveal a legitimate aspiration. Which is why the one elected by an undisciplined gang of fraudulent fools and pirates dares to openly declare that the time has come for those pirates, those fraudulent fools, to assault civilization. Let us not, then, be any less convinced of the truth than they seem to be convinced that they are frauds. Let us not discuss their system of evil while fearing to proclaim our system of goodness. And let us hasten to urge the alliance of the Latin races, without which there is no salvation for civilization, since they, surpassing our skill, have been able to turn crime into a religion as we appear to renounce our own.

And the proof that the immediate result of this alliance would unhinge all of evil's plans is in the infinite efforts it makes to break apart that alliance before it is formed: in the imminence of a fratricidal fight as skillfully prepared as it is ill advised. It knows very well that once the fight has begun, its victory is certain, the isthmus and the island are its captive, and nothing will hold back its invading march toward the south, its destructive onslaught toward Europe. "The time is not far off," says Mr. Soulé in Madrid, "when an American fleet will put ashore fifty-thousand Yankees on the coasts of Europe, who will swallow in one gulp your supposed civilization." This is why Mr. Buchanan's message should be considered a serious document . . .

The message is openly directed against the faith, against ideas, against principles, against the interests of Europe, which it slaps on both cheeks . . .

Mr. Buchanan and the nation he represents do not try to hide it. They covet Cuba, and the language used in the message is proof that they will not back off from achieving their ends. Accordingly, they are trying to occupy two provinces of Mexico, and in case the general that they are counting on to sell them the rest is not victorious, they declare that they will take over a part of the Republic, which is the same as saying that they will seize Sonora, Sinaloa, Chihuahua, Durango, Zacatecas, Nuevo León, Tamaulipas, Coahuila under the pretext that the first five offer incalculable metallurgical riches, and the last three would round off Texas. They proclaim openly that Nicaragua, Costa Rica, Honduras, San Salvador, and Guatemala are its property. *They should be mine*, they say, *and the reason is because I call myself a lion*. They need to extend their protectorate over Arizona because, according to them, it is a den of assassins. Not very long ago they shelled Greytown, on the pretext that the wooden city was a nest of pirates. Pirates, punished by pirates! But it should be understood, the only pirates were born upon the ships that bombarded them, not the city inhabited by peaceful merchants, foreigners for the most part. And if up to now they are only pursuing what we have mentioned, it is because, according to them, Mr. Buchanan's prudence and moderation stands in their way.

Encouraged by Europe's indifference, which they must believe is a front, and therefore dictated by fear; made arrogant by the concessions of England, whose navy they insulted in Greytown, and for which they have still not been asked to give satisfaction; wealthy enough to cover the world with their accomplices, it is not Mr. Buchanan whom they need, it is Mr. Soulé; it is not Cuba, it is not Mexico, that can satisfy their thirst for invasion; it is all of America, the rest of its continents, the ruin of everything that can form the universe of Catholicism and monarchy. Those who are fearful of seeing the start of such a fight, those whose self-interest makes them complicit in that evil, try to persuade themselves, and to persuade everyone else, that the United States does not condone the spirit of Mr. Buchanan's message, because the message is only a weak expression of the public's opinion in that den of pirates who are destined to punish humanity, if humanity does not pull back in time from the rapid descent pulling it into the abyss.

The triumph of the United States must be the sign of the dissolution of the Latin race . . . On the day that Catholic unity ceases to reign in Mexico and in Cuba, that day would be the fait accompli of the destruction of Latin society in America, and the only obstacles that today still oppose the invasions of the United States would crumble to the earth.

A Spanish-French intervention in America in favor of Latin principles would have, for Catholic civilization, the immense advantage of diverting Europe's attentions away from material transactions and toward a field of moral influence that is much more extensive than that which it believes it can exploit today in the New World.

The relations between Europe and the United States have only brought deplorable results for Europe, and this is easy to understand if we keep in mind that the United States continually conspires against it. Barely a few months have gone by since that crisis organized by the electors of Mr. Buchanan produced a disturbance favorable to its designs upon the world. Every single relationship between the United States and Europe has tended to bring about Europe's ruin; every time it has felt a disturbance under its feet, every time it strikes the mine, it discovers the Anglo-Saxons' powder. Commercial relationships have always favored the United States and disfavored Europe. Nevertheless, Europe can acquire advantages of every kind and create a debt of recognition that will one day be satisfied by establishing a counterweight adequate to *Yankee* aspirations, securing for us all the modes of universal traffic between the Atlantic and Pacific Oceans, lending Latin America a quarter of the attention we have given to Anglo-Saxon America, exercising our influence as benefactors to Central and South America, promoting commercial and industrial development in all the Spanish American republics, whose riches have very different sources than the riches of the United States.

A Latin alliance would force the electors of Mr. Buchanan to enlist under the flag of civilization and Europe to recognize that Central and South America are the natural theater where it should exercise its future influence and establish its transatlantic relationships. Nearly all the sons of Europe who go to the United States, scarcely have they stepped foot in that accursed land when the wind of ingratitude blows into their hearts, and like Soulé, repudiate the country where they were born. All of Europe that mixes with the Yankees immediately becomes the enemy of Europe. Something even stranger happens in North America, and it is certainly not the least curious or important thing. The true, formal inhabitants of the United States, those who are landowners, the descendants of those who courageously secured the independence of the English colony, not thinking that they would open up a refuge for the dregs of the revolutions, expressed opinions of order and morality, but found themselves lorded over by the new recruits from without who daily strengthen and swell the phalanx of certified democrats. There is no doubt that they would be indisposed to supporting Europe, if Europe with its indifference or its fear did not leave them at the mercy of their adversaries. Removed from power twenty-eight years ago, they are forced to sit silently at the orgies of the pirates and see their country transformed into a lair where all the political disgraces that threaten civilization are planned without penalty. These men are respectable; these men could revitalize their country if Europe would intimidate or overthrow their adversaries, but instead their influence is destroyed. Those Europeans who step foot in Central or South America continue to be sons and friends of Europe; if they behaved otherwise, they would lose all their prestige, and this is the difference that exists between the Yankees and those whose country they seek to invade. Therefore, Europe has someone there to protect . . .

. . . It is not in the United States in which the true sources of New World wealth are found, and that is why the United States is always attempting to reach out beyond its country . . . Americans from the North, like all the sons of Anglo-Saxon races, excel in the means of exploiting the work and fortune of others: they see their Indies in South America, and this drives them to pounce on the other side of the Isthmus of Panama . . . The hour for the United States will come, therefore, on the day when the Latin alliance gives them the order not to advance one step further on the road to invasion. The cancer that devours them, and which they nourish with the product of a new theft, will suddenly eat out their hearts. Their confederation will fall to pieces due to the force of events, and then Latin Europe will have the right to smile if its kindness does not oblige it to pity them. The United States only lives by invading, and its inhabitants, like bandits, can only exist by leaping frequently out of their caverns. Wall them in, and you will see how they eat each other like savages. Haven't they proved this already in Utah?

That would certainly be the fate of the United States when a Latin alliance reduces them to the state of existing by themselves alone, and no one can imagine how easy that would be. That fearsome adversary whose blows can be so terrible, whose triumph would mean the death of civilization, is only counting on the forces that are indifferent to it, or on the fear of those that it threatens. For the world, it is the same as those ghostly shadows that a child believes he sees pursuing him; if he runs away, fear will take him to the abyss, but if he stops and faces that shadow, the ghost will disappear. In them there is nothing but lies, weakness, cowardice. They think they have nothing to fear, nothing to lose, and that is why they risk everything and dare to do everything. They are huge because of the senseless fear they arouse. Is there anyone who does not remember the campaign they waged against Mexico in 1846? This country, which has only eight million inhabitants and was torn apart by civil war, and did not have a million in its Treasury, cost the United States twenty thousand soldiers and two hundred million *duros*, though it had a population of twenty-six million inhabitants and a Treasury with only a million more *duros*. What would have happened to them, what would happen today, if they had fought or had to fight any of the great European powers, and especially a Latin alliance? They have men for a sudden raid, but they could never have a brilliant general because one of two things would happen: Either that general would be an honorable man who would not lend himself to their plans, or he would be an ambitious egoist, and then they would have to fear for their institutions. Didn't that same war in Mexico bring about jealousy, and wasn't General Scott himself fearful also? Their naval power generates a good deal of noise, and they don't have one military squadron to present as a force. Their merchant ships are well suited for transporting pirates, but they cannot hold up against European frigates. They are forced to parley with rebels in the interior, and they cannot even gather an army capable of sweeping away a few well-trained madmen.

An examination of their forces could, in fact, prove that those who ridicule them are right, if impunity did not lend them the assistance of forces that are truly dangerous for the Latin race. It is these that must be conquered, demanding that the United States not take one step farther. What must be combated is the threatening aspect of the revolution, the universal revolution of which they are the symbol: What must be torn from them is their means of subsidizing their accomplices in Europe, forcing them to use other things than gratuitous threats and unpunished bravado . . .

The terrible moral influence that the United States wields over its European accomplices and their steady increase is undoubtedly the consequence of weak governments that bow to Yankee eccentricities and aspirations. How could we not believe that governments are forced to submit to the will of the electors of Buchanan, when we see how these men continually triumph over the laws and pacts laid down by common consent and respected by the world's greatest powers? Didn't the *Wabash* recently pass the Dardanelles with complete impunity, violating the terms of the Treaty of Paris, and declaring that

U.S. ships were not bound by that treaty? Haven't we seen a simple Yankee captain challenge Austria and even forbid them, right in the Mediterranean, to touch one hair of Kosta's head? There are innumerable examples of such abuses. That is why the fifth column of civilization says: "Europe, afraid of the United States!" Europe, which also believed that Yankee bravado was not worthy of their attention, allowed the United States, in 1846, to steal from Mexico, *one hundred ten thousand square leagues!*

And yet, to dispel the threatening phantom and stun the forces that its accomplices have placed at its disposal, there is no need to fire even one cannon shot. The United States has no Sevastopol, just as it lacks the army or weaponry. They know that there is no hope for them in the field of defense: A simple declaration would be sufficient to make them stop and think, and it would give enough confidence to the adversaries of American democrats to make them return to the power that they have not held for twenty-eight years. Such a declaration would be universally applauded, in the same way that Carlos X was applauded in another time with regard to that den of pirates called Algiers. The case is identical, and if the United States, when forced to explain itself, confesses that for them invasion is a matter of life or death, the world will decide if it wants to die so that the United States can live.

And don't doubt it for a moment: The conduct of the United States, the language of its presidents, of its diplomatic agents, of its ship captains, of all its citizens in whatever circumstances they see themselves in the world, their actions, like their language, ultimately prove that they see their right to be invaders whenever it is to their advantage. Cuba would be useful to them, so they have a right to own Cuba, and using this same logic, it won't be long before they make themselves the masters of all the European colonies that exist in those seas. It is not only Spain, then, that should fear for its Antilles; it is France, it is England, in fact, it is the entire world. When Peru discovered its wealth of guano, didn't it see the United States demand ownership of their islands? They have arable lands, so the fertilizer belongs to them. It is the same as saying that if a man walks by without knowing what time it is, his neighbor has the right to steal his watch, if he doesn't have one . . .

When justice, truth, order, reign in the universe: when weak nations have nothing to fear from strong ones; when religion proceeds with its regenerative work; when the adversaries of civilization, terrified by the dynamic hand of justice, are dragged over the ground; when France and its sovereign are respected and their legitimate influence is exercised to its fullest; when the conspirators dare not show themselves in the light of day and confess that their inaction makes them impotent. Your Majesty has said it: "The empire means peace." But when justice, truth, and order are unknown, insulted, and challenged; when the independence of the nations that are our brothers is threatened; when religion is publicly insulted and is cast out of a parliament where it should preside; when law is argued over, fought against, and violated by the adversaries of civilization; when France and its sovereign are barred from addressing important matters, their influence wounded, attacked for the principles they represent and profess; when the conspirators show their faces and have the courage to write messages like the one they have just thrown into the face of Europe, the Empire is the avenger of order, of truth, of justice; the Empire is the defender of threatened nations; the Empire is the arm that holds the sword of Saint Peter and vindicates the legacy of Charlemagne; the Empire is the champion of law when it has been violated, the great bestower of peace-making influence; the Empire is the form of government that acquits, challenges, and condemns those who have caused them harm; and if, to carry out this complex mission, it is necessary for the Empire to mean something other than peace, then let it mean war.

Selection 3

Another icon of transnational U.S. Latina/o *crónica* is RICARDO FLORES MAGÓN (1873–1922), editor and founder of *Regeneración*. He was born in Oaxaca, Mexico, and spent the last eighteen years of his life in exile in the United States, after the Mexican government forbade him to publish in Mexico. Having devoted part of his life to fomenting armed struggle against Porfirio Díaz throughout the northern states of Mexico, Flores Magón is considered today one of the intellectual forefathers and precursors of the Mexican Revolution and an important figure of international anarchism. His political ideology was published mostly in the journals *El Hijo de El Ahuizote* and *Regeneración*, in which he expressed his disagreement with Francisco I. Madero's political goals; as an anarchist, he was determined to eradicate both the state and private property. The continuing efforts to reconstruct the Magonista archive in the United States, above all Southern California, offers new evidence of the transnational reach of Mexican anarchism in the history of the Chicana/o Left.[1] Ernesto Galarza's classic autobiography, *Barrio Boy*, confirms, via recollected testimonies of exiled workers, the way the revolution's narratives and rhetoric echoed in California's Mexican labor agitation.

In the *crónica* included here, "La repercusión de un linchamiento" ("The Repercussion of a Lynching"), published in *Regeneración* on November 12, 1910, Flores Magón denounces the lynching of Hispanics in the United States, which was often condemned in the early Spanish-language chronicle. He also condemns the U.S. support of dictators such as the Guatemalan Manuel Estrada Cabrera and the Mexican Porfirio Díaz as well as U.S. intervention in the internal politics of several Latin American countries. While not directly blaming U.S. people, he nevertheless denounces the greedy owners of U.S. multinational companies as well as the mistreatment and oppression of Mexicans in the United States. More specifically, like Práxedis G. Guerrero in "Blancos,

blancos," he condemns the lynching of the Mexican citizen Antonio Rodríguez, who was burned alive after being accused (without a court case) of killing an American woman in Rock Springs, Texas. Flores Magón turns the tragedy to his own political uses by blaming capitalism itself for the lynching when he accuses it of dividing "the two races that populate this beautiful continent" (meaning Anglos and Latinos).[2]

The Repercussions of a Lynching

RICARDO FLORES MAGÓN

TRANSLATED BY ROBERT RUDDER

The daily newspapers of this city have been busy lately, telling their readers about alleged assaults inflicted on Americans by rioting mobs in Mexico City.[3] The stories in the press are indeed horrific; but we think they contain a good deal of exaggeration.

No one can deny that a reaction is taking hold throughout Latin America—against a United States imperialism that is a grave threat to the existence of those countries as autonomous nations. A sense of hostility, ever more marked, against the demanding politics of the U.S. government can be seen in all those nations.

It is not the people of the United States but, rather, the greed of great American millionaires. The hunger for gold by this country's plutocracy has been the cause of that sentiment that is making the achievement of brotherhood slow and difficult among the human beings who inhabit this continent. Because, while we men who have freed ourselves from racial prejudice work to create bonds of brotherhood among all men, the great businessmen, the bandits of finance, attempt by their actions to divide people, to open up abysses between different races and different nationalities, and in that way to keep their empire secure: *divide and rule*, said Machiavelli.

The attacks that have been perpetrated on the Latin people of America have been motivated by the ambition of great millionaires who make use of patriotism to affront peoples who have committed no other crime than to live on rich lands that have tempted the greed of the vampires of Wall Street. Is there anyone who does not remember the attack on Colombia's sovereignty?

Who can forget the intrigues by the great millionaires of this country against Venezuela's independence? Is there anyone who is in the dark about the fact that the policies of the White House toward the Latin nations of this continent are the policies of "takeovers," that, in addition, they are policies that tend to support insatiable tyrannies, like that of Estrada Cabrera in Guatemala and that of Porfirio Díaz in Mexico? And who could doubt that whenever a government appears that does not bow down to the shameful tutelage of the United States plutocracy, that that government will find itself best with internal rebellions, forged, directed, and fomented by rich Americans, with the ports of the United States being the places from which those pirating expeditions will be launched to make war as if it were a revolution against the Latin American nations that do not submit to this nation's capitalistic demands? Isn't it public information and widely known that the revolution against President Zelaya of Nicaragua was the work of North American adventurers paid with Wall Street's gold? And as if all this weren't enough, don't Mexicans remember that if their blood was spilled, fighting against the plutocracy of this nation, because the wealthy desired to possess Mexico's lands?

These are acts that speak with fulsome eloquence. These are acts that are in the memory of everyone, acts whose origin is in the insatiable thirst for riches of the great American millionaires, and that have raised a wall between the two races that inhabit this beautiful continent; and that will remain standing, upright, insurmountable, and that would end by turning two important factions of the human race into mortal enemies; if the literature of the libertarians were not lighting in the hearts of the landless peasantry of all races, sentiments of love and fraternity, which, as they grow stronger, will tear down that wall raised up by the crimes of capitalism, forging all these interests into one alone, a beautiful and great solidarity.

In Mexico particularly—it cannot be denied—there is a well-defined feeling of hostility against the grasping tendency of the government in the White House, a feeling that becomes more pronounced day by day because of the individual or collective actions of Americans against Mexicans who live in this nation. Everyone knows how disdainfully the Mexican race is treated in general; everyone knows that in Texas Mexicans are treated worse than Negroes. Mexicans cannot enter hotels, restaurants, and other public places there. The doors of public schools are closed to the children of our race. Semi-savage Americans use Mexicans for target practice. How many men of our race have died because a blond savage has gotten a notion to test his skill with weapons by firing at them, without there even being any dispute between them! In the so-called court of law, Mexicans are judged, generally with no formalities at all, and are sentenced to be hanged or to suffer harsh punishment, without there being any proof or even the slightest hint that they might have committed the crime for which they are being punished.

Everything is linked to the pride that wealthy Americans display in Mexico because they consider our unfortunate country a conquered country. Because the cowardly and tyrannical traitor who oppresses us gives them everything they want, concedes everything they demand, puts into their hands lands cultivated and owned by humble laborers—because it is always the poor who suffer—fully authorizes them to raze our forests, to exploit the riches of Mexican lands and seas for their sole benefit, to function as authorities that are nearly always more brutal than the indigenous population. All this has raised the barrier capitalism has placed between the two races even higher; all this has made the task of fraternity and love between all the world's races more difficult, a task that we as libertarians of earth have undertaken with our acts and our propaganda.

That is the way things are. And when the Mexican people see that the American plutocracy is the worst enemy of their freedoms, when they realize that the persecution and tortures we have suffered in this country are due to the desire of great American millionaires to remain in Mexico, when the conditions of tyranny and barbarity that make quick enrichment possible for those evildoers—remain as they are, we say we need only one act among many to arouse a storm of protest in Mexico. And the deed that caused the indignation reported by the newspapers in this city is one of many that have taken place on the savage plains of Texas and whose actors were a mob of savage whites that furiously attacked a humble Mexican: Antonio Rodríguez—accused of murdering an American woman and whose crime was not proved in the courts—was tied to a post by a mob of Americans and burned alive. This horrible crime took place in Rock Springs, Texas, on the third day of this month.

The students of Mexico City resolved to organize a protest against that lynching; they carried it out on Tuesday, on the eighth of this month. A large crowd gathered; several forceful speeches were made, protesting the assault. The large number of protesters went to the offices of the American newspaper, the *Mexican Herald*, which, as is well-known, supported by Díaz and is one of the main sycophants that his despotism relies on. The crowd threw rocks and shattered the building's windows.

The following day, Wednesday, the students, accompanied by an enormous crowd, went through the city's main streets, shouting in protest against the murders of Mexicans in Texas. The windows of several stores were shattered. An American flag was taken by the crowd and ripped to shreds, amid shouts of indignation against the abuses of Mexicans that are committed in this country.

The newspapers are publishing reports about an American who has been lynched and an American child who has had his head split open, but there is no proof that these acts ever occurred. It is all simply the desire of newspapers to attract readers by printing sensational news items.

Newspapers have also reported that the residence of the United States ambassador to Mexico was bombarded with sticks of dynamite. But that news item, like the lynching of the American and the child's broken skull, lack any basis in fact.

On Wednesday the crowd burst into the office where the most abject and lowest sort of newspaper in Mexico is published, *El Imparcial*, and began to tear apart the pressroom. Mounted police arrived and dispersed the protesters, with one man being stabbed by a sword of one of the Cossacks.

The most noteworthy events took place on Wednesday. The troops descended on the crowd, and some men were killed. When the crowd was dispersed from one place in the city, it would gather in another, and so on. There were many confrontations between these hatchet men and the people. The protests by the inhabitants of Mexico City had their repercussions in Guadalajara, where the students also organized a protest march. The crowds took over the city for several hours. Many stores owned by Americans were pelted with rocks. The entire garrison was fitted with arms; after several encounters between the protesters and the troops, the crowds dispersed.

The government of Díaz, with its usual barbarity, has arrested more than one hundred students in Mexico City; it has given categorical orders to the cops and the military to savagely put down any cry of protest. And with protests coming from the government of the White House, it has bent over backward with explanations, apologies, and promises that it will suppress all newspapers that, by having published articles protesting the lynching of Rodríguez, aroused the public to manifest its discontent.

This is all that is known up to the time *Regeneración* went to press. The Catholic newspaper *El País* is recommending a boycott against American products as a protest. Other newspapers are publishing powerful articles about crimes committed against Mexicans in this country, but not one of them dares tell the truth: none of them will open its mouth to say that capitalism—the voracious octopus that is sucking the strength of the people—is the cause of all these disturbances, of all these crimes. For it is capitalism that is fomenting hatred between races so that people will not come to an understanding, and in that way sit back and rule at its leisure.

Selection 4

The Colombian journalist BLANCA DE MONCALEANO, a fervent supporter of women's rights and revolution, worked for the Mexican leftist weekly *Tierra* and was married to Juan Moncaleano, a Colombian educator and Partido Liberal Mexicano (Mexican Liberal Party; PLM) member. As Emma Pérez explains in *The Decolonial Imaginary: Writing Chicanas into History*, Blanca de Moncaleano began publishing essays for *Regeneración* in 1913, often condemning, from a feminist perspective, women's subjugation to the patriarchal family. At the International Workers' Home in Los Angeles, she lent her support to the instructors, who "lectured party members' daughters against the 'bonds of female slavery' and its sons against the 'fetters of imperialist wars.'"[1] As Nicolás Kanellos explains, Blanca, expelled with her husband from Colombia, Cuba, and Mexico for their radical activities, also published a tabloid, *Pluma Roja* (Red Quill), in Los Angeles. Its motto was "Instruid a la mujer y el triunfo de la Anarquía será breve" (Educate women and Anarchy's triumph will be swift).[2] Many of her essays railed against patriarchy in all forms: institutional religion, the state, class oppression, militarism, and the fellow revolutionary men who mistreated women. According to Kanellos, her "Manifiesto a la mujer" (To Womankind, a Manifesto) "is a revision of history from women's perspective and a militant call for women to break the chains that have suppressed their progress over the millennia, and consequently the progress of the entire human race."[3] The publication of her September 7, 1915, manifesto seemed timed to oppose those who called the United States to join World War I on the side of the Allies. It also encouraged women to rebel against the church, state, and capital for forcing their sons to die in useless wars. The passage, "tear down that millennial wall that divides man into races and states," also carries special resonance for Hispanic letters. On the one hand, it echoed José Martí's landmark 1892 essay, "Our America," in which he denounced the concept of biological race as an invention of Western colonialism. On the other hand, her insinuation that unnatural political, religious, and economic laws prop up the nation-state's borders prefigure the cultural turn's late-twentieth-century deconstructions of the nation-state effect. Eventually, the de Moncaleanos parted ways with the Flores Magón faction over its uses of political violence. After her husband's death, explains Kanellos, she remained in Los Angeles, or what she called "the city of Anarchy," but changed her name to Lawson and went underground.[4]

To Womankind, a Manifesto

BLANCA DE MONCALEANO

TRANSLATED BY VICTOR VALLE AND NICOLÁS KANELLOS

I direct these words to you, sublime human form of which the Vedas called mother of Humanity some ten thousand years ago; to you, whom the church fathers denied a soul; to you, the unending source of life, the key to all that exists; to you, the slave of priests, governors, and the rich go my words; to you, who makes innumerable sacrifices to raise your children, and when they are all grown and robust with you at the doors of happiness, tyrants tear them away in the name of the fatherland, throw them into battle, where they are ripped to pieces by deadly lead, where they will become food for worms and crows: such a sad end for that immense treasure of your love!

And since for the thousands of years your sons have died on the battlefield, bandaged in religious prejudice, the source of patriotic zealotry, believing to fashion a true fatherland of love and equality, it is to you whom I direct myself; to you, exhausted mother, suffering without remorse that you have not had a single moment of repose, weeping from the moment the appearance of the sun's first ray until falling into the West of existence, into the black of night's immensity!

Reviewing the history of your long captivity is maddening; the convolutions of Dante's brain could not stand to pause over the immense mouth of the abyss and meditate upon the friar who tortures womankind, playing with her the way a cat entertains itself with its prey sold in the slaver's marketplace, and, in the temple, by the slave-owning friar who counted your love's worth in coins. The state then imitated the church, and now both sell you like a lamb; both rob and kill your children.

Why curse the slave's maternal fecundity in the presence of so much crime? Life and love, cries the bird in wingbeats of jungle sounds; life and love, answers the flower's perfume that hangs from the heavy bower; life and love, says the hurricane kissing the ocean's frothy shoulder; life and love, says the child in the first peals of laughter and flashes that shine in its innocent pupils; life and love, says the sun, embracing the earth with its fiery arms; life and love, answers the dewdrop as it falls from the rose-colored aurora into the flower's fragrant chalice; life and love, says the field that sustains its rich carpet of delicate herbs.

Hatred and death, screams the friar from his pulpit, ordering obedience to his slaver's precepts; sending believers to their deaths defending a god, lord of the celestial fatherland; hatred and death, says the autocrat who orders extermination in the terrestrial fatherland's name; hatred and death, says the mighty rich man who condemns the worker to suffer in the collapsing mine, in the field and workshop, or the filthy sty without light or bread, without instruction or warming shelter; hatred and death, says the schoolteacher, who shows his students the flag saying, "Abandon your fathers, friends, brothers and women, to glorify that rag with your deaths," that rag that represents the fatherland's laws, and whose emblem is "Die for god and king." Hatred and death, says the friar from the altar when he shouts to his flock, "The rich man who pays for masses, incense, rosaries, and who tithes the church may purchase the celestial fatherland's riches, after having enjoyed its terrestrial wares." "The poor may buy the celestial fatherland's wares with obedience and resignation to work, to patiently suffer in misery, stifling the least hint of rebellion against their master; and by making a small gift of your salaries to our cult; but, lo, those who harbor the least inkling of rebellion, who withhold their sin in the confessional shall be punished in the other life in hell's eternal flames."

These words of hatred and death have reverberated in the ears of humanity for century upon century; this lugubrious ecclesiastical brass band has prevented humanity from hearing the redemptive voice of Anarchy, which is life and love, as nature teaches us.

It has been fifty years since anarchism has shouted to thee; women, educate thy children for liberty and not for the yoke; educate them to live in harmony with nature's laws, free of tyrants who oppress and exploit you, because all those who pretend to call themselves the representatives of divine or human right are nothing more than freeloaders who wish to idle eternally at the expense of your suffering, robbing you of the wealth of your strength. Know that you may live in a world without the borders that divide us, where human beings, who are the owners of the wealth of their labor, may enjoy the well-being that is possible in common, if educated with mutual respect, the foundation upon which Liberty must rest!

Humanity has not flourished and progressed because of the church's commandments or the law's penal code. The judge's writ, the president's and the friar's, have nothing to do with the natural turning of the seasons that tell the laborer the most provident time to sow. The law and the church's commandments have only served to slow down human progress. The miner, the seaman, the scientist, has no need to consult divine or human laws because nature, an affectionate mother since our birth, has indicated the good and bad, pleasure and pain, to us. The nameless crime of war that now stirs the world, which fills our eyes with tears and the fields with blood, is the unavoidable lesson of religious teaching.

Womankind, poor slave of unconsciousness, who raises her eyes to the millennial altar, break that heavy religious chain and enter the sanctuary of rational science, where liberty will crown your brow with a reward for your mighty effort. Hear me! I approach you, not as Veronica, who approached Jesus to soak up his cowering tears in her dusty robes; nor do I come crying like the mother of the crucified Jew; I have no patience for desolation, nor do I come smiling like the convent's Safos and Mesalinas because my bitter lips can only curse, not bless. I am not here to whisper into your ear, as the reptiles in cassocks do; I'm here to address you like a thunderstorm; a rebel am I, and as such I beseech you. I'm not here to speak of the peace that debases the slave nor to murmur sorrowful words; I'm here to speak of rebellion and vengeance, to explain the cause of the evil that sickens you and the fear that prevents you from avenging yourself with dignity. So, listen!

A horrible reptile, the very worst, nests in your heart and brain; the one who will not leave you for an instant, who has lived in you since birth, speaking to you of a God whose lie, in eating him, is digested. I am speaking of that loving and vengeful being, the cause of good and evil who is the creator who punishes you for the very defects with which he has molded you. He, of the omniscient eye from which nothing escapes him, not even your brain's most fleeting thought is invisible to him. But such a wise being needs a spokesman of the earth and heavens to tell him about your sins; he lives with you everywhere, in the filthy sty, where the worker and his children die of hunger, in the brothel and tavern; a being who needs sumptuous cathedrals of marble and gold, to which the believers pay tribute with their talents; he calls himself "Jehovah, god of armies," a benevolent being who orders the razing of cities and the throttling of the old, the children and women. Jesus Christ calls you, commands you to patiently suffer; he offers the fatherland's celestial riches so that you may forget its worldly ones; always preaches chastity yet violates the chaste consciences of your daughters and rapes them again in the church or convent; preaches humility and poverty though he lives in luxury, his coffers overflowing with gold and his towering arrogance. Well then, he, the one who speaks of this anthropomorphic being, and whose throne is ensconced over yonder . . . . in heaven, who they call the king of heaven, creator of earthly kings, that cassocked reptile, that libertine friar who officiates in his altar of lies, is the cause of your pain.

Pagan from birth, he believes in nothing; yesterday he was a priest of the sun god; he takes different forms and is the same: police, president, king judge, soldier; Egyptian, Chinese, Russian, French, German, American, and Japanese; he is, in sum, a parasite that exists everywhere. He was Salomon, Moses, Saul, Joshua, later Torquemada, Ignatius of Loyola, and was also called Borgia; at first a king, his arrogance pushed him to become the king of kings and then made himself pope. He lit the inquisitorial bonfires, distributed scepters, staffs, gallows, miters, and crowns, training the world for slavery.

He was the first tyrant, who said, "Obey me," the first thief, who said, "This is mine"; the first violator of consciences who told the world, kneel before me; who said, I rule the gods of Olympus, and in hell, heaven, limbo, purgatory, and on earth; all doors open to my voice. He was the first to divide the human race into slaves and lords, the inventor of the first flag; he who loved the fatherland's terrestrial wealth was the enemy of god and, therefore, distanced himself from his celestial wares, and the patriot of heaven was the planet's enemy; so began the origin of nations, cause of the wars that today afflict humanity. And the peoples of the earth devour each other, some because they reach for celestial positions; others, because they do not believe in those offices, have waged bloody battles down below, and the fruit of all this: hunger, misery, and thousands of epidemics that have lashed the world, and spread the plague of militarism. It was the friar who, with his venomous word, poisoned the crystalline fountains of life.

Womankind, come with me and hesitate no longer; take my rebel's hand and climb with me to the heights of the sublime ideal; from there I shall show you the battlefield where the ones responsible for that crime now officiate; come with me . . . let us climb, look, over there . . . the immense battlefield, where mankind, transformed into to a beast, tears at its entrails.

The explosive detonates and mutilates, shreds and pulverizes the fierce fighters; youths, the elderly, children and women, fall into its whirlwind of death. Though they speak different languages, wave different flags, never speak to each other, never see each other, yet hate each other because the tyrants have ordained it; each believes to have a fatherland, well, that's what they were taught in school, not because they really do. For what fatherland can deny workers the freedom to enjoy the product of their labor? What do the nations that devour themselves gain, what are they defending? The chain of slavery, which makes the palace its prison and whose glory is a death from hunger, these are the sacrifices that build the marvelous city. Can you see the perpetrator of which I speak? Look at him over there, sanctimonious and priggish, resting upon a tripod of Talmudic bayonets: the Bible, the Koran, and the other sacred books with which he has brutalized humanity.

Look at the way he blesses the horrific butchery. His hands, which look like claws, drip blood. All the armies kneel before him, imploring his blessing of absolution. Some in the name of Christ, who pray for the victory that exterminates all the rest; the others guarantee battlefield success in Jehovah's name. Those, over there, die believing they please the grand Allah; those over yonder implore Buddha for a victory. Each of the assassins of conscience, God's priests, bless the military assassins and their mainstays, the government that robs, enslaves, and kills the industrial worker. It is these three terrifying deities, clergy, government, and capital that are responsible for the evil that annihilates you.

Look at how they carve the fields, level cities, blow up ships, railroads, and bridges. And though they destroy, what do they build? Nothing!

While the world becomes filled with widows and orphans, smoldering ruins and people disabled for industrial production, while the arts and industries are turned into skeletal ruins, the high and mighty, the impresarios of war, dance in their palatial ballrooms and clink their glasses in insolent libation as they count the millions of workers yet to be sacrificed in the slaughterhouse of war. Who shall gather up the millions of mutilated men to give them sustenance, who is capable of healing so much evil? What awaits our sons if they survive the disaster? Shall you line up with the privileged who show off their riches and shiny medals? Ah! no; you and your children will join an army of beggars who, weak from hunger, will approach the marble steps of the lordly mansion pleading to the powerful for charity, and they will answer with a strident, demeaning guffaw that stifles the anguished cries in your throat. And your daughters will enter whorehouses after having lost their innocence in the arms of those same gentlemen who harangued the ignorant masses, painting a beautiful future full of honor and glory that awaited them if they fought on behalf of the fatherland's laws. Look yonder . . . see how their bodies now crumble, how they fall as if into a human volcano that spouts fire, smoke, blood, and mutilated flesh, how its crater thunders and moans; it thunders with explosions and groans to ask for protection against the claws of death, an unfathomable chaos where the watchful thinker is drowned in the world's idiocy.

You tremble in horror, and I see that you ask yourself what purpose can all this sacrifice of feeding and giving life to your sons have? Why invest our greatest love and grandest hopes in them if the voice of the first functionary undoes our beloved son's life before our eyes, bursting it like a soap bubble that leaves us sad and disconsolate upon the cliff of our disgrace and from which we ask the "Infinite mute" who ignores our bitter plaint? Rearing sons so that "the crows" may feed upon them is indeed a horrible thing!

What can be done to avoid so much crime and safeguard your children's lives? Destroy the tyrant, hurl ourselves against the palace where the jailor of liberty resides, unite ourselves to forcefully conquer the rights we are born with; by destroying the religious yoke that makes women submissive slaves and workers vile pariahs. Yes, demolish that den from which the rich, the governor and the priest officiate and feast on proletarian blood; sweep away the evil briars that obstruct our triumphant march, lopping off the executioner's head to the rhythm of our libertarian songs.

To die breaking the chains is more dignified than kissing them. To die liberating the world's children is to live eternally. Giving them a beautiful world where humanity, redeemed by education, will labor for its own welfare, without soldiers, priests, the wealthy, and governments. An anarchic world in which your children will be safe!

Yes, women, fill your breast with ire; dry the tears in your eyes and light them with the torch of vengeance; make a fist and help me land the mighty blows that hammer down that enormous fortress gate of unconsciousness that imprisons the ignorant masses groaning under their heavy chains.

Help me, and be not afraid to tear down that millennial wall that divides mankind with races and borders. Help me show the children that road that leads to the port of Anarchy.

Dither no longer! Gather your strength and courage to help me destroy palaces and tyrants, jails, military garrisons, churches, and convents. Help me build the eternal city of harmony and goodness, the city of Anarchy.

Selection 5

Switching to life writing, our anthology includes an excerpt of the unpublished memoirs of ALFREDO COBOS, the grandfather of this anthology's coeditor Victor Valle. Alfredo's recollection of the Mexican Revolution begins when José Inés Salazar, one of the last of the surviving *magonista*-affiliated generals, pressed him into service in the winter of 1916. Alfredo's account illustrates the way *magonista* anarchism continued its echo in Southern California. We hear them when Alfredo's daughter, Lilly, linked his story to a string of social justice memories: the week she walked the picket lines with her father during Southern California's wildcat dairy strikes of 1933; the time her barrio filled Downey's public plunge with trash when the city segregated its swim days for Mexicans and African Americans; her adult efforts to fight for Mexican and Chicana/o civil rights in the schools. Her younger brother, Robert, attributed his sense of social justice to Alfredo's story, but also his "source of bewilderment." How was the pointless destruction of a failed revolution supposed to help his generation claim a new national identity? On another level, Alfredo's Spanish-language memoir, which he orally related to his scribe and wife, Matilde, is a Hispanic immigrant text, which Nicolás Kanellos defines in his 2011 work *Hispanic Immigrant Literature* as "the literature created orally or in written form by immigrants from the Hispanic world who have come to U.S. shores since the early nineteenth century." In this case Alfredo's account confirms what is known of the intimate relations the Villistas cultivated with northwestern Chihuahua's landowning families. Read now, his memoir also suggests a recurring theme in Latina/o literature. The landscape Cobos describes with such intimate knowledge is remembered in another place, the one in which he remembered his losses. For many Mexican and other Latina/o immigrants and their U.S. descendants, the memory of this trauma becomes unbearably poignant whenever the danger of displacement or expulsion threatens their attempts to stake claims to place or citizenship.

Excerpt from "The Memoirs of Alfredo Cobos"

ALFREDO COBOS

TRANSLATED BY ROBERT RUDDER

The story I'm going to tell was heard and greatly appreciated by my wife, my children, and their children when they were small. Now they are my grandsons and granddaughters. It goes like this.

My name is Alfredo Cobos. I am sixty-five years old. I am going to tell you a tale, a short episode of the Mexican Revolution that happened to me. Back in the year 1916, I was living with my parents and all my family in the State of Chihuahua. My father had been the owner of a ranch with large numbers of cattle, horses, and everything a good ranch should have. He sold part of his cattle, and then he went into partnership with a wealthy rancher, Mr. Urrutia. The Revolution came along, and this destroyed their business, so they split up. My dad took his share of cattle and the rest of his family to live in a little [logging] town that at that time was called Pearson, still in the state of Chihuahua. One day my dad learned that General Murguía had given the order to round up all the cattle near the train line and load them onto it. My dad decided to send me and my brother Arturo to the Sierra de Sonora [in the western Sierra Madre] to protect his cattle: that was the place along the line where the State of Chihuahua and the State of Sonora met. The little ranch we went to was called The Chimneys. There were about ten or fifteen families there. We struggled to take our cattle there because we had to walk a lot; it was far away, and it was getting very cold since it was December. The animals were tired when we got there. We put them in a place where we thought, were very sure, that revolutionaries or bandits wouldn't be able to steal them. Then, in a few days, I made some friends. There were plans to celebrate the coming New Year with a dance at the little ranch. It seemed like everything was going along all right when one morning I decided to ride out to go have a look at the cattle. We were surprised at the ranch by some men on horseback. They were revolutionaries, followers of Pancho Villa. They asked who the cattle and the horses around there belonged to. I told them that I was their owner, and then they immediately took my leggings, my leather jacket, my spurs, since it seemed like they really liked my saddle. I gave them all my riding gear, my good saddle. For my own part I asked them who their commander was so that I could talk to him to see if they would give me back what they'd taken. A couple minutes later I found myself with Colonel Ramón Vega, a friend of mine from Casas Grandes. After greeting me, he took me to the generals, General José Inés Salazar and General Silvestre Quevedo, who were also from Casas Grandes and acquaintances of mine. Before that they had gotten horses from my father's ranch. They were very glad to see me. After talking with them a good while, I told them why they'd found me there. I told them the truth: I told them that my fifteen-year-old brother was with me. After hearing this, they looked at each other and told me they weren't going to bother my brother or my cattle but that, like it or not, they were taking me. I told them, All right. They knew I knew the terrain very well and the mountain range and the hills, there ins and outs. I was brought up on the ranch, you see. Horseback riding, breaking colts, and roping heifers, well, all that rodeo stuff, was like my favorite sport. I could do it in my sleep. They immediately ordered the soldiers to give me back everything they had taken from me, except for my spurs, and they gave me a horse. They told me his name was El Pabellón, and he was truly a good horse. So my horse and I were set; I was now a revolutionary soldier in Pancho Villa's band, even if my heart wasn't quite in it. It was true that I sympathized with Villa's cause, but I didn't want to join the Revolution. At that moment I was assigned to the personal guard of General José Inés Salazar and General Silvestre Quevedo, generals who under General Francisco Villa's command. Generals José Inés Salazar and Silvestre Quevedo were great horsemen and were well respected by their troops. General Quevedo was very handsome, tall and fair, with sidewhiskers, and he had especially good schooling. His father was wealthy and always held good government posts.

I said good-bye to my brother and told him to wait. I would find a way to tell my father so he could go and get him because I knew I would be passing close to where my parents lived. So then, the next day, when the sun was up, we went out, heading for Ciudad Juárez. There was no one to stop us from entering the city; there were no government soldiers. So we provisioned ourselves with everything we needed, especially sugar and coffee, because that's one of the things that's really good out in the countryside: a cup of coffee. We also pressed some men into our service.

Then we headed out for Pearson, my town. I was the guide. I had to tell them how to get in and where the soldiers were quartered. And we went up against our opponents there: the *federales*. They were well trained and armed. For our part we were about ten thousand men strong. Every day we grew in number, some volunteers and others conscripted by force, but there were lots of us.

At about two in the morning we stealthily surrounded the garrison; not even the dogs in the nearby houses heard us. But then the sentinels noticed something and shouted out, "Who goes there?" The cry "Long live Francisco Villa" was heard everywhere. We heard the general's order, "Boys, attack." The sentinels were the ones who died first. Then the soldiers in the barracks, the ones who came out running and shouting; you could hear their cries everywhere. It was terrible; they were caught by surprise. For the first time in my life, I found myself in a sad reality, which was unbearable at times. The soldiers put up strong resistance. They shot at us, but we prevailed. Some were taken prisoner, others were killed, and some were wounded. Our side lost men in the field too. And right afterward they gave me a few minutes to go to my house. When my mother saw me come in, she thought I was coming from the place where I had hidden the cattle, and she quickly told me: "Come inside, dear boy, and hide before they see you. Last night they were fighting here; it's Villa's men." I was smiling. I didn't want to make her sad, but I had to tell her the truth. "Mamá, Villa's men brought me here. I only have a few minutes to say hello and to tell you to go and get Arturo." She began to cry, along with my brothers, and my father was so sad and forlorn because of what had happened.

I had lunch with them, and then my mother, crying, tried to fix me some food that I could take with me, whatever she could. She gave me some money, and the most important thing for me, her blessing. I left quickly. We knew that they [the federales] would be coming for us from Casas Grandes since the general and chiefs of staff who were in the town had escaped along the riverbank heading to Casas Grandes. We left Pearson at ten in the morning. We had not gone more than a few kilometers when we saw a carriage, pulled by a team of horses, coming at us at a full gallop. I had no idea who it could be. It was my mother, my brother, and a girl who had once been my sweetheart. Her name was Angélica Ponce, the daughter of don Guadalupe Ponce, the town judge. She made an offer to my mother, "I with you [unintelligible] up [very early in the morning] to talk to General Quevedo, because he's a very good friend of mine and of my father, and he can let Alfredo go." She was very much mistaken. General Salazar and General Quevedo stopped and talked. They told them that there was no way they would let me go and that they had put themselves in very great danger by coming there since they expected to see the enemy at any minute. They told them to go back immediately, and they had not even reached town when we heard rifle shots from the Villistas who warned us [of approaching federales]. But there was no combat because the government soldiers went back to Casas Grandes for reinforcements. We headed for the town of San Joaquín. We set up camp; we dug in and sheltered there and prepared to meet the enemy. We were expecting them to come at any moment. And the moment arrived. We saw hundreds of soldiers coming down the mountains trails, heading toward us. The fighting began. It was a terrible battle. Many men on both sides died. But always more of them because we were well protected, because they had to bring the battle to us. So then, the trumpet calls for their withdrawal. The victory was ours. We broke camp. Many prisoners were taken and immediately put in front of a firing squad and shot. That's what I hated most, killing men in cold blood, men who had surrendered and were defenseless. They cried out, their heads down, begging not to be killed for God's sake, for the sake of their parents, their wives, their children, but there was no mercy. War was war. I kept thinking more and more about getting out of all this. That's why they told us every day that if anyone deserted, troops would go and burn, destroy, our homes and families. As a result, I kept thinking, I couldn't desert without telling my father to make plans to go to the United States, and that's what I intended to do. Somehow

I managed to send a letter to my father. Then he had my brother Manuel, the eldest, who was in El Paso, Texas, come and sell everything they had. My father took his best dairy cows along, and they went to the United States. They went by way of Columbus [New Mexico] until they got to Douglas, Arizona, where they stopped and waited to see what was going to happen to me: they were expecting me to arrive at any minute. Meanwhile, I kept going along. It was my good fortune that the generals took a liking to me; they seemed to think highly of me. They gave me a .38 special revolver, a real pretty one for sure. Then one day, while I was on my horse, running after some mares, my pistol fell onto a rock and broke. The generals were rather disappointed in me, but they didn't give me any chances to leave them.

We went to the town, Valle de San Buenaventura. The government soldiers had recently evacuated the town's plaza. There hadn't been many of them, and they weren't waiting for us. We went into the town. We gathered a sufficient supplies for the troops, and we set out for the hacienda they called the Willow [Sauce]. There we took on about twenty-five volunteers—very brave men. We headed for the train station a few kilometers away; we were going to wait there for the train coming from Chihuahua to Ciudad Juárez. We knew that it was coming with the pay for the government troops. My generals wanted to meet the train and make off with the money, but their plans failed. About thirty men were sent off to set up an ambush behind a big wood pile. Then they ordered that a section of rails be pulled up to derail the engine before it passed by; everything was supposed to be very easy. But it didn't turn out that way. The soldiers needed to hold their fire until the train passed the spot where they hid. And the train was full of soldiers guarding the paymaster. The soldiers waiting for them got antsy, as they say, and began to shoot before the train reached them. The train stopped, and the battle began. Our men behind the logs were killed by the soldiers on the trains, and the rest of our men came forward. It was closely fought, man to man; the Villistas were mowed down with machine guns. The federales targeted all of them, and they fought desperately until General Salazar and General Quevedo, seeing what was happening, went to their aid, but it was impossible. They beat us back. We mounted our horses. One of the captains got his horse shot out from under him. When I saw him fall, I turned back and pulled him up on my horse's haunches. A bullet came right at me. It struck my saddle horn and blew it to pieces. It was a terrible battle. You could hear wounded soldiers cry out. They had taken our horses, and the frightened men dropped their rifles and wouldn't turn back even if we threatened them with our pistols. Finally, we learned that three enemy soldiers got away with three horses. The train started backing up, little by little, with its soldiers, and we were forced to break camp. We lost a lot of men and gained nothing. Of the poor soldiers who had volunteered at the hacienda, hardly one was left alive. We left with three carts full of wounded men. The carts were from a nearby mine; the wounded were cared for, but nearly all of them died. Shortly after this, the mothers and daughters of the soldiers came up on foot, asking what had happened to their men; General Quevedo told them that they were fine and that they had gone on ahead.

From there we set out for Sierra el Nido [Sierra's Nest], a place that the Villistas always went to. It's beautiful countryside. There's an abundance of water, trees, very tall hills from which our sentinels can look out over long distances to see if the enemy was approaching. A great silence settled over everything. At night you could only hear the neighing of a few horses or the sound of water as it ran tranquilly down the arroyo. We rested very well for a week. Then we took to the road again, until we crossed another mountain range. We went into a very large canyon that they call Juan el Largo [Long John]. We made camp there, for the enemy was still on our trail. We could not sleep easily now. That was where I made my decision to get away, and I was resolute; two of my trusted friends and I made our preparations. These were the Sosa brothers from the Juárez neighborhood [of Casas Grandes]; the Villistas had also recruited them by force. But these poor boys knew nothing about the countryside. They had never left their town or taken part in the Revolution.

On a cold, dark night, at about eight o'clock, the generals—Salazar and Quevedo—saw me out walking, and asked me where I was going. I told them that I was going to talk to some boys who had a campfire. They told me to come back right away, to not stay long. I told them, All right. I was tired of that sad life, so I had made up my mind to do whatever it took. When I was alone, I asked for my mother's prayers to help me. I did not go back to my spot to sleep.

My companions made plans to get food and rifles to take along. I couldn't do any of this. My rifle was on the bench where they put them, and the bench was very close to where the generals slept. So I couldn't get anything, except for my jacket and some matches. My friends and I made arrangements for where they'd wait for me. So I started doing what I had to do and what had to happen. At about eleven o'clock at night I tried to mount a horse that had no saddle. The horse wasn't used to having a bareback rider. When it felt me, it let loose and threw me off, which made a very loud noise. The sentinels shouted, "Who goes there?" And the camp was put on alert. I lay there, where the horse had thrown me, until everything was quiet again. I waited about an hour, and then I started out again, but this time I went on foot until I reached the place where my companions were waiting for me. They couldn't hear me; I threw stones at them. They were very frightened by the noise that I had made with the horse. I joined them, and we walked all night long, as fast as we could, crossing the plain. We knew very well that if we'd tried during the day, the generals would be able to see us with their binoculars and that they'd come after us the next day. Tired, exhausted, and very thirsty, we went into some woods at about eight in the morning. There we rested a good while and then started on our way again. We passed through a good part of the woods, afraid that we'd run into the Villistas or the federales. The animals, on the other hand, which wanted to make us their prey, were all around us by the thousands, and we could find nothing to eat there. We decided to stop at a place that had once been a camp-site. We were very hungry because the boys hadn't brought any food or rifles. With rifles we could have shot something to eat, even if it was only a bird. But none of that. So I kept looking around, and finally I found a piece of animal hide that was more or less fresh. I put it on the fire and made a kind of pork rind out of it. My companions and I shared it. We had water, which made for a great feast. We took what was left along for lunch. The ammunition we had with us helped us a great deal one night when we were surrounded by seven or eight wolves. We lit a fire near a tree and then climbed it. From there we threw bullets into the fire and scared the animals away with the noise. On another day we came upon the San Lorenzo River. It was completely frozen over because it was so cold. We broke through the ice to cross over. By now our clothes and shoes were in very bad shape. But we kept going, now [illegible] sad, especially my companions. One of them didn't want to go on any farther; he wanted to stay there; he felt absolutely hopeless. Our feet were very swollen from walking so far. I encouraged them, telling them that we'd come to a town soon and we would get help, but that town never appeared. I told them that we would get to a road that people traveled, but that was all imaginary because we were in the deepest part of the mountain range. After we had gone through the woods and mountains, their spirits picked up a bit one morning, at about ten o'clock, when we came upon a road that showed signs of recent cart tracks. We got very excited and hurried to catch up to it. There was a good man. We caught up with him because he'd stopped by the side of the road to have lunch. We greeted him and briefly told him what had happened to us and where we'd come from. He made us feel welcome and gave us some of his lunch, but he wouldn't let us eat much because our stomachs were empty. We asked him where he was going, and he told us to San Buenaventura. We asked him if he could take us in his cart. He said nothing. We saw that he didn't trust us because we were deserters. Finally, he answered that he would. We told him we would let him know when we reached the outskirts of the town so that we could get off the cart and go on foot.

The Valle de San Buenaventura is a settlement that's well-known for its great agriculture. It has many orchards that produce sweet fruit; it has a nice plaza with its kiosk and a nice garden; you can see its church tower from far away. Finally, we got there. I had a friend there, Patricio Cadena. So we asked the first person we met where my friend lived. He told me. We were very close to his house. We knocked on the door, and Patricio opened it. He recognized me immediately. He let us in, and we were very embarrassed because we were in such bad shape. My hair uncombed, I had not shaved in at least a week and was nearly without shoes or clothes. He kindly did what he could to help us clean up and gave us some clothes. Afterward he introduced us to some friends of his; there had been a dance that night, and they had just gotten up.

We spent a day there. We told Patricio our story, and afterward he took us to the home of one of my future wife's sisters, where they made us feel welcome, too. Now that we were rested, we could find no one to take us to Casas Grandes. They gave us a few centavos and some lunch, and we said good-bye, thanking my friend, Patricio, and Matilde's sister, before we set out on foot again. My companions told me that they had an uncle in [San Pedro] Espindoleño who could get us some horses. The ranch was far away. It took us days to get there. When we arrived, we found the uncle without any animals to lend us because the revolutionaries had taken them all. So we set out on foot again, following the path we had already gone over, until we got to the road to Casas Grandes. There, from time to time, we were given rides in carts. After many mishaps we finally reached Casas Grandes. From there we found acquaintances to take us to Colonia Juárez because that's where the boys' parents were from. When they saw us, their sons, they were very happy. They told my companions that if it had not been for me, they would not know what would have become of them. Their parents, nearly in tears, thanked me. They prepared a meal for us. That was the last day I spent with them. I said good-bye to my companions, promising never to forget these hardships and the suffering we had gone through because of the Revolution, because this business of being Villistas had taken its toll on us.

I went to see a friend who lived in the Colonia. He took me to Pearson, which was very close by. I discovered that my parents and my family had gone to the United States. I had not known any of this [while I was in the sierra]. I went to the house of another friend, Marcos Flores. Then I went to visit all my friends. I sold the animals, a mare and a cow that my father had left behind. I got the money together in a few days. I set out for the United States, following my parents, who were in Douglas, Arizona. I really surprised them. They welcomed me very happily. We stayed for some time there, with my father always dreaming of his beloved Mexico.

So we returned to Mexico, and I think that my destiny was always calling me back to that town, Pearson. And here I end my story of the Villista revolution of General Francisco Villa, which holds an indelible history for Mexico and for that northern state, our beloved State of Chihuahua.

Selection 6

ANAÏS NIN, born Angela Anaïs Juana Antolina Rosa Edelmira Nin y Cul-
mell (1903–77), has not been traditionally identified as a Latina. She was
born to privileged Catalan Cuban parents in France, where she was raised,
and spent some time in Spain and Cuba but lived most of her life in the
United States (New York and Los Angeles), where she became a writer. The
selected excerpts are taken from her journal writing while Nin lived in Los
Angeles, the city where she died. She began writing her journals, to which
she owes her writing fame, at age eleven and would continue writing them
until her death. She also published three novels, a five-volume roman-fleuve
(continuous novel), short stories, essays, erotica written during the early
1940s, three novellas, and critical studies, much of which was published
posthumously. Her writing was influenced by surrealism and psychoanalysis. Yet surprisingly, Nin remains absent from anthologies of Los Angeles
Hispanic writing and U.S. Latina/o writing in general while retaining her
literary purchase as an important feminist precursor. Marisela Norte, for
example, acknowledges the influence of Nin's journaling style in her poetic
diaries of Los Angeles bus riding.[1] Nin's views of Los Angeles move from
the stereotypical image of the city toward a more personal attachment with
the place where she lived for long periods of her life. Nin never denies her
connections with Hispanic culture. Her upbringing in Spain and Cuba and
her frequent trips to Mexico are recurring reference points in her diary, as
is her struggle with Spanish Catholicism. Her diaries of gay, bisexual, and
heterosexual experimentation precede and complement John Rechy's, each
"sexual outlaws" of their respective times. Her 1966 *LA Free Press* review of
a UCLA screening of Jean Genet's 1950 sexually explicit short film, *Un chant
d'amour* (*Song of Love*), in celebrating the surrealist poet's overtly homoerotic
aesthetic (and which a U.S. Supreme Court decision banned from commercial
circulation), helped open an expressive space for gay and feminist artists.[2]

Excerpts from *The Journals of Anaïs Nin*

ANAÏS NIN

From *The Journals of Anaïs Nin, 1947–1955*, ed. Gunther Stuhlmann
(New York: Quartet Books, 1974), 24.

I return to Los Angeles for another book-signing party.

Los Angeles is not as deeply natural or joyous as Mexico, but the white houses, the palm trees and the sun give a feeling of lightness; people are tanned, they seem carefree, they prefer the beach to an exhibition, the beach to a concert, the beach to a theater. The cars shine and carry surfboards on their roofs. Or the drivers ride in bathing suits, with the top down, hair flying. There are parts of the beach which are deserted, rocks to sunbathe on. I am awaked by the singing of the mocking birds. They sing at night like Keats' nightingale. It is a forest of billboards, each bigger and louder than the next. It is Nathanael West's Hollywood, a fair, grotesque vaudeville, a grade B film. The people of Hollywood Boulevard dress as though they bought their clothes in a thrift shop, a fur coat and sandals, slacks and gold shoes, satin waists and sports skirts. Dyed hair tired of being dyed. They live in boardinghouses, awaiting roles, jobs, stardom.

*

From *The Journals of Anaïs Nin, 1947–1955*, ed. Gunther Stuhlmann
(New York: Quartet Books, 1974), 34–35.

Life in Los Angeles is not as toxic as in New York. The proximity of the Orient and to Mexico has made people less obsessionally ambitious and more in love with life. Everyone has a garden, and people are not enslaved by the clock.

The Japanese have designed the gardens, the Mexicans influence the rhythm. You feel the presence of the desert when people speak of the Santa Ana winds, which recall the simoom in Mallorca. You feel the fruitfulness of the canyons, and the presence of the sea. The sun pulls you out of the house. The artificial presence of filmmakers does not seem part of the land. The surrealists would be pleased with the sudden appearance of a subway station on a truck being taken to a studio, by the movie villages Nathanael West wrote about, the reproductions of Western towns, of Swiss villages, of Southern mansions. As you are walking along a street suddenly you see a whole house approaching on wheels; it fills the streets. It is being moved. I thought it would be marvelous to film a party going on as the house moves; it reminded me of the Haitian stories about the trees which moved from place to place in the night. One never thinks of a house moving.

*

From *The Journals of Anaïs Nin, 1955–1966*, ed. Gunther Stuhlmann (New York: Quartet Books, 1988), 96–98.

Watts Towers.

When Simon Rodia arrived from Italy he was twenty years old. His father had been a mason and had taught him his profession. He settled in a flat, sparsely built section of Los Angeles, next to a railroad track, because the gray wooden shack, built on an odd triangle of land, was inexpensive. He began to work.

He traveled in a dilapidated old Ford truck and returned each night to the lead-gray, wooden house. The patches on each side of the railroad track were neglected. Weeds, tin cans, broken bottles were the only flowers on these dismal gardens. A few discarded automobile tires attracted the neighborhood children to play. The only trees round were bare telephone poles. The landscape ran from burnt brown wild grass to the dirty brown of oil wells. The other houses were like his, wooden planks hastily nailed together, with toothless fences sheltering Negro and Mexican families. The doors whined on rusty hinges. Old newspapers fluttered like dying birds.

The Italian mason was not dressed in dark blue denim. His care was gray and dusty. But he was a skillful mason and had enough work. The radios were loud and harsh, and under the pretext of sharing news, told only of crimes, malice, gangsters, and never registered acts of devotion and sacrifice.

Only salesmen came to his door. One wanted to sell him a burial lot.

"No thanks," he said, "I want to be buried in Italy."

He worked hard. House after house, day after day. At the end of each day there was much to discard, broken tiles, broken mosaics, broken glass, which he brought back in his truck.

During his meals of red wine, sausage, spaghetti, he dreamed. It was almost always the same dream. It was in color. He remembered the tile floor in the kitchen of his childhood home, laid by his father. He remembered the intense midnight-blue of it. He remembered the fountains in the square of his village, decorated with mosaics. The ceiling of his church, and the scenes of heaven in gold and blue mosaics. He remembered the church steeple decorated with gold tiles which shone in the sun. Memories of color. Memories of arches, colonnades, steeples, stairways, patios, squares where the mosaics were delicately painted.

What he had collected in his yard were fragments, as if all the beautiful things he had seen in Italy now lay wrecked. But the fragments, discards shone in the light even when broken. He began to see he could no longer live with such squalor around him. He cleared his own yard, erected a skeleton of iron, similar to the Eiffel Tower, and upon this he began to cement the broken pieces of tiles, glass, and even pottery he found in garbage dumps. It was not a reproduction of what he had seen in Italy. It was his dream of color, of light-catching fragments, diffused by time and memory. It was his very own creation, resembling none other, but capable of giving the same delight as the contemplation of the finished ceilings, towers, plazas of Italy. The fragments would be patterned, abstract floral designs, abstract mandalas, with the bottom of a bottle for a heart. There were turrets, archways, ogival passages, all richly encrusted with whatever had color and could catch the light. It was a Byzantine city seen in dreams, slightly blurred by time, as if the campaniles of Venice, the minarets of Rome, were all reflected in water, built of light, losing their sharp contours. Standing out from the flat masonry surfaces were strange lyric shapes: the swan neck of a broken teapot, the lyre-shaped handle of a cup. His Italian cities had left imprints of gold, green, red, silver, his churches the memory of colors seen through painted glass. Assembled lovingly in spiraling towers, they were more miraculous, built by one hand, in the midst of barrenness, rising among telephone poles and dead, brown devil grass.

The salesman came every year to sell him a burial lot.

The mason was forty years old. Two towers rose as high as oil rigs. Artists came from all over the world to see them.

One day when the salesman came to see him, the mason, now eighty years old, had gone. He had returned to Italy.

*

From *The Journals of Anaïs Nin, 1966–1974*, ed. Gunther Stuhlmann (New York: Quartet Books, 1980), 278–79.

I am beginning to appreciate Los Angeles. True, Frank Lloyd Wright called it a lot of suburbs looking for a city (he also said the United States tilts to the southwest and everything loose ended up in Southern California), and I still resent the long drives on the freeways. But I now feel this is the only large cosmopolitan city where I can be warm all year, close to the sea and still create my own small paradise just five minutes from downtown.

Selection 7

BERT CORONA was one of the most prominent members of the Sleepy Lagoon Defense Committee and one of the present-day founders of the immigrant rights movement. We learn in Corona's recollections that this community activist, labor organizer, and organic intellectual was another child of the Mexican Revolution shaped in the Depression's labor struggles. It is his not-so-disguised formation in the Left politics of the pre– and post–World War II era that will color his recollections of the notorious Sleepy Lagoon case. As Raúl Homero Villa acutely observes, this *testimonio* represents one of several texts offering "longer views of historical presence and struggles for place-rights that have helped construct the social space of ethnicity among working-class barrio residents."[1] Corona's *testimonio* recalls the 1970s as an exciting period in which he nevertheless perceived the limits of Chicana/o cultural nationalism and anticipated an immigrant Latina/o working-class majority's turn toward an urban politics of class struggle. Along these lines Laura Pulido, reflecting on Corona and Los Angeles's Centro de Acción Social Autónomo (Autonomous Social Action Center, CASA), writes, "Former members of CASA had not only created a network of like-minded people but seeds of resistance within the 'old' labor movement that would blossom with the advent of greater institutional support."[2] These seeds, she argues, would bear fruit in the 1990s, when former CASA members trained under Corona assumed leadership positions within the local and national labor movement, the legal arm of the immigrant rights movement, and the political class that would reshape Los Angeles's political culture after the 1990s. Rather than simply respond to the material conditions of the late 1970s, their practice would create the conditions for another struggle, the one that filled the streets of Los Angeles and other major cities in 2006 with arguably the largest collection of U.S. street demonstrations since the early twentieth century.

Jesús Mena, as Corona's *cronista*, continued the organizer's pro-social legacy. A founding member of the Los Angeles Latino Writers Workshop, Mena edited the anthology *201 / Two Hundred and One: Homenaje a la ciudad de Los Ángeles / Latino Experience in Literature and Art* (1982) in which Corona's *testimonio* was published. Already an activist in LA's emerging immigrant rights movement, Mena looked to the Latin American *nueva crónica*'s experiments that tried to reverse the self-aggrandizing power relations of the journalists who appoint themselves the "voice of the voiceless." Instead, like Elena Poniatowska's *Hasta no verte Jesús mío* (1969) and Miguel Barnet's *Biografía de un cimarrón* (1966), Mena subordinated his desire for self-expression to Corona's, a role reversal that created a space for his subject to put his life story to print for the first time. Mena's interviewing and editing experience would serve him well, as it provided him the opportunity to launch a journalism career that eventually made him director of communications and public affairs for Harvard University's Kennedy School of Government.

Bert Corona's "Struggle Is the Ultimate Teacher"

JESÚS MENA

I first met Bert Corona at a rally in downtown Los Angeles in February 1971. A coalition of Chicano activists spearheaded by casa (Centro de Acción Social Autonóma) had organized the rally to protest the harassment that the Latino population in East Los Angeles was suffering at the hands of the Immigration and Naturalization Services (ins). The demonstration marked the first time anyone had tried to mobilize undocumented people in a militant street protest. Even the organizers were uncertain as to how massive the turnout would be. Much to everyone's surprise, more than five thousand East Los Angeles residents gathered at the corner of Olympic and Broadway on the sunny Saturday morning. Bert Corona, founder of casa, spoke angrily to the gathering at the steps of City Hall, where he documented the abuses of civil rights that the ins was guilty of. A motivating orator, Corona received a thunderous applause when he proclaimed that the Spanish-speaking population would not sit idly by as their rights were trampled upon.

Corona has been a public spokesman for the Latino social movements in this city since the days of the infamous Zoot Suit Riots. His persistence in the struggle for equality has earned him a massive following in the barrios of East Los Angeles. His influence, however, extends beyond the Spanish-speaking community—he has been a union organizer since he was a teenager. Despite the broad base of support he enjoys, Corona has never run for public office, choosing instead to influence local politics through periodic shows of force on the streets. Undoubtedly, he has been one of the most prominent men in LA politics over the decades.

Getting an interview with Bert Corona requires a great deal of patience. While the man is sixty-three years old, he keeps a schedule that would tire a man thirty years his junior. Only when I combined the interview with a social gathering was I able to spend the time with him necessary to learn about his complex life's story.

As I later sat across from him at the dinner table, I was struck by his relatively short stature. Undoubtedly, his eloquence as a public speaker gives one the illusion that he is a much larger man. Yet the strength of presence he projects as an orator is apparent in his hand gestures, which he uses skillfully to emphasize his comments. His bushy white hair helps to dramatize his emphatic voice that never falters, flowing smoothly from English into Spanish and back again.

Corona was an inspiration to those of us who were active in the Chicano movement in the 1970s, when his charismatic personality consistently motivated both his followers and his opponents into action. While most of my activist contemporaries have dropped out of the movement altogether since that time, Corona seems to have found the secret of longevity in the politics of protest. Understandably, my first question concerned the reason behind his consistency in struggling for justice for the Latino population.

Corona insists that to understand the motivation behind his activities, one has to know the Corona family history. Bert Corona was born in 1918 in El Paso, Texas, into a recently immigrated family that had a rich history as political activists in Mexico.

According to my grandmother, my great-grandfather came into Mexico about 1854–55, when the country was in the middle of a civil war. Arriving penniless from Spain, he joined the army and fought some of the battles. He settled in the Sierras of Chihuahua after the war, where he married my great-grandmother, his first wife.

Chihuahua was still in turmoil at the time my great-grandparents settled in the area. Many of the generals who had fought with Benito Juárez in the war against the French came to settle in this state, where they just stole whatever land they wanted. That's how my family lost their land. The hierarchy that these generals formed was very powerful, and they succeeded in forcing most of the small settlers from the foothills into the higher Sierras. Some of the people wound up in land that was rocky. It was very difficult to survive in this type of land.

But the poorer families began to fight back. They organized guerrilla bands that raided the large landowners. These bands were led by such figures as Enrique Parra and the original Pancho Villa—not the more commonly known Villa from the Mexican Revolution. The federal troops were helpless against these indigenous fighters because they knew the terrain so well. It was their land to begin with. Wherever the troops dared to pursue a raiding party into the Sierras, they were usually ambushed.

In 1892, after many years of violence, the government proposed that a peace "mass" be held so that some settlement could be arrived at. The mass was convened in the village of Tomochi by a priest who had the confidence of the mountain people. And so many of the resistance leaders came down to bargain in good faith. While the peace mass was in progress, federal troops surrounded the village and set fire to the church. Hundreds of people were killed. From that point on, my family was on the run.

My family went to hide in the Cañón del Cobre in Chihuahua, where the Tarahumara Indians lived. My grandmother talked very vividly about those times. My clan lived there for five or six years, and my grandmother came to speak their language fluently. Until the day she died, she insisted that she was Tarahumara.

The fighting against the *hacendados* continued into this century, leading up to the Mexican Revolution. My father joined Pancho Villa's forces at a young age—about thirteen or fourteen. He fought with him for many years and was finally killed when some of Villa's forces were ambushed in Chapingo in 1924.

In many ways my family was victimized by the Mexican Revolution. They lost their land, their cattle, and were finally forced to seek refuge in the United States. Yet my family never took it as a defeat. They always spoke of the principles that we fought for and continued to believe in the cause, confident that it would eventually triumph.

Though we fled from Mexico, we actually carried the Revolution with us. There were many refugee families in El Paso other than ours. They were either friends or foes—they either fought on the same side as my father or fought against him. So we related to these people in this fashion. So, as you can see, politics has always been an important influence in my life.

Corona's concern with politics as a youngster led him to choose law as his career. He came to Los Angeles in 1936 at the age of eighteen to attend the University of Southern California.

I had a so-called scholarship. They didn't give you money in those days. They just gave you a job while you were attending school. I was assigned to the Brunswig Drug Company, a large laboratory of some thirteen or fourteen hundred workers. As a matter of fact, the building we worked in is still there at La Placita, near the Pico House. I hadn't worked there three or four months when some organizers from the International Longshoremen's Association (ILA) of the AF of L came to our workplace. They wanted to organize us into a local. So I became active, and we began the long process of convincing our fellow workers to join the union.

The dockworkers were on strike at the time. It was a very violent struggle in which the bosses were trying to destroy the longshoremen's union altogether. The newspapers never mentioned the violence, except once, I think.

Sporadic disorders flared along the Los Angeles Harbor waterfront yesterday and last night in advance of the threatened strike due at midnight tonight.
—*LOS ANGELES TIMES*, OCTOBER 28, 1936

The longshoremen badly needed the support of the inland warehouse in order to win the strike. Since the union was short on organizers, those of us active in the Brunswig plant decided to help out in recruiting new locals inland. We formed what were known as flying squads. Our responsibility was to visit workers at other warehouses early in the morning before our own shift began. Then, after work and on weekends, we would join the picket lines on the docks. Young people nowadays don't understand how united workers were in those days. We didn't go because we had to. We went because it mattered to us even if it was dangerous business. The police attacked us on several occasions, swinging their clubs as they attacked the picket line. They tried to destroy our spirit. But we held out, and after ninety-nine days of fighting, we won. We did it.

In the spring of 1937 the Brunswig Drug Company was successfully unionized. Corona was elected recording secretary for the new local, only to become its elected president two years later, at the age of twenty-one. Corona quickly came to realize that union politics could be fraught with danger.

The national leadership of the International Longshoremen's Association was very corrupt. They had not had an election since 1922. All of the important decisions were made in New York and imposed on the membership in the locals. Understandably, we often had heated debates in our locals that turned into brawls. It was madness. The way the locals settled the arguments was by issuing union books. You see, the union had a hall on the docks. In order to be assigned a job, you had to report to the hall and present your union book to show you were a member in good standing. Well, whenever you disagreed with the leadership in those local meetings, you were not issued a book and therefore could not get a job. You can imagine how frustrating it was.

In 1937 we decided to deal with the situation by running a democratic and progressive slate in our local. Since the leadership in New York was backed by mafia elements like Frank Scalise and Joseph Anastacia, they saw our slate as a threat to their power. They sent in goons to intimidate our people. When the elections took place, our slate won, but the national union refused to recognize us.

We had pitched warfare with the national leadership for about a year after the election. Even though they did not recognize our elected officials, they still sent in gangster types to try to collect our dues and relay orders from national headquarters. When we refused to comply unless they recognized us, the goons would try to physically evict us from our headquarters. Vicious fights broke out. We were forced to post armed guards at our office on Second and Los Angeles, twenty-four hours a day. The harassment continued for almost a year. The thugs would often wait in their cars outside our union meetings or near the plant, and whenever they saw any of our people by themselves, they would jump out of their cars, strike the person with the sap, and run from the scene. You know what a sap is? It's a rubber bag filled with sand. They preferred those to sticks because they made less noise but caused serious injuries. Many of our members were beaten up.

After a year of violence, we couldn't take it anymore. We decided to withdraw from the ILA altogether. We had a convention in 1938 and formed the International Longshoreman and Warehouse Union Independent, affiliated with the Congress of Industrial Organizations (CIO). We elected Harry Bridges as our West Coast regional director. We were finally able to get to the business of organizing workers rather than fighting the goons.

Corona's union activities took him away from his studies, and he dropped out of college altogether. He went on to become a prominent organizer in the CIO, helping to organize Spanish-speaking workers in low-paying jobs such as scrap iron junkyards, canneries, and warehouses at the end of the 1930s and in the 1940s. His work with the lowest-paid workers gave Corona an insight into the social conditions in which Latinos lived. Corona was saddened when he related how little things have changed.

Even though things have improved for our people over the years, the social problems remain the same. Racism has always existed in Los Angeles. There was racism on the docks. The black and Mexican workers formed gangs and were forced to segregate themselves from the rest of the crew.

The population as a whole was segregated. The barrios were like islets in Los Angeles. There were places, like Glendale, where Mexicans were not tolerated. There were no barbed wire fences keeping us out of those areas, but blacks and Mexicans who were not servants were escorted by the police out of Glendale if they were found on the streets after dark. We got similar treatment in Santa Monica as well as other places.

There was segregation in the theaters and the motion picture houses. The large Paramount Ballroom, for example, was set up so that Friday was Mexican night and Saturday was Anglo night. It was a popular place where the big band sounds performed—like Glen Miller and performers like that.

We experienced discrimination on a daily basis. I remember an incident when a friend of mine and I went to the Bimini Swimming Pool on Third and Vermont. As a matter of fact, I went with Henry Nava, brother of the former ambassador to Mexico Julian Nava. We got into line to get our towels, locks, etc. I was ahead of Henry and went on in, thinking he was right behind me. When I got to the gym, I noticed Henry was missing. I went back to the line and found the attendant asking him for his birth certificate. They were threatening to detain him if he could not show proof of citizenship. Well, he was so outraged he was almost in tears.

Perturbed by the memories, Corona stroked his bushy hair as he leaned forward to the edge of his seat. The wrinkles on his forehead became more pronounced as he continued to paint vivid pictures of the injustices he has spent more than forty years trying to eradicate.

There were many cases of police brutality, many documented cases of beatings in jail. The maladministration of justice was certainly a key social problem. There was brutality in the schools, with many cases of severe beating of Mexican kids by the coaches and the principals. But I guess the biggest problem for Mexicans was the economic problem. The economic conditions for Mexicans in this city were deplorable.

We represented a smaller portion of the city's population than we do now, about 18 percent or 19 percent of the total. Since a large sector of the Mexican population was employed in agriculture, the population fluctuated with the seasons. In the summer our percentage would go down to as low as 15 percent when people left for the harvest, only to rise to 23–24 percent in the wintertime. The wages these workers got on the road were barely enough to keep body and soul together. The wages for the Mexicans employed in the city were about as bad. Mexicans worked as janitors, busboys, railroad workers. The ditchdiggers were Mexican, as were the cannery workers and the food processors. In general all of the dirty, seasonal, and unsafe jobs were left to the Mexican population. We could be found in the lumber, the chemical mixing rooms, flour and cement mills, in the foundries and in the hearths in the steel industry and in the scrap iron industry. The scrap iron industry was especially big in those times because Japan was buying all our scrap iron. That country was at war with China but did not have the steel to build the weapons essential to conduct its offensive. Mexicans have always played a vital role in this city's economy, but our economic and political needs have never been fulfilled.

Corona pointed out that the injustices prompted concern in the Catholic Church, the radical groupings and the Mexican nationalist groupings. Yet because of disparate interests, it was often difficult to build united protest actions from these forces.

The Citizens' Committee for the Defense of Mexican-American Youth, better known as the Sleepy Lagoon Defense Committee, was a classic example of how united action could be formed to defend our rights. It was the first effort organized by Mexicans themselves to resist the police attack that had been launched against our community.

Throughout the year of 1942, the press had been reporting that East Los Angeles had been experiencing a crime wave involving juvenile gangs. Those of us who lived in the area knew that was not the case. The death of José Díaz at the Sleepy Lagoon Ranch was used by the media to prove that Los Angeles was being overrun by Zoot Suit gangs. José Díaz was a youngster who had been found dead on a road in the ranch one night. He had been run over by a car and was apparently intoxicated when he died. There had been a gang-related incident in the area, but there wasn't any evidence that the death was gang related. Of course, the newspapers reported the death as another gang casualty.

ONE KILLED AND 10 HURT IN
BOY WAR: BOY GANGS OPERATING
WITHIN THE CITY
One person dead . . . another believed dead
. . . 10 others beaten and injured was the
grisly toll early yesterday as juvenile gang
warfare flared anew in Los Angeles County.
—*LOS ANGELES TIMES*, AUGUST 3, 1942

The reporting was terrible. The hysteria the newspapers whipped up was so bad that the soldiers stationed in the area decided it was time to take matters into their own hands. These enlisted men would form caravans that would invade the barrios on weekends and would beat up any kid that they saw on the streets wearing a zoot suit.

Corona recalls the assaults by the soldiers and sailors on the Latino community with bitterness, contending that they represented the most brutal treatment that any minority has received in this country. *Time* magazine would concur, as it reported in its issue of June 21, 1942: "The police practice was to accompany the caravans (of soldiers and sailors) in police cars, watch the beatings and arrest the victims. The press, with the exception of the *Daily News* and the *Hollywood Citizen News*, helped whip up the mob spirit. And Los Angeles, apparently unaware that it was spawning the ugliest brand of mob actions since the coolie race riots of 1870, gave its tacit approval."

Josefina Fierro, a longtime agricultural trade union organizer and secretary of the National Congress of Spanish-Speaking People, was the one who called and asked me to help her organize the Sleepy Lagoon Defense Committee. Even though I did help her in the initial stages of the work, the credit for organizing the committee belongs to Josefina.

Josefina Fierro was a marvelous organizer with a dramatic family history. She was married to a Hollywood writer by the name of John Bright, who became one of the Hollywood Ten during the McCarthy inquisitions. Her mother participated in the Mexican Revolution, and she was related to the Flores Magon brothers. At the same time, however, she was related to the Amador family, one of the most prominent Mexican families in Los Angeles. They owned the biggest restaurant on Olvera Street—the Amador that was behind the Pico House. But Josefina was a rebel at heart. She remembered her early childhood when her mother had driven a cart from labor camp to labor camp. Her mother would serve food to the farmworkers, would wash clothes for a fee, and would write letters home for those workers who could not write. Inspired by her mother's concerns for other people, Josefina dedicated her life to union and political organizing.

The respect that this woman had acquired over the years because of her work became apparent when she undertook the organization of the Sleepy Lagoon Defense Committee. She was able to put together a coalition that included prominent church leaders as well as Hollywood personalities like

Anthony Quinn and Orson Welles in support of the Zoot Suit victims. She gained the endorsement of the Mexican consulate as well as of the Mexican Chamber of Commerce. She was also able to involve communists, radicals, and blacks in the work of the committee. With such a broad base of support, the committee was able to mount a good legal defense and successfully stage demonstrations in support of the defendants. During the trial, for example, the committee organized a rally at La Placita that was four blocks long and was one of the largest political gatherings of Mexicans up to that time in Los Angeles.

The Sleepy Lagoon case had a great deal of impact in Latin America. Most people were not aware of this. At the time of the Zoot Suit Riots, the Allies were already at war with the Nazis. The Axis powers were trying to win over the allegiance of the Latin American countries. When the riots took place, the Nazis transmitted the news throughout Latin America, broadcasting editorials to whip up resentment toward the United States. A radio statement broadcast by the Axis powers all over Latin America on January 13, 1943, announced: "In Los Angeles, California, the so-called 'City of Angels,' twelve Mexican boys were found guilty today of a single murder and five others were convicted of assault growing out of the same case. The 360,000 Mexicans of Los Angeles are reported up in arms over this Yankee persecution. The concentration camps of Los Angeles are said to be overflowing with the members of this persecuted minority. This is justice for you, as practiced by the 'Good Neighbor,' Uncle Sam, a justice that demands seventeen victims for one crime."

Their tactics were effective. The students in Mexico City, for example, staged a strike in support of the Zoot Suit victims and wound up setting fire to the U.S. Embassy.

The Allies were upset to see such hostility toward the United States since they needed the support of the Latin American countries. The European Allies pressured the White House to intervene in the Zoot Suit affair so that some settlement could be reached whereby the Latin American countries would feel that justice had been carried out. Under the international pressure, Vice President Wallace appointed a committee to come to Los Angeles to investigate the matter. By this time the Mexican consulate was actively involved in the case. They insisted that negotiations had to be carried out with the Mexican government before the matter could be cleared to their satisfaction.

Since Josefina had done such a good job on the Defense Committee, she was called on to mediate the negotiations that took place in Mexico City and in Washington. When the mediations were completed, the White House and the War Department sent orders to the naval commander and to the air force commander, informing them that they were to keep all soldiers out of the Mexican community or they would face a court-martial. Now, this is the *real* story of the Sleepy Lagoon Defense Committee. It's the story of the Mexican community organizing itself and successfully fighting for its rights. It is a far cry from the story that emerges from Luis Valdez's play *Zoot Suit*.

I must admit that I was very disappointed with Luis Valdez's play. The play implied that it was the Jewish woman, Alice Greenfield McGrath, and not Josefina Fierro, who was the main organizer for the Defense Committee. Alice did work on the committee, but all she did was the secretarial work, and she'll be the first to admit it. Instead of concentrating on the community organizing that went into the Defense Committee, Luis chose to present the story of the case as a romance. What's worse is that the romance between Henry Leyvas and Alice Greenfield McGrath never even took place. His portrayal of this romance offended some of the original defendants in the case. Now, there is plenty of room in literature for works that are strictly the product of a writer's imagination, but when one pretends to base a work on historical fact, he has to remain true to the facts. As far as I'm concerned, the case is still open for some decent literary and dramatic treatment.

> The intervention of the federal government finally put an end to the racial strife that was blatant in the East Los Angeles barrios throughout the early 1940s. While locally there was peace, the rest of the world was at war. Incensed by the atrocities that the Nazis were committing in Europe, Corona volunteered for the air force in 1941, hoping to be sent to combat duty. Although he graduated from Santa Anna Air Force Base with honors, he never received his commission.

My history as a political activist followed me into the service. Just weeks before I was to graduate, I was interrogated by Intelligence. They wanted to know my views on Russia, communism, and on the labor movement. I answered them the best I could and told them that my biggest concern in life was fighting for democracy. I told them that was why I had volunteered and why I wanted to fight the Nazis. Well, by the time they were finished interrogating me, I was blacklisted. It's the kind of thing that follows you all your life. When I got out of the service, I was surprised to find that even some of my old union coworkers thought I was a political militant. The Merchant and Manufacturer's Association had my name on the blacklist that they kept so I was unable to find a job.

Blacklisted in the Southern California job market, Corona moved to San Francisco, where he went to work for his father-in-law, Abraham Taff, who had a small jewelry business.

I have been very fortunate in having both a wife and a father-in-law who sympathized with my activities. I met Blanch on a picket line in 1941. We were married after a brief romance. Her father, Abraham, had been a political activist in the Jewish Bund in Russia that was fighting for freedom against the Russian czar. When I was unable to find employment, Abraham hired me as a traveling salesman. He kept me on payroll, off and on, until 1957, even though I really never earned my keep.

I say that I never earned my keep because I was regional organizer at the time for the National Association of Mexican-Americans (ANMA [Asociación Nacional Mexico-Americana]) and most of my time on the road was spent organizing local chapters instead of selling like I was supposed to. ANMA was a very significant organization that came into existence in 1948. It was the first group to consciously call itself Mexican, choosing to fight for the right for Mexicans to speak our native language, struggling to preserve our culture. Since I was traveling through the smaller towns in the Southwest, most of my work was with migrant workers. We had a broad base of support among braceros, whom we often represented in negotiations whenever the growers would try to cheat them out of their wages. ANMA was especially significant because it was an organization that flourished during the reactionary McCarthy period. It was one of the few organizations to actually grow in those conditions.

The fifties was a very difficult period for political activists in this country. The prosperity that this country enjoyed after the war made the white workers very content with the status quo, very receptive to the anticommunism of

Senator Joseph McCarthy. McCarthy's House Un-American Activities Committee tried to purge this country of all political dissidents. Anyone who disagreed with the government, no matter how mild his criticism, was subject to persecution. Many of the most prominent Mexican leaders were deported. Josefina Fierro, Refugio Martinez, Armando Davila, all were militant leaders who were deported. And these were people whose documents were in perfectly good order.

I was a little more fortunate. The worst that happened to me was that I was bullied by the FBI. Between 1948 and 1953 I received several letters asking that I present myself before various committees that were investigating subversive activities in the state of California. Since they were not subpoenas, I just ignored them and never bothered to show.

Then, in 1953, two FBI agents came to my house. They had been there before, but they had never found me home because I was always on the road. So, when they came to the door, I let them in. They asked me to give them the names of the leaders in the Mexican community who had Communist ties. I told them that I would never give them any names and that they were gravely mistaken in thinking that the Communists had an important influence in the Mexican community. They asked me if I was refusing to cooperate. I repeated my statement. They threatened me, telling me they had ways of making people talk, and then they left. They continued to make calls for a couple of years, but I was never subpoenaed.

> Corona found it difficult to survive as a political organizer in this period
> of political reaction. In 1956 the tough-minded organizer was forced to go
> into business himself, opening an emporium of import goods that stocked a
> variety of exquisite merchandise, from Philippine carved ivory to Mexican
> lacquered cabinets.

My business did very well so long as I made it my main concern. When I began my business, the country was in a period of reaction, so there was little that a political activist could do. In 1960, however, I became involved with MAPA (Mexican American Political Association).

MAPA evolved out of the Minorities Coordinating Committee, which was a part of the Democratic Party. While the blacks were getting some concessions from the Democrats, we, the Mexicans, were being defeated on every resolution we put forward. So we decided to form an independent organization. After several unsuccessful attempts, we were finally able to put together a regional convention in Fresno in 1961, where we elected Congressman Edward Roybal as president of the newly formed MAPA. In 1961 I was the regional organizer for Northern California, which meant that I again had to travel from town to town. Needless to say, it became especially difficult to run my enterprise when I was elected president of MAPA in 1965.

By 1965 I had pretty much closed my business. I had suffered some terrible economic losses. I had been forced to sell a house I had built in Contra Costa Country because I was unable to make the payments. I then built another house in the Oakland Hills on some land I had acquired when my business was doing well. The bank foreclosed on this house as well because my financial situation was so bad that I was unable to keep up with the payments. My wife had to get a job in 1962 as a legal secretary to keep us going. I would say that my wife supported us from 1962 to 1970. As I've already said, I've been very fortunate to have married such an understanding woman.

In 1966 MAPA became involved with Cesar Chavez and the United Farm Workers [UFW]. Chavez had initiated an aggressive organizing drive that year, and we took it upon ourselves to support his movement, especially in the urban areas, where he had no base and we did. But as we began to work more closely with Cesar, we found that we had some principled differences. The main point of disagreement centered on the undocumented worker issue. It was a difficult problem because the undocumented people were very much a part of the workforce that wanted a union, but at the same time, whenever there was a strike, they were the ones who were used to break the strike. The issue came to a head in the 1968 Coachella grape strike. Even though that particular strike had been well organized, it lost a great deal of strength when the INS permitted the growers to openly bring scabs in from Mexico. The reaction of the UFW was very primitive. They decided that the best way to deal with the undocumented scabs was to intimidate them. So they rented some airplanes; they would fly over the fields about two hundred feet from the ground, and they would scream at the people through the loudspeakers:

SALGANSE DE AQUI!! HAY [sic] VIENE LA MIGRA!!

GET OUT OF THE FIELDS!! THE MIGRA IS COMING!!

Well, some of us could not stomach this. How could we go around threatening our own people as if we were the very authorities who persecuted the Mexican population? It was the kind of mistreatment that we had been fighting against for years, and yet here we were doing exactly the same thing.

So in the fall of 1968, those of us who were unhappy with the UFW policy on the undocumented workers had a series of meetings in Los Angeles. Most of the people who participated in these meetings were primarily labor organizers who understood the complicated nature of the problem. It didn't take long to come to an agreement. The only practical solution was to organize rather than intimidate the workers without legal papers. We tried to sell the idea to the union movement but were met with a lot of skepticism. You see, it was an accepted myth that the undocumented workers were not organizable. In fact, most professional union organizers contended that Los Angeles County would never be strongly unionized because there are too many wetbacks in the area. After some initial rejections, we finally got the National Maritime Union to support us.

> With the limited funding from the National Maritime Union, Corona opened up El Centro de Ayuda on Whittier Boulevard near Atlantic. The small office was staffed on a volunteer basis, and Corona was able to get the legal assistance that he needed for his fledgling organization from the Raul Magaña law firm.

When people heard that we could help them with their immigration problems, they literally flocked to our office. While we did help people to file their papers, our center was not simply a social service organization. Anyone who wanted help from us had to commit themselves to helping with the everyday work in the office. They also had to be ready to recruit other members. We were trying to get people to organize themselves. Our operation became large enough that we were forced to move to a larger place in 1970. When we moved to the building on Vermont near Pico, we also changed our name to CASA, El Centro de Acción Social Autónomo (Autonomous Social Action Center). In spite of the fact that we were having such a success, many of the professional organizers continued to be pessimistic about our ability to organize the undocumented. "You may be able to get them together to get their papers," they said, "but you'll never be able to get them to go to picket lines and demonstrations." But we proved them wrong.

The National Chicano Moratorium of August 29, 1970, provided CASA with its first opportunity to mobilize its membership in a militant action. The moratorium was to have been a peaceful antiwar demonstration, but it terminated in a violent confrontation with the police.

An East Los Angeles parade and rally that attracted about 20,000 persons to demonstrate Mexican-American opposition to the war in Southeast Asia erupted into a riot Saturday, claiming the life of one of the city's leading spokesmen for Chicano rights.

The dead man was Ruben Salazar, 42, award-winning *Times* columnist and news director for the television station KMEX (Channel 34).

—*LOS ANGELES TIMES*, SUNDAY, AUGUST 30, 1970

At the peak of the turmoil, a dozen fires burned out of control along Whittier Boulevard and about 500 police and sheriff's deputies were involved.

—DR. ARMANDO MORALES, *ANDO SANGRANDO*

It started innocently enough with almost a festive atmosphere to the march and rally. Many of the CASA members came to the demonstration with their entire families. The children were ecstatic as they helped to carry the banners on the way to the park. It was really a touching scene of solidarity. At the rally we sat at the edge of the park to listen to the speakers and musicians who were to perform that day. Then, the next thing we know, many of the people sitting in front of us started standing up and staring in our direction. A squad of armed riot police was lining up in military formation right behind us. They were preparing to attack the crowd. Our first concern was for the women and children. We tried to safeguard them, but the area we were standing in soon became the main battleground. Chaos broke out when the police shot tear gas into the crowd. Our people ran frantically from the park grounds. We regrouped in an adjacent residential area away from the stinging gas fumes. Then a few of us—myself, Ruben Salazar, the Reverend Father Casso, and Rudy Acuña—went up to the police lineup and tried to reason with the deputy in charge. We asked him to hold off until people were given a chance to disperse peacefully. But he wouldn't listen. They were declaring war just like that. Well, after the initial shock, the youngsters began to fight back, throwing bottles, rocks, even returning tear gas canisters. Even though the police were prepared for combat, the kids forced them to retreat several times.

I certainly regret the loss of lives on that day, especially that of Ruben Salazar, who was a good friend of mine. Still, I can't help but feel a certain pride at the tremendous courage that our youth showed that day when facing a well-armed opponent. It was obvious that the police were intent on crushing this protest movement. It represented an organized defiance to the injustices that the Mexican people had suffered in this country. Our youth showed the police that they could, on the spur of the moment, fight back and take control of their barrios if need be.

If the intent of the police was to defuse the Chicano protest movement, their brutal attack had exactly the opposite effect. According to Corona, the confrontation taught the participants how unjust this country could be to the Mexican population. It also reinforced the need for self-organization. Committees of all types sprang up all over East Los Angeles, focusing on all types of social issues.

I know that our group really grew after the moratorium. With our renewed forces we stepped up our campaign against the Dixon Arnett bill that had just been passed by the state legislature. It was a law that was similar to President Reagan's Employer Sanction bill that made it illegal to knowingly hire undocumented workers. Well, we saw this as a slap in the face because any employer could then justify not hiring Mexicans out of fear of breaking the law. We had tried pressuring then-governor Reagan into vetoing the bill, but he had turned a deaf ear.

You know, there was an interesting meeting between us and Reagan just before the Dixon Arnett bill got passed. As a part of our campaign, casa was picketing the Marina Hotel, where a banquet was being held in honor of then-governor Reagan. The fact that we had some three to four thousand people surrounding the hotel really shook up Mr. Reagan. He sent Judge Alarcon out to the picket line to tell me that Governor Reagan wanted to talk to me. Now Judge Alarcon was an old friend of mine, and he was really upset when I told him I didn't want to talk to Mr. Reagan. But the other people on the picket line thought it was important to keep the channels of communication open, so we chose a delegation to meet with him.

Stepping into that banquet room from a picket line was a very strange experience. The banquet was organized with the center of the hall being left for the dance that was to follow the dinner. And everybody was the guest of honor, I guess, because there was nothing but head tables, four tables, all generously decorated with small American flags. So they took us to the table where Mr. Reagan sat in his tuxedo with large flags hanging on either side of him. He was friendly enough, telling me that he wanted to work out some kind of agreement with my people. I told him that the only thing we wanted was for him to veto the Dixon Arnett bill. And he said: "Well, Bert, you know that I couldn't do that. Those illegals are stealing the jobs from the American worker." I argued with him on the issue, and it really upset him that I did not stand in awe of him. After all, I'm sure he thought, I was talking to the governor. Needless to say, we came to no agreement, so we went back outside to join the picket line. Three to four weeks later he signed the damn bill.

We decided it was time to take more aggressive action. We called for a march and rally through downtown Los Angeles on February 1971. Since it was the first protest we were to organize by ourselves, we were not quite sure how big it was going to be. We worked feverishly for a whole month, setting up committees in the Harbor area, the Valley, Orange County, as well as in Los Angeles proper. I guess the myth that undocumented people would not participate in street protests out of fear of being apprehended was beginning to affect even us. We were cautiously hoping to bring out at least one thousand marchers. But lo and behold, we wound up with a march that was massive. Since we did not have a parade permit, we marched on the sidewalk down Broadway. A lot of people joined us spontaneously from the streets. The spirit was fantastic, and when the head of the march reached First and Broadway, the end was still leaving Olympic. Well, after this experience we made demonstrations a routine part of our activities. We called even larger actions in 1972 and 1973, when the INS was harassing the Mexican population in East Los Angeles.

Our movement became so successful that we got calls from all over the country from community centers that were trying to deal with the problems of the undocumented workers. By 1974 we had centers in New York, San Antonio, and Oakland.

We were not the only ones who were building successful movements in that period. The seventies was an exciting period for Mexican activists. La Raza Unida Party, the Welfare Rights movements, the nationalists like the Brown Berets—all were finding popular support in the barrios. The Mexican population in this country had become openly proud of being Mexican. Whereas in the 1940s and 1950s the activists had argued vehemently over whether to call ourselves "Mexican American" or "Latin American," the generation of the 1970s was expressing a pride that bordered on chauvinism. The tremendous strength that this rediscovery of our identity created really bolstered our movement.

The movement of the 1970s was a youth movement. That was the secret of its strength, its vibrancy and vitality. Unfortunately, it was also the reason for its decline. Youth is very transitory. We were not dealing with a class but with an age, a chronological period in people's lives. It had very valid roots and reasons for being, but so long as it did not recruit the workers as a class, it was bound to burn itself out. I was very aware that this was going to happen.

Don't misunderstand me. I regret its decline as much as everyone else. Certainly, it is much harder to fight injustices when the forces at our disposal are so diminished. But other forces will rise up to play similar roles in the near future. I see that young people who participated in this movement are workers today who are more politically aware than their white counterparts. I am encouraged by the strong rank-and-file movement in the United Auto Workers, the United Steelworkers, and even in the Teamsters, where the Latinos are playing such an important role. It is these elements who are responsible for the mobilization of September 19 [1981], in which the unions rallied tens of thousands of people against Reagan's policies. For myself I am very optimistic for the future, and I will continue to fight for justice whenever wrongs are done.

And Corona remains true to his words. He is currently facing termination of his teaching position at the California State University at Los Angeles, where he has been teaching Chicano Studies for the last ten years. While the administration claims he is not qualified to teach the course, Corona insists that the threatened dismissal is politically motivated.

I have been teaching there for more than ten years, and they had never questioned my credentials. It is only when I publicly denounced the administration's policy toward the Iranian students that I was brought up on charges.

The current administration is very racist. They had adopted a policy of encouraging the deportation of Iranian students. A few weeks ago the campus police went so far as to direct the immigration authorities to a classroom, where they apprehended an Iranian student. The INS went to his desk, handcuffed him, and dragged him away. Well, we organized a picket line around the vice president's office, and she called the police. Fourteen of the participants were arrested. A few days after that, I was informed by the dean of my termination.

At the age of sixty-three, Corona continues with his zeal for the struggle. He has gotten the Chicano Studies Department to file a departmental complaint protesting his termination. The Campus Defense committee, which he helped to organize, has just filed a lawsuit against the university. One can only marvel at the enthusiasm he maintains at his age. When asked his secret for his zest for life, he replies with a chuckle.

Well, it never ceases to amaze me. I guess if I don't know by now, I never will know. Seriously though, I guess I've always seen life as a challenge. It never ceases to amaze me how most people can take such a simplistic attitude toward life. They feel that they can learn about life from a few textbooks. As far as I'm concerned, formal education is but the beginning of an education. The sooner the youth of this country understand this, the better off they will be in their understanding of life. For Latinos in this nation, life is filled with struggle, and struggle is the ultimate teacher. If the majority of Latino youth can take this attitude, then we will be well on our way to bettering the lot of our people as a whole.

Selection 8

HELENA MARÍA VIRAMONTES was born in 1954 in East Los Angeles to Mexican American parents who maintained an immigrant outlook, as she states in the selected text. She is currently a professor of creative writing in the Department of English at Cornell University and lives in Ithaca, New York. Viramontes has published a collection of short stories, *The Moths and Other Stories* (1985), and the novels *Under the Feet of Jesus* (1995) and *Their Dogs Came with Them* (2007). In "Beach Blanket Baja," published in the *New York Times* on August 16, 2008, she reminisces about her life in the underprivileged East Los Angeles of the 1950s and 1960s and about her mother's fears while crossing the international border into the United States, even though she was an American citizen. Her childhood recollection charts the spatial contours and social universe of a working-class and thoroughly urbanized Chicana chronotope but in the guise of a family vacation epic. It begins in the 1960s, the decade in which the auto and tourist industry market a recently completed national highway system and the shiny v-8 sedan as promises of a hedonistic enjoyment of postwar consumer freedom. But because this family's journey heads southward, instead of toward the habitual West of Manifest Destiny and its map of nation building, it cuts against the grain of a heroic individualism and a Utopian idealization of nature. The narrator's outward-looking subjectivity, which focuses upon a family's communal and dysfunctional dynamic, and the story's parody of the Hollywood beach movies, a simulated Eden of teenage sensuality, betray its dystopic coordinates. Camping on the beach, for a family that lives outdoors each raisin grape–picking season, combines the necessities of work with its supposed opposite: a retreat to nature. In fact, the only vacation the family ever takes from work and East LA to its non-city idyll must pass through Tijuana's hellish thicket of postcolonial poverty. On their return the family must invert Mexico's welcome. Crossing the border into the United States requires the native-born family to subject itself to a national surveillance that questions their belonging. All these themes suggest claustrophobic entrapment and a critical awareness of it perceived from a much older Hispanic and Mesoamerican gaze that reads the hemisphere's spaces from the verticality of genealogy.

Beach Blanket Baja

HELENA MARÍA VIRAMONTES

In our East Los Angeles working-class neighborhoods of the 1950s and 1960s, no one thought of summer vacations or sleep-away camps as a possibility. Right after the school year was over and before we were driven to the Central Valley to pick raisin grapes for the summer, we'd hunt down discarded bottles to redeem for the deposits, roll up our swimsuits in a towel *taquito*, locate our one Esther Williams bathing cap (mandatory in the public pool and which we had to take turns wearing), for our sojourn to the Belvedere Park plunge located a quarter-mile from our home. One dime paid for our admittance, while a precious nickel bought a Big Hunk candy bar, which, later on when we were sun-toasted, sugar-starved, and spent by hours of water play, delivered the energy for us to walk back home.

My parents grew up in one of the largest and oldest Mexican American communities in the nation. Immigrant belief prevailed, despite the fact that both Mom and Dad were born in the United States. We were poor, but it was a poverty that we were unaware of since everyone around us was the same. The fact that our family was Catholic and large once made the headlines of the *East Los Angeles Tribune*, where a photo of my smiling mother announced the birth of her eleventh child at Beverly Hospital.

Work was a given, and labor of any kind was highly valued. My father was a hod carrier who bore the weight of sixty pounds of wet cement on his back while expertly climbing scaffolds braced against buildings under construction.

My mother was our cook, consoler, healer, launderer, and caregiver. I became a dutiful daughter, like most of my sisters. We all felt strong empathy for her. We howled whenever we'd watch Donna Reed on television vacuuming in stilettos and full petticoat dresses. If we were lucky enough to catch an Annette Funicello and Frankie Avalon *Beach Party* movie, my older sisters would remark to one another in frustration and with a hint of jealousy, "Where do they get all that free time?"

Our Tío José was a great drinking friend of my father's. He was a stout man who had a fondness for whiskey, a frequent visitor who arrived with pocketfuls of lollipops that he distributed to the younger ones. Sometimes he brought along his two handsome teenage sons as an added bonus. My older sisters were prohibited from dating, so they entertained mutual crushes on Larry and Joe Junior while playing their 45s on the turntable and munching potato chips. On one such visit, in 1964, when I was ten, my father announced that we were all to spend a weekend in Ensenada, Mexico, with José and his family.

My mother was at first skeptical: It would be no easy feat to transport a total of sixteen people, the majority of them children, but Tío José had worked out a plan. He would drive his Pontiac, accompanied by his wife, Tía Lola, and his children. My father would drive Joe Junior's clunky Chevy, and my oldest brother, Gil, would be in charge of driving our father's white Ford pickup.

Gas and food? Everything was much cheaper across the border. Lodging? Camping under the stars!

Grumbling ceaselessly, my mother packed her good menudo knife, along with her tamale pot for the slow-cooking tripe, and most of her kitchen setup. She had grown up in the fields, traveling with our grandparents, who were following the California crops. And although she still used her own mother's cast-iron stove, the one with removable legs for easier transport to migrant labor camps—it still amazed us all that Grandma made both tortillas and bread in this odd-looking apparatus—the stove was kept home.

We children quickly became stupid with vacation delirium. At dawn on the day of departure, we scuttled to pile the truck with our clothes-filled paper bags (we did not own luggage), cardboard boxes containing bread and peanut butter, coffee, chips, snacks, and other nonperishables, including a set of dishes and a metal bucket to wash them in. Like Steinbeck's Joads heading out for something better, we joined the caravan for the two-hour drive to cross the border to Tijuana, then another two-hour drive along the bumpy, winding, and ill-repaired Carretera 1 to Ensenada.

I was the fifth to the youngest, the invisible child, and for a reason I cannot recall, my mother allowed me to ride with her inside the truck. This is what I remember: the alacrity with which we were waved across the border by a Mexican immigration officer, the muddle of the Tijuana streets and the astounding poverty of the Mexican children as we stopped to buy more groceries, then the unknotting of the streets into the main highway where we passed the shantytowns, or *las colonias*, on the outskirts of the city. Seeing houses molded from cardboard and garbage, tins and bushes, children whose filthy faces were snot-smeared, men without legs scooting themselves around, brought on a terror larger than my empathy. And although I could not turn away, I sat closer to the warm folds of my mother.

Once we entered the winding *carretera*, my mother's nerves shot up. "Slow down!" she demanded of my brother. "Watch out!" But I caught my mother's proud smile—her first-born son, as thin as wire, sitting upright and rigid, eternally focused on the road, light sprigs of a mustache, a young man now.

Finally, the caravan of vehicles drove into an empty stretch of beach, parked side by side with trunks facing the surf, and the tedious work of unloading began. Our father prepared the campsite, while my older sisters paired off with Larry and Joe Junior to find firewood. My father and Tío José opened a bottle of tequila and took swigs back and forth while working.

We younger ones ran over a series of dunes and into the surf with absolutely no regard for time. We bodysurfed, built sand castles, chased the waves as if they were monsters and we were their intended victims, body slammed our nakedness against the froth, buried one another—on and on our illustrious and profound play went.

By late afternoon, caped in our towels, we returned to the campsite, trembling and hungry. Apparently, my mother had sent my father to find firewood since my sisters had not returned, and by then annoyance had replaced her worry. In the meantime we ate cold bologna sandwiches and Ho Hos and drank Kool-Aid, but we remained hungry until my father returned with planks of wood so uniformly cut that they could have easily been a section of a picket fence. (They were.)

Already boozy, Tío José started the pit fire, and we roasted marshmallows or hot dogs. In between the licks of flame, my lost sisters and the brothers returned, and I saw patches of sand on MaryAnn's hair. Words were exchanged. Later, as MaryAnn sat beside me, her face held such beguile against the crackling of the fire, I thought her more beautiful than Annette Funicello.

Our collective trance broke when Tío José, in a fit of alcoholic anger, got ahold of my mother's menudo knife and threatened to kill my aunt. His wobbling roars and verbal assaults were almost hilarious (he could barely stand up straight) had he not been wielding the huge machete.

His swings to and fro forced all of us, including Tía Lola, to dodge behind the dunes while my mother and father tried to settle Tío down. These were things that adults did all the time. The affliction of split personalities, the mysterious explosions of emotions, nuclear rages that we were often exposed to—confusing and terrifying—made us into children who wavered in their faith in God because He, too, was an adult and prone to similar fits. Crouched behind a sand dune, Larry told us quite calmly, "My dad does this every Saturday."

Perhaps it was the pot of strong coffee and Kahlúa or simple exhaustion that lowered my Tío into a deaf-defying snore. Then we all readied for bed as if nothing out of the ordinary had happened.

In the truck bed seven of us lay atop thick Mexican blankets. Even at such a tender age, my younger brother Frank's sinuses rattled like marbles in a jar, hence the nightly bickering as to who would sleep next to him. This night it was to be me, and I considered myself lucky since he kept me awake to witness the stars, inhale the scent of the sea, and listen to the smoothing mellow waves broaching the shore. From the truck I admired the shattered bits of moon on the skin of the water.

While others slept soundly, I could hear Tío's snores in the distance and my sweet brother's gurgling, and I felt as if I were the only person in the world who was awake. I thought about the stars and the beyondness of them, and the darkness, which made up the unknown.

We have no photos of this one family vacation, but the images of Gil behind the steering wheel of the truck, the sand on MaryAnn's hair, and Tío's machete threats are easily summoned and deliver a sense of gratitude. Unfortunately, upon our return to the United States, the long lines at the border crossing allowed anxieties to grow to monstrous proportions.

At the gateway a United States immigration officer studied us. He remained silent even as he reached over and grabbed away a piece of sugarcane I had been sucking on. I began to cry. My mother said nothing to him about his rudeness, and I could see by her trembling as she handed over the documents that she was afraid of something.

"Are you an American citizen?" he demanded. Gil knew to stare straight ahead as the officer deliberated whether to search us or allow us to cross into our own country, while I complained and whined. All my mother could muster during the two-hour drive home was: "Behave next time." Since that day I never have.

Selection 9

The first two chapters of ALEJANDRO MURGUÍA's *The Medicine of Memory: A Mexica Clan in California* (2002) give us one of the best Chicana/o critiques of the San Fernando Mission and of Fray Junípero Serra and the other Franciscan *cronistas*. His excerpt provides this anthology with a sense of unity via dialectic negation in which the reader discovers a long-ignored Chicana/o dialogue with seventeenth-century writing rooted in the *crónica*'s three hundred–year literary genealogy. His portrayal of the California mission as an intrusive, racialized, and repressive system for eradicating the indigenous culture thoroughly problematizes Fray Junípero Serra's beatified image. Indeed, this very system would unintentionally enable a genocide and an epistemicide. More than a mere rhetorical denunciation of this trauma, Murguía gives us a chronotope of postcolonial critique. The time-place he creates establishes the space for him to reexperience his sense memories of the aptly named "Memory Gardens" and the evolution of his critical faculties, which reach an apotheosis in Brand Park when he reflects upon Serra's vandalized statue. Murguía's narrative thus creates a sensory path to a critical and moral Latin American space. The reader who follows him risks discovering what it feels like to embody the troubling intimacies of capitalist conquest of the Americas hidden within the San Fernando Valley's suburban sprawl—and one of LA's enduring clichés.

The chair of Latina/o Studies at San Francisco State University was the founding editor of *Tin Tan* magazine, a 1970s era literary-cultural tabloid named after the Mexican comic who mixed the Chicana/o zoot-suiter's caló and fashion aesthetic, Marx brothers absurdist slapstick, and Cab Calloway's performance style in B-films that subverted the Mexican government's myth of a national culture. The magazine's nod to this borderlands bricoleur expressed the many ways it deployed a Latin American anti-imperialist critique of U.S. military intervention in South and Central America. San Francisco's sixth poet laureate has written or edited eight books, including *Southern Front*, an award-winning memoir of his stint as a Sandinista guerrilla who helped to topple Nicaragua's brutal U.S.-backed dictator Anastasio Somoza.

"The 'Good Old Mission Days' Never Existed"

Excerpt from *The Medicine of Memory: A Mexica Clan in California*

ALEJANDRO MURGUÍA

If you were raised in Fresno, Bakersfield, or Sacramento, you don't have a connection to the California missions. Yes, you recognize the oxidized iron bells along the highway marking their relative location, but you don't give them much attention. When you visit a mission, as everyone in California does sooner or later, it is merely an ethnic curiosity left over from two centuries ago that has nothing to do with you or your growing up in Sacramento or whatever. To you the missions are relics of a romantic past lit by the sunset's rosy glow. Like all relics, they are not a part of your life. But if you grew up in a mission town, near any of the twenty-one California missions, they leave a definite impression—you wonder about their history, you try to make them fit into the historical landscape of your memory, and you are not impartial to them.

I grew up a hop and a skip from Mission San Fernando, so I have my own sense of the "mission days." From the age of ten till I leave my father's house at eighteen, I am within the sphere of the mission, its myth, and its history. I also had as a neighbor, the respected archaeologist Dr. Mark R. Harrington, curator emeritus of the Southwest Museum of Natural History, who played an important role in the restoration of Mission San Fernando in the 1930s and 1940s. On Saturdays I often worked for him, earning a few dollars by cleaning up the thick wall of opuntia in his front yard or splitting oak for his fireplace. He loved to talk about his work, which had taken him all over North America, including Cuba. With his thick bifocals, a weathered hat, and a hobble caused by one leg being several inches shorter than the other due to polio, Harrington was my original source on mission as well as California history. Through him I learned firsthand about the process of building the missions, their ruin, and their restoration; I also received a top-notch guide to the Indian communities that existed before the missions and the rancheros and ranches that followed. These two quirks of fate, the proximity of Mission San Fernando and my interaction with Dr. Harrington (plus a dash of curiosity), instilled in me an intimacy with California missions that had nothing to do with schoolbooks or classroom lectures or tourist maps.

As a young man, I often wondered what my place in the mission system would have been. I don't fit into the racial category of light-skinned *gente de razón*, the Spaniards who were the creators and supporters of the missions. Instead, I despise the concept that Spaniards were people of reason, people who could think, whereas Indians were considered savage, nonthinking beings, children incapable of critical thought. Since I am dark, I'm not *gente de razón*, which doesn't bother me; I'd rather be a wild, crazy Indian, free to bare my ass on Hollywood Boulevard if I want.

Now, had I lived during the mission days—say, in the same locale where I actually grew up—I would have been a mission Indian. And my short life would have been a tight regimen of work, work, work, and in between work periods, religion, with the threat of whipping or lashing if I stepped out of line at work or church. Some life.

I must confess I have never cared for religion or for the doctrine of the Catholic Church. To begin with, our working-class household wasn't all that concerned with the sins of the flesh. The way my father saw it, we weren't supposed to sin, period, so religion wasn't essential; it was more of a cultural remnant he clung to as a reminder of Mexico. He seldom attended Mass, though our house was a gallery of saints' photos in the living rooms and bedrooms. But neither the concept nor the practice of religion moved me. To be honest, religion scared me. I was deathly afraid of it—the fiery torments of hell seemed to have been created for boys with vivid imaginations, just like me. Even heaven scared me; I couldn't conceptualize eternity at the side of God back then, and I can't conceive of it now. I think the idea of eternity in heaven, more than the fear of hell, caused me to break with Catholicism.

In general I just seemed to be a bad candidate for sainthood. I flunked out of catechism and never made my First Communion, as my older brother did; his Communion photo, proudly displayed in our living room, shows him in a white shirt, with his hair slicked back, holding a taper candle. And in the fourth grade I committed one of the worst sins of all time. My father still had hope for me, so he enrolled me in after-school catechism. But my heart wasn't in it, so I mostly skipped the class. Then, when Easter came around, I failed to qualify. Instead of coming clean with my father, I decided to make up a tall tale. I told him that there wasn't going to be any big ceremony, just me taking the host along with everyone else that Sunday. He seemed a bit suspicious of that, and I can't blame him. After all, the ritual of the first Holy Communion plays a big role in our culture, especially for boys, since we have no ritual of manhood, unlike the girls, who have their *quinceañeras*. I guess we're expected to be men from birth.

Unfortunately for me, my father had big plans for my Communion. He'd brought a camera, had even bought me a new white shirt and a pair of slacks. With all this pressure, it became harder and harder to tell him about the nuns' decision, and postponing the dreaded moment only made it worse. On Good Friday my conscience got the best of me, and I couldn't go through with it. I didn't even know the Act of Contrition that I'd have to say to the priest. And I was not willing to take Communion without confession. I may not have been a good Catholic, but I knew that much. So that night I hauled my own cross to my father and told him there would be no Communion, that, in other words, I had been bullshitting him. Let me tell you, my father's belt sang a bloody *corrido*—and for days after, I could contemplate the bruises on my butt as a small reminder of what Jesus must've felt.

I guess you could say I've always had a love-hate relationship with the California missions. About once a month, sometimes less frequently, I'd walk from our house, cross Brand Boulevard, go through Memory Gardens to Mission San Fernando, and there I was in another world. If I came to Sunday Mass at all, it was because the mission grounds had a peacefulness that attracted me. I liked walking through the gardens lush with bougainvillea and citrus trees, especially after it had rained and the richly scented earth seemed alive. Inside the church I felt in touch with a part of myself that was Latin American; the polychrome statues of the saints on the main altar reminded me then, as they do now, of every church in Mexico I've ever stepped in. The liturgies were still sung in Latin during my youth, and although I didn't understand it, I knew that Spanish was derived from it. After Mass I'd walk in the cemetery out back and read the Spanish names on the gravestones. All this made me romanticize the mission days, a nostalgia that was more myth than reality.

*

In front of Mission San Fernando stands Brand Park, built in the 1920s by a real estate developer on what had been part of the mission orchards. Some of the original mission olive trees still line the main walk that cuts through the center of the park. On the west of Brand Park is Memory Gardens, shaded by aged lemon trees and dotted with palms. In the Gardens two fountains, originally built in the 1820s, create a contemplative mood, making this the most beautiful spot in the San Fernando Valley. But despite the beauty and the elegiac mood of Memory Gardens, it was here where one day I sensed another facet of mission life.

In the center of Brand Park sits a small mound with a rectangular stone structure on top. These are the tallow pits of the old mission, where cow fat was boiled for use as candles. The Indians, as usual, did all the work, and one Saturday as I played there, I imagined myself working in the tallow pits, stirring the cow fat with wooden poles, filling the leather *botas*, and the stench I imagined made me sick. Another day, while horsing around in the Gardens, I jumped onto the bigger-than-life bronze statue of Junípero Serra that stands next to one of the fountains. Junípero Serra has a staff in one hand, and his other hand rests on the shoulder of an Indian youth, as if walking him to the Promised Land. I pretended to be that Indian youth, the hands of the good padre on my shoulder. I wanted to see the world from the eyes of the Native American boy, who in this case is supposedly Juan Evangelista, one of Serra's first converts. (Only through a miracle could Serra have converted anyone in San Fernando, since he'd been dead for thirteen years when this mission was founded.) But the imaginative leap did not happen. Life as a pious Indian neophyte seemed phony to me. I jumped down from the statue feeling unsatisfied and rebellious.

Eventually, I realized, little by little, one small insight at a time, that as nostalgic and romantic as the images of the missions are, they are not historical memories that I cherish. I tend to see the missions and the missionaries as oppressors, even if in their own eyes they were benevolent. For the Indians the missions meant a virtual turning over of their lives to the friars, who then controlled their time with work and prayers. In my imagination, had I lived two hundred years ago as a young Indian trapped in the mission, I would have run away, chancing the soldiers' whips, because only in the *cañones* would I have been free. But that's just me. Some of my friends in the same barrio saw themselves as priests baptizing the pagans.

I have other memories of Brand Park. As a teenager, my friends and I came to the park on Saturday afternoons to wash our cars or to smoke *yesca*, Mexican pot that we bought for ten dollars an ounce; or on Sundays, to cruise around and around in our lowriders playing oldies music. Sometimes a girl would come with us at night, and we'd scare her with stories of the headless woman who supposedly haunted the Gardens. If the moon was full, rising between the palms and the olive trees, or if the girl we were with got scared by our ghost story or if we were lucky, the girl would snuggle up to us, and we'd make out, practicing our sloppy kisses.

For a while—just after I'd moved away—most of Brand Park was heavily tagged by the *vatos* of San Fernando. All the benches, the fountains, the walls, were scrawled with spray-painted graffiti more important to us than whatever history was implied in the mission and Brand Park. The stone sundial in the center of the Gardens was vandalized and its bronze face removed. It was as if history didn't matter to the new generation of Chicanos, as if we didn't care what the mission represented. I understand that feeling.

Still, Mission San Fernando left an impression on me. Even now, in every mission town from Sonoma to San Diego, I find my bearings according to where the mission is located. Eventually, I discovered that the mission system created in California had previously existed in Mexico, in Querétaro, Sinaloa, and all the way up Baja California. So, for me the California missions are intimately linked with that whole colonial period of the continent. By extension, then, I consider the missions to be part of the Latin American experience. That's the good thing about the missions: they make the Latin American roots of California familiar to me; I see them in Mexico, and I understand the concept of being both oppressor and oppressed.

Selection 10

HARRY GAMBOA JR. (b. 1951) is a Chicano essayist, photographer, filmmaker, and performance artist. Along with Gronk (Glugio Nicandro), Willie Herrón, and Patssi Valdez, he cofounded Chicana/o performance artist collective Asco (1972–87; the Spanish word *asco* means "disgust" or "revulsion"), which reacted against the socioeconomic and political oppression of the Chicana/o community, particularly in the East Los Angeles where Gamboa Jr. grew up in the 1970s and 1980s. Asco also challenged the marginalization of Chicana/o artists from Los Angeles's art world with its now infamous Los Angeles County Museum of Art (LACMA) installations. In 1972, for instance, the group protested the exclusion of Chicanx artists through its "Spray Paint LACMA," a graffiti in which they spray-painted their names, Herron (Willie Herrón III), Gamboa (Harry Gamboa Jr.), and Gronkie (Gronk), outside the LACMA, which is famously depicted in a photograph Harry Gamboa Jr. snapped the following day of Patssi Valdez posed by the three names furtively looking away. As Max Benavidez explains in his 2007 book *Gronk*, the piece was a reaction to Gamboa Jr.'s meeting with the LACMA curator, who assured him that Chicana/os only did folk art, not fine art: "Gamboa reported this to his Asco cohorts, and they decided that if their work would not be exhibited, they would sign the museum and call *it*—the whole publicly funded museum, including bricks and mortar and everything inside—their artwork."[1] Asco's multi-genre performances and conceptual art in public areas of Los Angeles responded to the marginalization of the Chicana/o urban community and the violence it suffered. As a high school student, Gamboa Jr. participated in the 1968 "East LA Blowouts" to protest the deplorable conditions of public schools in the area. His work tends to reflect the alienation of Chicana/o life and to denounce white hegemony. The setting of his art is usually urban. Among his most significant works are the mail art of the 1970s, Asco's "no movies"

(*Tumor Hats* [1973], *First Supper (After a Major Riot) / Instant Mural* [1974], *Cruel Profit* [1974], *Á la Mode* [1976], and *Search and No Seizure, La Dolce, Waiting for Tickets* [1978]), and the "urban operas" *Ignore the Dents* and *Jetter's Jinx*.

In "Light at the End of the Tunnel Vision," from *Urban Exile: Collected Writings of Harry Gamboa Jr.* (1998), Gamboa Jr. contextualizes the book's photographs and other visual texts. As Richard T. Rodriguez points out in his review of the book, in the essay "Light at the End of Tunnel Vision," Gamboa Jr. "recounts how he was inspired to create the series of photographs entitled *Chicano Male Unbonded* upon hearing a news announcer on his car radio declare: 'Be on the lookout for a Chicano male. He is probably armed and very dangerous to society.'"[2] Gamboa Jr. exposes the media's bias against the Mexican American community and how this affects its members' self-esteem: "Millions of Chicanos are ignored, stereotyped, and denied by the mass media of television, cable TV, radio, Hollywood movies, popular magazines, educational curriculum textbooks, and a new generation of personal computer-based multimedia software."[3] For him that regime of media nonrepresentation had turned Chicana/os into a phantom presence (or absence) in Los Angeles, and he was determined to document their presence in the urban environment with his photography.

Light at the End of Tunnel Vision

In Memory of Gerardo Velázquez and Ray Navarro

HARRY GAMBOA JR.

Partial Eclipse

During the 1950s, when I was a young boy, I stared at the partial eclipse of the sun through several strips of negatives that had been folded over and layered so as to create a montage of reversed images of family events, local landmarks, and portraits of people who have vanished from memory.[4] The silhouette of the sun appeared to be consumed by an eroding shadow as the photographic impressions were literally burned into my unconscious. The shadow receded as the sun regained its awesome brilliance, but my vision of place, time, and self was permanently altered. The persistent "spots" that danced before my eyes during childhood and teen years corresponded/collided with my visual experiences of everyday life at home, school, or the streets of East Los Angeles; television, the movies, and with an imagination that was focused on the possibilities of the present.

Erasing the Spectrum

By the fall of 1972 I had witnessed the sequence and series of personal/social events that caused me to self-identify as a Chicano in a country that actively held people of Mexican descent in low esteem. At that time I believed that it was urgently necessary to photographically document the existence of Chicanos in the urban environment and to disseminate the images across the cultural borders within the United States. I purchased a Minolta 101 35 mm camera and fifty rolls of film with the intent to complete the documentary project within a couple of years. During the process of shooting countless images of faces, crowds, the streets, violence, spontaneous elegance, I became acutely aware of the power of pre-visualization and selective imaging. Within several months of looking at life-through-the-lens, I was convinced that the black-and-white of concrete reality was obscured by the absurdity of an infinite gray scale of perception. Incongruous visible patterns emerged from the cyclonic social and demographic changes that typified the ongoing destabilization of Los Angeles. It was necessary to illuminate the internal impressions that I had accumulated during my first twenty-one years and to confront a vast array of contradictory beliefs, ideas, and concepts. I realized that the documentary project would have to be extended indefinitely as well as complemented by an interpretive approach to creating photographic images that would reflect my understanding of the contemporary Chicano experience.

Focus on the Invisible

It is impossible to exist in a vacuum of awareness. Distortions flourish when there is only rumor and innuendo to fill in the chasm that is widened by ignorance. Confusion is in the eye of the beholder when one looks into the mirror and sees nothing. Millions of Chicanos are ignored, stereotyped, and denied by the mass media of television, cable TV, radio, Hollywood movies, popular magazines, educational curriculum textbooks, and a new generation of personal computer-based multimedia software. In the United States, Chicanos are viewed as a disposable phantom culture. In a country that is dominated by the white-versus-black frame of reference, Chicano culture is systematically excluded and separated from the collective "American" experience. The individual Chicano who successfully traverses the subtle and complex maze of dominant media acceptance is an anomaly.

It is possible to divert public opinion, common knowledge, laws of physics, rules of order, social norms, and cultural expectations. All one needs to oppose reality is a camera, film, and a concept. The manipulation of content and context is an expression of power over the perception of the viewer. If an event is created and designed for photographic documentation, it can provide persuasive "proof" that the event actually occurred in time and place. However, all events, whether they are natural occurrences, political accidents, manufactured social productions, or the repetitive activities of faceless humanity, can be the source of greater factual understanding as well as the catalyst of mass disinformation.

Drowning in the Mirage

If the smog is not too severe when you stand atop nearly any rooftop in Los Angeles, you can see the Hollywood sign as it beckons to the world with its multibillion-dollar myth. When you climb back down into your own backyard and walk along the streets, everything can be considered a facade, everyone can be acknowledged as an "extra," and you can be the brightest burning star. There are thousands of stars who spin out of orbit as they try to reach Hollywood. They drift away into a perpetual void of dysfunctionalism. Others lose their luster as they scratch away in vain at the locked entry door. The urban desert is filled with many venomous creatures and toxic plants. It is difficult to survive in such a harsh environment. When you set out to reach Hollywood, beware of the cracks in the sidewalk, avoid the emptiness of most promises, and deflect the accolades of strangers who may be clutching rusty switchblades. The illusion of Hollywood is harmful, but the delusion is fatal.

I have stated in various public forums that the Hollywood sign is the ugliest example of graffiti in North America and that it should be whitewashed and replaced with a simple neon sign that points the way to Aztlán. Such heresy has been responded to with personal attacks by individuals who have invested their lives in perpetuating negative stereotypes as well as those who value the glittering falseness of playing a "bit part" in the nullification of the important history of Chicanos and Mexicans in Los Angeles. There have been many who have been invited to drink at the fountain of the oasis only to discover that they have quenched their thirst with the sands of a vast hypnotic wasteland.

Collapse of Memory

Since 1972 I have maintained a photographic diary that continues to capture the evolution of my expanding and collapsing universe. The diary includes: an unexpected album of the dead; a collection of cherished moments in wide angle; the serialization of mundane events; portraits suitable for blackmail;

frozen incidents of schizophrenic responses to multicultural stimuli; close-ups of poseurs-in-waiting for the next déjà vu; blurred snapshots of fractured asphalt, broken jaws, and shattered windows; blow-ups of minor emotional injuries; hundreds of Polaroid sx-70 instant photos that have recorded the uniqueness of what should have been immediately forgotten; dozens of muti-lated composite color prints that fail to reconstruct the true meaning of a particularly significant gray day; many pictures that say the same thing to no one; and finally, the visual identification of selected individuals who emerge as survivors from a nocturnal urban abyss.

However, the diary is incomplete. Many of the original negatives as well as numerous original one-of-a-kind prints have been lost, stolen, burned, buried, or in some way transformed into questionable confetti that has added to the post-quake/post-riot decor of the city. I can always count on a distorted journey whenever I go down photographic memory lane. The disappearance of images from my past provides ample opportunity for revision, speculation, and the blinking effect of temporary amnesia. If a picture is worth a thousand words then sometimes no picture is worth its weight in gold.

A Violation of Refraction

I am occasionally reminded that certain photographs continue to circulate in unwanted circles. Names and faces are attached (oftentimes intermixed) so as to create an indelible persistent fantasy of an alternative Chicano art group of the 1970s and 1980s. Guilt by association is compounded when relationships that have been dead for nearly a decade are suddenly brought to life before a mass audience. The viewer must beware that several zombies do not constitute a living or relevant art group. Even the most narcissistic of the dead will not make a pretty picture.

There have been numerous published accounts of Asco (Spanish for "nau-sea"), including my essay for the *Chicano Art: Resistance and Affirmation* exhibition catalog,[5] in which the Chicano art group is credited for creating works that challenged the stereotypic notions that are oftentimes attributed to contemporary Chicano culture by mainstream and alternative cultures of the United States. The incorporation of street performance, mural paint-ing, drawing, costume design, and photography, which was utilized by the group in creating a collective public image that would generate notoriety, continues to inspire a certain amount of nostalgia for an East LA lifestyle that may or may not have been in existence during 1972 through 1987. Academicians, young artists (or would-be terrorists), students, and many of the hard-core devotees of an imagined social apocalypse have sifted through the rubble of the aftermath of the fatal implosion that destroyed Asco in the late 1980s. The tangible evidence that remains of Asco is supported by hearsay and conflicting memories of plausible events. The works of Asco were often created in transitory or easily degradable materials that crumble at the slightest prodding and fade quickly upon exposure to any glimmer of hope. It is unlikely that the objects, historical accuracy, or spirit of Asco will ever be recovered.

Sticks and Stones and Skin and Bones

On the day of the birth of my son, Diego, in 1978, there was a tremendous windstorm that felled trees, scattered the urban refuse into the air, and tossed polluted dust into the faces of the innocent bystanders who littered the pavement of downtown LA. I was elated when I held my son in my arms for the first time at 5:30 a.m. and was surprised to find myself, only a few hours later, on the streets shooting pedestrians who were in the early stages of pink eye. As I walked along Broadway in the company of my Nikon F2, it occurred to me that life is as precious as it is absurd. I took refuge from the harsh winds by entering a favorite landmark, Clifton's Cafeteria. As I sat with a tray of pancakes and coffee at a table on an upper tier, I witnessed an enclosed society that offered membership into the circus of mankind or the snake pit of despair. As I ate the late breakfast, I saw: a plainclothes policeman choking a homeless man over a stolen crust of toast; a woman spoon-feeding red Jell-O squares to her surrogate daughter (which upon closer inspection was a discolored doll); ten street preachers, each presenting a separate boisterous sermon with different interpretations of the Last Supper; a young boy loading bullets into a polished revolver; and a distraught couple who were arguing violently in an unfamiliar language. I drank the last drop of bitter coffee and rushed toward the exit without taking a single photograph.

Throughout the course of the following ten years, until 1988, I rushed toward many exits during a thousand days of wandering the downtown streets with my son, my camera, and a shadow that inched closer with every step. I continued to photograph the anonymous population who posed and performed as though they were professional actors in an unnamed play gone berserk. Many of the antics and routines of the general public were worthy of a standing ovation, but before they could take their bows, they were oftentimes swept away by an overflow of shoppers or accosted by strangers, or they intuitively boarded the nearest bus. My primary focus was to continue the contemporary urban Chicano experience documentary photography project that I had begun many years earlier. However, other elements of the city that had been of peripheral concern were now at the forefront of visual awareness. The psychological and demographical time bomb of Los Angeles was ticking faster and faster toward disaster. I intended to rush toward the nearest exit, but there was seemingly no way out.

Brown in Black-and-White

In 1982 I exhibited sixty black-and-white photographs that I believed at that time best represented my interpretation of documentary and conceptual images of the Chicano urban experience during 1978 through 1982.[6] Many of the images captured the essence of downtown LA and its people.[7] I included many portraits of Chicano artists and several portraits of deranged street people. The conceptual works were designed to provoke the viewer to commit acts of perceptual sabotage. The opening reception of the solo exhibition was an experiment of mass hysteria that involved several thousand people who had decided to come without a proper invitation. The crowd was composed of the "Who's Who of the Obscure." Upon encountering family, friends, and foes during the reception, I entertained criticism from unknown traditionalists, who complained that my work was not a true reflection of Chicano culture. I managed to escape their grasp and moved to a different end of the gallery. I was then cornered by several avant-garde types who accused me of being too Chicano because I had included some images of cholos, Anthony Quinn, and Rufino Tamayo. The demarcation between documentary and conceptual work was apparent in the way two separate lines had formed as people waited their turn to offer suggestions, threats, compliments, and insults. The reception ended short of violence with a mysterious note having been slipped into my pocket that I discovered before leaving the gallery; it read, "KILL YOUR CAMERA!"

Self-Portrait on Fire

Whenever I write about the 1980s, I am always certain to use invisible ink. It was a protracted decade of disappearances. Many people, places, ideas, ideals, and images are gone forever. In 1989 I decided to induce historical blindness by destroying all of the visual trivia that resembled pieces of a puzzle that were impossible to fit into a coherent picture. I led my way into the nineties by laying down a trail of scraps and ashes.

Chicano Male Unbonded

In 1991 I was engaged in a four-hour conversation with a man who could easily have passed as my double. I had never met him before, nor have I seen him since our intense discussion. We talked about the politics of silence, the love of self-loathing, the aesthetics of blindness, the dynamics of punitive control, and the daily ephemeral experience of sinking quickly into the hot asphalt of LA. As we spoke, I unconsciously bit my tongue whenever I mentioned, "phantom culture," "police state," or "performance art." However, I was conscious of the fact that we were both dressed exactly alike and that he wore a doomed expression on his face that reminded me of someone who had vanished long ago. We never exchanged names or shook hands, but we both laughed and cried as we walked away from one another without ever looking back. I recall walking aimlessly through darkened streets until I reached my parked car, which was located in a secluded dead-end alley. As I drove toward the nearest on-ramp, I turned on the radio as a news announcer stated: "Be on the look-out for a Chicano male. He is probably armed and very dangerous to society." The statement was followed by commercial announcements and synthesized western music. I stepped on the accelerator and merged into the fast lane of the Hollywood Freeway. The freeway intersects with other freeways to form a concrete ribbon that binds the city into an explosive package. I drove across several freeways in an attempt to figure out how to untie a concrete knot. I exited at Oblivion Boulevard, not far from where I had begun. I had nearly gone full circle without arriving at a conclusion. I was concerned about the man with whom I had shared so much in so little time. I was worried that he or the many other Chicano men who had played a role in influencing my life, including my son, father, brothers, uncles, friends, and colleagues, were also in danger of being apprehended or assaulted by societal authority based on the radio alert that played loudly in an atmosphere of ethnic intolerance and racial hatred.

The following day I was invited to participate in *L.A. Iluminado*, a group exhibition of Chicano photographers at Otis Parsons Gallery.[8] I was intent on exhibiting new work, which would be created for the exhibition. I decided to counter the issue of negative stereotypes by introducing a B&W photographic documentary project that would be based on my interpersonal encounters with the Chicano men who impact my life. I composed an initial list of one hundred men who could possibly represent the various concentric and overlapping social circles that define my subjective experience. I was interested in photographing each man as an individual as he is confronted face-to-face in a dimly illuminated and isolated urban setting at night. I photographed the first twenty-five men on the list and placed the images on exhibit as the series *Chicano Male Unbonded*.[9] Each work is titled as the name of the individual who appears in the photograph and by his respective self-defined occupation— for example, *Eloy Rodriquez, Ph.D., Phytochemist (UCI)*; *Humberto Sandoval, Actor*; *Victor Gamboa, Intermediate School Teacher*; and *Max Benavidez, Artist/ Writer*.[10] The remaining seventy-five names on the list have been adjusted and realigned over the past few years as the conceptual-visual linkage is clarified by realities that go beyond the borders of photography. A photographic update is required of certain individuals who have undergone definitive physical or personal changes that enhance the dramatic impact of the series. *Chicano Male Unbonded* is a series in progress that continues to establish the individuality of the members of a group.

NO DETOUR

In 1994 I have decided to eliminate more pieces of the puzzle in the hope that I can build a better memory. The earthquakes, riots, deaths, and denials have a way of removing the sheen from glossy photos. I have discovered permanent tattoos on the foreheads of urbanites that read, "Victim," "Killer," "Unemployed," "Nobody," "AIDS," "Fate," and "Temporary." Many of the freeways sway and shake at the slightest rumble of social awareness. I read the *Los Angeles Times*, and my vision becomes blurred by words that are written to neutralize or modify critical focus. The TV set supplies an endless array of mind-numbing narratives, vignettes, and artificial flashbacks. Homicidal and suicidal children are rewarded with movies, recordings, and video games that glorify the excesses of popular nihilism. There are multiple conspiracy theories that attribute all that is wrong in LA to its newly arrived immigrants. Anarchy is worn as a designer label that is stitched directly to the skin so that all who dare may try to rip it off. Police shoot rubber bullets for crowd control at Chicanos and Mexicans in downtown. Surreality begins to resemble the movies except that the *extras* are bleeding on the sidewalk.

TOTAL ECLIPSE

I am looking for a photograph that may not exist. I recall many details of an image but cannot piece them together so that the picture may come to mind. Sometimes events, pictures, and dreams are all integrated into a misdirected recollection. I have already looked through the family albums, newspapers, wanted posters, picture books, identification cards, museums, and daily obituaries, without any clues to where I might find the photograph that I am seeking. I am beginning to feel that the photograph was burned in any number of fires or that it has been placed into the hands of a vicious critic. Maybe the photograph is floating as a superimposed projected image onto the urbanscape, where it can be camouflaged and exert its subliminal influence without ever being discovered.

I have been told by many experts on the subject that one needs light in order to make a photograph. I have also been informed by advertisers that a camera and film are very necessary. Curators have mentioned platinum and archival paper. I have wondered how long should a total eclipse last because it is what has prevented the photographs from being seen. It is not necessary to stumble through the darkness before one can see the light. The sun will return, and the images will not fade under intense exposure. Perpetual darkness is a hoax.

Light at the End of Tunnel Vision

I have been blinded by the positive and the negative. It has forced me to lose sight of 1972 through 1994. I am looking into a mirror, and although the reflection is unfamiliar, I must confess that I have seen that man before. I know that he exists because I carry his photographic image in my wallet. The process of self-awareness involves a series of reversals, refractions, and the elimination of impressions that would otherwise burn holes into the eyes of the person who gazes back through the mirror with a lapsed sense of recognition. I am in the early stages of seeing what has been invisible for so long. I will continue to photograph the phantoms even with the slightest ray of light. Out in the immeasurable distance, I can perceive that there is a source of incredible illumination. One day I will reach the end of the tunnel, even if it is only so that I may look up and stare vacantly into the sun.

Selection 11

GUILLERMO GÓMEZ-PEÑA (b. 1955) was born in Mexico City and moved to the United States in 1978. From 1983 through 1990 he lived in the San Diego / Tijuana border region, an experience that would influence his cultural production, often concerned with border culture and politics. A performance writer, artist, and activist, he has worked, like Harry Gamboa Jr., with different media, including performance, installation, photography, video, and experimental radio. With the selection in this anthology, we attempt to underscore the importance of the post- or non-mimetic stance of his performance art. Gómez-Peña has published poetry, essays, performance scripts, and chronicles in English, Spanish, and a combination of the two languages.

He is also a founding member of the art collective Border Arts Workshop / Taller de Arte Fronterizo and serves as director of the performance art troupe La Pocha Nostra. Among his performance art pieces are *The Couple in the Cage* (with Coco Fusco, 1992–93), *The Crucifiction Project* (with Roberto Sifuentes, 1994), *Temple of Confessions* (1995), *The Mexterminator Project* (1997–99), the Living Museum of Fetishized Identities (1999–2002), the *Mapa/Corpo* series (2004–9), *Corpo Ilícito* (2010–11), and *Corpo Insurrecto* (2012–13).

Guillermo Gómez-Peña wrote the selected text while living in Los Angeles, a geographic fact (writing from the heart of a global metropolis) that is reflected in the author's positionality. We can contrast his gaze to the imperial turn-of-the-century railroad barons who oversaw their industrial domains, to the west and to the south to Mexico, from a then-emergent industrial metropole. Gómez-Peña, by contrast, looks out more than a century later from the metropole of neoliberal globalization to critically assess the result of that imperial trajectory. Stylistically, as with Gamboa, we are looking at a *flânerie* from below. This piece, in commenting upon and describing a theatrical event, establishes the performance as an empirical event, which he "reports" on and interprets through his nonfiction metanarrative, hence his position as a postmodern flâneur.

"Deported to the North"

Excerpt from *Dangerous Border Crossings: The Artist Talks Back*

GUILLERMO GÓMEZ-PEÑA

I remember that cold afternoon in Buenos Aires vividly. It was mid-August 1993, and my colleague Coco Fusco and I were performing a version of our project, the *Guatinaui World Tour*, right on the corner of Callao and Corrientes, one of the busiest intersections in the city. As part of our performance projects subverting pseudo-ethnographic exhibitions of humans and the colonial format of the "living diorama," we spent three days inside a gilded cage displaying ourselves as "exotic primitives" from a fictitious island in the Gulf of Mexico. On the second day, suddenly, from within the crowd, a mysterious character in a black trench coat approached me, threw some kind of liquid at me, then vanished. Seconds later I realized I had been the victim of a physical assault. My stomach and legs had been burned with acid.

One of the theories circulating in the Buenos Aires artistic community was that this attack involved a political misunderstanding. There was speculation that the assailant was an ex-military man who felt implicated by our performance, probably because he believed that our project was a direct commentary on Argentine military culture, which jailed thousands of youths before the alleged democratic transition of 1987. It makes sense.

For politicized artists experimenting with the tenuous and ever-fluctuating frontiers between art and life, real danger is always present, especially when the art event takes place outside the protected space of cultural institutions. It's one thing to carry out iconoclastic actions in a theater or museum for a public predisposed to tolerate radical behavior; it's quite another matter to bring the same work into the street, where it will be exposed to unpredictable social and political forces. In the street the artist faces far greater risks. Some are obvious, such as the danger of confronting the intolerance of police and, in certain countries, extremist groups or the military. Others are more random, like a surprise encounter with a lunatic who happens to cross your path. Performance artists are well aware of these risks, but every now and then we don't accurately gauge the volatility generated by the combination of the context in which we choose to perform and the symbolic weight of our actions. Then, as we say in Mexico, "the devil shows up."

In mid-July 1994 I received a disturbing telephone call. The artist Hugo Sánchez (who shares his name with a Mexican soccer star), a native of Ciudad Obregón, Sonora, and longtime resident of Tijuana, had just been deported to—not from—the city of San Diego, California, for "desecrating the Mexican flag" in a performance. The newspapers, including the infamous Mexican tabloid *El Alarma*, published incendiary photos and headlines portraying the *norteño* artist as a psychopath.

The facts, hallucinatory as they may seem, are the following:

On July 11 Hugo Sánchez arrived in Tijuana to participate in the filming of *Fronterilandia*, codirected by Rubén Ortiz (from Mexico) and Jesse Lerner (from the United States) and sponsored by the Fundación Cultural Mexicana (Mexican Cultural Foundation). The filmmakers describe the work as "an experimental chronicle, half documentary and half poetic essay, of the mythical perceptions which both sides of the border have about each other."

The directors planned to shoot a performance by Sánchez, using the streets of Tijuana as a backdrop. The portion of the work to be filmed focused on the topic of migration. The hybrid persona played by Sánchez was an "undocumented Zapatista/*charro* (cowboy)," decked out in a mariachi sombrero à la "Tj curio-style," a ski mask, a flag wrapped around his chest, with a cow's head, representing (in the artist's words) "the pain of the immigrants who cross the border daily, and who are sacrificed like animals by an inhuman work/police system."

Filming began early on July 12. The crew consisted only of a cameraman, a photographer, and a sound technician. The two opening scenes were filmed without mishap, the first in front of a strange edifice known as the "Wadah," in the shape of an Ionic column, and the second next to the Monument to the Freedom of Expression—a curious foreshadowing of what was to come. After these sequences were filmed, the group made its way over to the Monument to the Textbook (located in front of the Lázaro Cárdenas School). The crew prepared to shoot a scene in which Hugo was to insert nails into the cow's tongue (which came out of his mouth, appearing to be his own tongue) as a commentary on "the pain engendered by the linguistic misunderstandings between races and countries." Lights, camera, action. Suddenly, Ricardo Luna and Jorge Nava, two agents from the municipal police, appeared. The filmmakers showed them a letter from the Binational Foundation, one of the sponsors of the film, explaining that it was "a cultural project, not a political action." A long discussion ensued. The policemen lost their patience and their sense of humor and decided to arrest Hugo Sánchez under suspicion of "disrespect for the flag." Numerous patrol cars arrived, and all hell broke loose.

Since Hugo was being charged with a federal offense, he was immediately transferred to the office of the federal prosecutor (PGR [Procurador General de la República]). Tabloid photographers surrounded the "Zapatista cowboy" and captured his rage and confusion—flash, click, *Alarma* style. Eagerly, they took close-ups of the cow's head and of the sacrosanct "bloodstained" flag. Subsequently, the police transferred the performance artist to a clinic for drug addicts and people with psychological disorders. Fortunately, after a meticulous examination, the doctor declared that the artist was "neither a drug addict, nor mentally-ill." Upon being returned to the cells of the PGR, Hugo was subjected to a full body search amid the constant insults of the law enforcement officers. As a protest, he decided to go on a hunger strike.

The deputies found a United States passport in the artist's clothes. Hugo explained that although he was born and had always lived on Mexican territory, his mother made him a nationalized North American when he was young, just like millions of other border Mexicans. The officials confiscated Hugo's passport and decided he was Chicano (a U.S.-born Mexican), not a Mexican.

On July 13, through the desperate efforts of Hugo's friends, various organizations got wind of the situation. Representatives of the National Committee of Human Rights, the Casa de la Cultura de Tijuana, and the Tijuana Cultural Center began to pressure the PGR for Hugo's release. Also on that day, the artist had to present his version of events before legislator Socorro López. Hugo contended that he never had any intention of desecrating the flag and that, paradoxically, the performance had been conceived as "a patriotic gesture of symbolic defense of the Mexican immigrants who daily risk their lives crossing the dangerous border." Ms. López burst out laughing.

The PGR authorities got in touch with agents from Mexican immigration, and together they decided that the artist (who has devoted much of his life to defending undocumented workers) was "illegally" dwelling in Mexico (his native land). Hugo's risks were multiplying. As he was considered a "foreigner," the insult to the flag would have more serious consequences for him than it would for someone recognized as a Mexican citizen. He was alerted to the real possibility of becoming "persona non grata" under article 33 of the Mexican Constitution, which would forbid him from ever setting foot in Mexican territory again. He was transferred to the sinister prison known as "La ocho" (No. 8), where they locked him up with other "foreigners." His deportation proceedings began.

On the morning of July 14 a (Hispanic) representative from the U.S. Consulate visited Hugo Sánchez in his cell. Hugo was told not to worry, that soon he would return to his country. Hugo tried to explain that "his country" was Mexico and it was there that he wished to remain. The consular envoy didn't get it.

On July 15, accompanied by an agent from Mexican immigration and a deputy, Hugo was transferred to the Customs Office of the City of Tijuana. There he was required to pay a fine for being a foreigner and acting in a Mexican film without being in possession of the appropriate permits. Fortunately, a curator from the Tijuana Cultural Center telephoned the agents and convinced them not to fine the artist, arguing that "people don't make money doing this type of art (performance)."

Hours later Hugo was finally handed over to the U.S. Immigration and Naturalization Service authorities. "*Maestro*," Hugo told me, "for the first time in my life, the *migra* [the U.S. border patrol] gave me a hero's welcome. They even gave me lunch money. It's like I just walked into a mirror where reality's turned upside down."

Later, on the very day of his deportation, the exhausted and humiliated artist decided to return to Tijuana "illegally" and confront the Mexican authorities.

He went to District Court No. 7 to inquire about his case and the whereabouts of his passport. He was told that the judge was on vacation. An employee who had read about the "case of the lunatic" in the newspaper assured him that he would receive a summons to appear in court and warned him that he should be prepared to receive, according to the judge's discretion, either four years in prison (in Mexico) or permanent deportation.

As befits the hair-raising paradox of this binational thriller, Hugo's first court appearance was set for September 18, two days after the celebration of the Mexican Declaration (*Grito*) of Independence. When September came, he was notified of a change of date; this time he was set to appear in court on October 11, one day before the alleged "discovery of America," which is known in Mexico as *Día de la Raza* (birth of the mestizo race). A few days later Hugo's court date was postponed indefinitely. Desperate and penniless, Hugo decided to cross the border and await the new date in his (fictitious) country of origin. Mexico, his true country, had been transformed into a juridical nightmare out of a Chicano secret service *pochonovela*.

Hugo Sánchez's case is unique: a Mexican deported to the United States for doing a performance. Why? Perhaps it had to do with the politically charged context and time. It was indeed an extremely tense period in Tijuana: The recent assassinations of the ruling party's presidential candidate, Luis Donaldo Colosio, and of Tijuana's chief of police, Benítez, had created a pervasive climate of melancholy, mistrust, and fear that affected everyone. Perhaps it was the timing of the incident, one month before the Mexican elections scheduled for August 21, which the opposition party had a real possibility of winning (Tijuana was in the hands of the right-wing opposition at that time). But other, inescapable, extra-contextual factors are also part of the picture. The intolerance of the police for alternative culture and the heavy restrictions on freedom of expression in Mexico definitely contributed to Sánchez's Kafkaesque nightmare. Sadly, in an authoritarian society (even one that so desperately wants to be seen as the eternal protagonist of a transition to democracy) the borders between art and illegality are becoming increasingly thin.

In a letter of support for the Mexican artist, the Chicano artist and writer Rubén Guevara wrote: "Hugo Sánchez's performance was as 'offensive' as the social conditions that inspired it. The artist is nothing if not a catalyst of

social and cultural forces, and his work is a stylized reflection of reality . . .
The shameful judgment passed on Sánchez is a test of the new government's
(Zedillo's) democratic image . . . The test consists precisely in allowing *any*
cultural gesture, however radical or strange it may seem, to be not just tolerated, but respected."

Thanks to media pressure (including publication of this essay in Mexico's
national daily newspaper, *La Jornada*), the judge decided to dismiss Hugo's
case in December. The passport disappeared mysteriously from the Mexicali
archives. (Maybe now there is a third "Hugo Sánchez" wandering the streets
of San Diego, Los Angeles, or San Francisco.)

The challenge for performer Hugo Sánchez now is to overcome his fear of
using the street as a laboratory for artistic creation and to recover his fragile
and bruised Mexican identity. As for me, only a scar on my right leg remains as
a sinister memory of the dangers involved in doing performance in the 1990s.

Selection 12

NYLSA MARTÍNEZ (Mexicali, b. 1979) lives in Los Angeles. She was a member of the narrative workshop of the department of literary studies of the Universidad de Guadalajara until 2006. She is the author of the short story collections *Roads* (2007) and *Tu casa es mi casa* (2009). In "Lights" Nylsa Martínez remembers how much easier it was, in the 1980s, to cross the border on a whim. She recalls her childhood memories of trips to Disneyland and Los Angeles before the tightening of international borders, including her reaction after seeing black people for the first time, and her comparison between Mexican and American graffiti. At first her visits would not meet her expectations. She remembers her family getting lost in the freeway, and those memories blend with the present experience in the city, still the same mirage of her childhood. In the present time, one day she enters a restaurant called Mexicali, like her hometown, but cannot recognize the food on the menu. That is, in her view, one of the idiosyncrasies of Los Angeles: nothing is what it appears to be.

Lights

NYLSA MARTÍNEZ

TRANSLATED BY IGNACIO LÓPEZ-CALVO AND VICTOR VALLE

In the 1980s some of my world's existing borders had not yet been hardened to the point they are now. Back then it was okay to use the slightest pretext to jump the fence: to look for a new appliance, buy tennis shoes, or, my city's favorite excuse, grab a pack of weenies. Crossing was such an ordinary and graceful event that only the idea of traveling beyond our comfort zone—that kilometers-wide world straddling both sides of the border—made us feel as if we were truly entering another country.

I lived through the times when the only purpose for traveling was to go Los Angeles; our forays into the United States typically required more than twenty-five-mile travel permits. Just as we never lacked for shopping excuses, it was just as common for people like us to maintain close or long-distance relationships with people we knew in other California cities—"some acquaintance," we casually said of those who lived along that concrete ladder that led to its highest rung, which for us was Sacramento—that imperfect polygon that several centuries earlier, and past a challenging ocean, the Spanish had imagined as a great booty.

We always had someone to visit in LA—only there and nowhere else. Yet all of us, including the immigration agents, knew that our stories were a sham, a big lie we were all in on: "And where are you going?" "I'm going to Los Angeles," "Oh yeah, are you going to visit any relative?" "Yes, my sister," "And where does she live?" "In Fontana," "And how many days are you staying there?" "Only the weekend," "Oh, very well! Here is your permit." And then the agent would give to the person in question a little yellow paper he scribbled on for the other agents to supposedly recognize when the traveler got to a sort of camp that suddenly appeared in the middle of the desert, the exact point where everything became strange enough to become an adventure. "Are you going to Los Angeles?" "Yes, that's where we're going," "And what are you going to do there?" "We're going to Disneyland," "Oh, very good! Here is your permit." "Are you going to Los Angeles?" "Yes," "Are you visiting anyone?" "Well yes, we're going to a wedding. A cousin is getting married in Long Beach." I belonged to a generation that grew up listening to these time-saving geographic "misunderstandings": Getting to our destination simply required a permit and some freeway driving.

I knew Los Angeles since I was a child, and I use the verb *to know* here in its most general and austere sense. I do not remember exactly when that realization became a fact, but the photographs I began to collect the moment I reached it showed that I had managed, during my adolescence, to turn the city into a deformed and frightening imaginary. Then several years in which I stayed away from the border passed and, as a result, a period in which I was freed from further detentions in that country, thus no more chances for me to rebuild that amorphous painting in which I assigned my memories their own geographic locations.

One time I can't forget was when my mother heroically threw herself into driving a freeway she claimed to have mastered; I don't remember who was traveling with us, but the car was a 1977 Ford Granada. I want to believe we made our exit from Mexicali before sunset. So there we go: to Los Angeles. There were probably no stops in between, maybe one in that obscure town well-known to us on our side, our cultural landmark: Indio, California. You always stop there because it's halfway. Halfway to what? That's still unclear to me.

After several hours the lights lit us up. These were not the mere reflections of cities we were passing through. No, these were impressively grand and beautiful. Then I thought that things would be different and our constant trips there would finally make sense. Neither cell phones nor GPS were part of our lives. It was a time when people stubbornly relied on their map-reading abilities or guessed their location from wild hunches. "I know I'm going the right way," said my mother, to dispel any doubts circulating among the passengers. And we advanced and advanced, the lights growing bigger after each mile until, as I grew happiest because we had finally neared a place that interested me, my mother's cry suddenly dashed our hopes: "We're lost."

We got off the freeway, and still touched by the fountain's luminous rays, she looked for a place to park the car: "We're going to have to call your uncle." She must have said something like that. The point is, our recently begun adventure that had seemed as promising as our other California trips began to turn sour. We got off at a McDonald's. That's where my mother made the fatal call to that terrible uncle, the same one who would guide us to his horrible house.

"We're close to Dodgers Stadium," I'm sure my mother said. Dodger Stadium, I thought, first time my eyes saw that place I used to hear about on television—a stadium, a real one, with huge lights and a lot of people coming out of it. I remember I told my mother that we should go there instead of Uncle's because I wanted to have a real adventure. I had the feeling I'd find the famous pitcher Fernando Valenzuela, one of the few international celebrities to hail from my town, under some bench or at the stadium's entrance, once we got inside there. At least that's what I thought.

Nothing. Instead of my dreams, the uncle arrived in a white van as plain and nondescript as any other. After engaging in a kind of ritual that instantly challenged my good luck, he took us to his house. We went navigating a sea of red lights that went out from time to time to allow us to advance a few meters, and then we stopped again. Only exits, entrances to unsuspected routes. We finally descended into a street that can go unnamed. We had already arrived when I woke up. Not 'til the next morning did those gray images that still scare me begin to clothe and populate that place. The uncle's house was part of a row of narrow buildings that appeared to go on forever. Not even sure if I had reached the sidewalk before they let me know I'd be staying in it. The weather tempted me to run down the streets to see if the lights that had fascinated me the night before would reappear.

Later, and after having all I could take of the adult conversations, we went out with our relatives. Then I remember seeing groups of dark people everywhere—but so dark I could not fathom what it was they called them: *morenos*. I was sure the adults were making a big mistake. They were not; my schoolmates were brown, all my neighbors were, but not them. They told me to shut up.

I still vaguely remember the reason for that visit, something to do with wedding preparations. That's why all the household's women were tossed into an enormous store the next morning. I remember that the uncle had dropped us off at a McDonald's again and that what caught my attention was the graffiti on its walls. I thought that the one back home was prettier. Then they told me to keep an eye on my bag and made our way through alleys full of people and clothing.

I heard people speak in unknown languages, and I wanted to look at them carefully to understand what they were saying; then they warned me not to do it. I saw a parade of women who covered their heads with robes and another group of people who looked very strange to me. I wanted to observe them, to listen to them closely. But no, my family kept rushing me along, insisting I not stare at anyone. Hurry, hurry. That's what we did for several days in different places. There were no lights in any of those places, however, nothing compared to the first night's splendor.

Sometime later these family relations waned, and there were no more visits. I didn't complain. That all seemed so threatening to me—I preferred my safety.

I was in Studio City some time ago—one of those well-to-do areas full of cafés and gourmet establishments. Curiosity got the best of me, and I could not resist walking into one of those restaurants called Mexicali. Despite the terrifying alley stroll I had once taken with my family, I now held out the hope of an uplifting experience of their confines. I scanned the menu and could not recognize any of my city's typical dishes to justify the restaurant's name. That's how it was: a matter of random circumstances and imaginaries. Afterward, just as we were about to leave, I saw a fainted woman splayed out on the floor; she was at the back of the rear entrance: she was a fallen diner who, until that moment, had not been missed by the people inside cutting their chimichangas with sharpened knives. We told the waiters to take care of her and left the place. Then I asked my companion, "And when do I get to know Los Angeles?" "What do you mean?" "Well, the other one." "What other one?" "Yes, the other one, the ugly part." I smiled as if that would tell her where to find it. "Sure?" "Sure," after I had finally seen the lights.

Selection 13

SESSHU FOSTER (b. 1957) has taught composition and literature in several American universities. He has published *American Loneliness: Selected Poems* (2006); the experimental prose poem *City Terrace Field Manual* (1996); the novel *Atomic Aztex* (2005); and the poetry collection *World Ball Notebook* (2008). In our selected text Foster plays with the contrasts between lived reality in Los Angeles, particularly East LA, and the filmic renditions of it Hollywood exports to the world. In an effort to acknowledge a Latina/o writing aesthetic that transcends questions of ethnic or racial authenticity, Foster has written about LA in an overtly Latina/o style, including the use of code switching and subversions of the ethnographic gaze that has dominated film representations of this community. He can be considered a Latino author through social proximity via lived culture and aesthetic preference. In "Movie Version: 'Hell to Eternity,'" Foster deploys ironic, synesthetic rejoinders to the objective "facts" of the film's scenic inventions to suggest how Eastside residents might embody their viewing of the film.

Movie Version: "Hell to Eternity"

SESSHU FOSTER

Guy Gabaldon, born in 1926 and raised in East LA, shined shoes on skid row from the age of ten. At twelve he moved in with the Nakano family of Boyle Heights, where he learned Japanese. When the Nakanos were sent to camps in Arizona, seventeen-year-old Gabaldon joined the marines and used "backstreet Japanese" to capture fifteen hundred Japanese troops on Saipan. In the movie version, he was played by a white actor named Jeffrey Hunter, who in 1969 suffered a stroke, at age forty-two, and died falling down the stairs.

In the movie version, skid row was played by 1960s Bunker Hill, and age twelve was played by a grasshopper flying in a summer field. Sweetness careened down the streets in buses and trolleys.

In the movie version, a ten-year-old boy shining shoes was played by Route 66, and the relocation camps were played by cars going by. Packards were played by Dodges.

In the movie version, the cold beer is played by country music nasal twang, and Jeffrey Hunter was played by slight nausea and nostril flare. His headache was played by the twentieth century.

In the movie version, the actual colors of the rushing ocean were played by a whirr of a strip through the machine, and the sizzling palm leaves were played by folded taco smell. Somebody was played by nobody.

In the movie version, the present is played by an off-camera past with seagulls added or removed and palm trees painted on a canvas backdrop of night. Popcorn smell was played by cotton candy.

In the movie version, wishes were played by a voice-over of broken dishes, and bouts of influenza were played by old magazines in the back. Smoke in a funnel over the hills was played by extras dressed like citizens.

In the movie version, East LA was played by the blood bursting an artery and dust specks thrown into a ray on the stairs. The golden moment balking.

Selection 14

HÉCTOR TOBAR (b. 1963), born and raised in Los Angeles, is the son of Guatemalan immigrants (his father was a leftist military police officer in the Guatemalan army) who moved Los Angeles in 1962. In 1992 Tobar won a Pulitzer Prize with the *Los Angeles Times* for his reporting on the Los Angeles riots. Before that, Tobar had been exploring urban violence and Central American homelessness for the *Times* when he came up with the idea for a novel: "a social worker at the agency El Rescate told me a story about a client of hers who had spotted a death-squad member in MacArthur Park" (www.hectortobar.com). *The Tattooed Soldier* (1998), a finalist for the PEN USA West Award for Fiction, is currently in its fifth edition in paperback. More recently, Tobar published *The Barbarian Nurseries* (2011), a novel about class and ethnic conflict in Southern California, and *Deep Down Dark: The Untold Stories of 33 Men Buried in a Chilean Mine, and the Miracle That Set Them Free* (2014).

This excerpt from *Translation Nation: Defining a New American Identity in the Spanish-Speaking United States* (2005) explores what it means for Los Angeles to be a twenty-first-century Ellis Island. While its first pages present Tobar's Guatemalan family's migration to LA as pioneers of a recent Central American migration, the shortwave radio broadcasts of Radio Havana he hears with his father introduce a young Hector to Ernesto "Che" Guevara as a revolutionary antidote to cultural assimilation. The north-south orientation of the Americas symbolized by Che not only reminds us of the grand sweep of José Martí's incipiently post-national "Nuestra América," but also redefines the meaning of U.S. liberal democracy. The radio's revolutionary wavelengths carry the anarchist and Mesoamerican ghosts of the peasant commons with which Héctor begins to question Jeffersonian liberty's enslavement to private property. Along the way the author recollects his family's attraction to and repulsion for American culture.

Americanismo

City of Peasants, Los Angeles, California

HÉCTOR TOBAR

Long before I understood what the word *revolution* meant, when I was a five-year-old boy growing up in the seamier half of Hollywood, California, I knew the face of Che Guevara. In the same way that other boys believed in Santa Claus and the Tooth Fairy, I knew that Che, with his Christlike martyr's gaze and mane of wavy black hair, had come to help the poor and to make things right in the world. In real life he was a knot of contradictions too complex to explain to a kindergartener: he was a poet who carried a gun, a dreamer known for his ruthlessness, generous to his friends and intransigent with both allies and enemies. He was a Robespierre in olive drab who wanted to bring socialism to the Americas. But to me, behind that beard, underneath that black beret and its red star, there was a benevolent savior. Plenty of other people around me believed the same thing: it was the late 1960s, and my father, like most men in their twenties, was an idealist. My mother, his slightly younger wife, was too. Like Che, they were ambitious romantics, although neither one could appreciate this quality in the other.

"Che died for us," my father would say. "He went into the hills and fought as a guerrilla." I was small enough then that I didn't understand the difference between a guerrilla and a gorilla. I imagined a man jumping about the jungle, in imitation of an ape, ambushing the purveyors of evil.

My parents had brought Che with them when they left Guatemala in 1962. He came in their luggage, a spirit of adventure tucked in between their layers of clothes, next to the English dictionary my father brought along, the devotional cards of saints my mother depended on to protect her and her unborn baby. Like my parents, Che was a risk-taker, a man with an impulsive streak. As a teenager, he would not hesitate to accept an outrageous dare, like walking on an irrigation pipe suspended over an impossibly deep gorge. A similar impetuousness had placed the young people who would become my parents in the back of a delivery truck one spring afternoon in 1962, slipping off their clothes just long enough to conceive me while a driving rainstorm beat on the roof of the truck. A few weeks later they were pregnant and married and planning to run away to California. They arrived the week of the Cuban missile crisis, on a Pan American Airways flight that dropped them off at Los Angeles International Airport. Stepping for the first time into the California sunshine, they were greeted by the striking image of the airport's new Theme Building, a structure suspended between two giant arches suggesting the orbits of atoms, the coming "Space Age." My parents, a pair of young adults with a baby on the way, would soon embrace that uniquely California élan that wove together modernity and an incipient rebelliousness. In this new land of cat's-eye sunglasses, my mother quickly learned to beehive her hair and to channel the allure of wool dresses that rose suggestively toward her kneecap. She outfitted my father in argyle sweaters no Guatemalan had ever worn before. Che was the most chic thing they had of their own to add to this American stew of coolness. Long before his face started popping up all over California—carried aloft on placards at Los Angeles City College rallies and on dorm room walls in Berkeley—he had been a hero to my father.

"El Che was from Argentina, but he fought in Cuba, and he lived in Guatemala too," my father would say, which would lead me later to ponder a map of the world, wondering how a man could travel such great distances swinging from tree branches, across mountains and jungles.

One of the first secrets I ever kept from my father was that I admired Maury Wills, the shortstop for the Dodgers, and Jerry West of the Lakers as much as, if not more than, El Che. For me the United States was a land ruled by sports heroes and astronauts, where arenas were filled with cheering crowds and rockets zoomed into space with fiery ascents that caused hundreds of necks to crane upward and mouths to open in awe. I had never seen Che on my television, unlike my other heroes, who sank baskets from the half-court line and sent baseballs over the fence at the brand-new Dodger Stadium or walked on the moon as fuzzy silhouettes. I was becoming an American, another species, different from all my ancestors. My mother and father would become Americans too, taking the oath as U.S. citizens within a decade of their arrival, even while believing and telling any Spanish-speaking person they met that they were still *guatemaltecos*. My father, I see now, embraced Che as an antidote to the lure of American culture, to its overwhelming power to amaze and intimate, especially back then in the 1960s, when America gleamed and dazzled like the chrome bumpers and tall fins of the Fords and Chevrolets he longed to win. To prove he had not become a total gringo, my father became a more devout Guevarista, an armchair rebel with a single, loyal follower—me.

An especially self-confident brand of American identity had reached its apex in the United States, the Anglo-Saxon Protestant worldview celebrated by writers like Samuel Huntington, a civil religion whose holy trinity was the Protestant work ethic, individualism, and an obsession with orderliness in all matters, public and private. Back then, an immigrant like my father needed to be stubborn to keep the person he had before from being washed out in the laundry. It took work to hold onto the idea that you could be an outsider. "Never forget where you came from," my parents told me, but this was not an easy command to follow since I was an only child, cut off from all my grandparents, my uncles and aunts, and my cousins by thousands of miles and by a cultural and language gap that seemed to grow wider every year. Well into the 1970s, I could still count the number of Guatemalans I knew in Los Angeles on one hand. Che stood for the beliefs my family had left behind, a symbol of our Latin American identity during the long years we lived as cultural prisoners, a lonely crew of *chapines* (as Guatemalans call themselves) planting a flag with Che's face on the 34th parallel of North America.

Everything is different in California today. In the decades since my family arrived in Los Angeles, several accidents of geopolitics and macroeconomics brought millions of people like us to the United States, all to experience a similar kind of attraction and repulsion to American culture, all to remake the idea of themselves and their community with icons like Che or the mustachioed Mexican revolutionary Emiliano Zapata, or more recently, the hooded Subcomandante Marcos, who led the Mayan Indian uprising in Chiapas. We have come in so many numbers to California, America's most populous state, filling its cities and towns with our flags and pictures of our heroes, our language, our parades, and our prejudices—and so many other things that are uniquely ours that even the notion of what it means to be an "American" has begun to change completely. You can see this transformation most dramatically in my hometown, where the Stars and Stripes still flies over the government building of the Civic Center downtown, an island of English-speaking culture encircled north, south, east, and west by a sprawl of *latinidad*. Latinness. Billboards for Mexican deejays in excessive Stetsons loom over the thoroughfares, and the Virgin of Guadalupe, the patron saint of Mexico, is posted outside countless liquor stores as a sentinel against graffiti and armed robbery. If you go to the flat plain of South Los Angeles on a Saturday night and stand under the milky light of the streetlamps or visit the arroyos of Echo Park on a Saturday afternoon, you can close your eyes and feel the rural provinces of Mexico and Central America come to life in the acoustic university that surrounds you, in the voices and the music of the people who live there.

In the most recent census, the number of Spanish speakers in the city of Los Angeles (1,422,316) was roughly equal to those who spoke only English (1,438,573). The city's top-rated newscast is the Spanish Univisión *noticiero*, and the city parks are beginning to resemble the exhausted public spaces of Mexico City. In 1995 Los Angeles County parents registered the name José most often on birth certificates for baby boys. At Griffith Park, where I played as a child, the city Department of Parks and Recreation has placed enormous boulders in the center of the lawn to discourage the most popular municipal pastime, the playing of soccer, a sport unknown in the California of my childhood. Che is stencil-painted across the city more than ever, almost always staring back with the dreamy eyes of his most famous portrait, from a 1960 photograph taken at a funeral in Havana. Four decades removed from that time and place, it is an image ever more stylized, a sort of George Washington in negative image, a Latin icon from the founding of an altogether different republic, staring back at his progeny not from the dollar bill but from countless printed T-shirts, posters, and postcards. Che is the "founding father" symbol of the anti-WASP republic, a nation that embraces informality, excess in emotion, the dissembling force of rebellion, and the idea of strength in collectivity.

Today Los Angeles and California are quietly exporting their people and their way of life eastward across the continent. The city is the starting point of a new identity that is at once Latin American and—though it may not be immediately apparent—intertwined with North American traditions, with Jeffersonian ideals and the civic culture molded in the United States over the past two centuries. Los Angeles is to the twenty-first-century United States what New York City was to the twentieth. It is the crucible in which a new national culture can be seen most clearly. Once upon a time it could be said that every American city had a little bit of Ellis Island in it—or even a bit of Little Italy or the Bronx or Harlem. Something similar is happening in the twenty-first century, in which each new day sees another Spanish-speaking Angelino set off on Interstates 5, 10, 15, from the overcrowded metropolises of our state to the greener pastures of places like Pasco, Washington, or Fayetteville, Arkansas, or even New York City itself, and in so doing helps bring a bit of Los Angeles to those places too.

In the United States and the Los Angeles I knew as a child, there was only one way to become American, the method perfected in New York and other eastern cities. Most immigrant families stuck to the formula, the one people had followed on a path to Americanness for a century. They stopped speaking Spanish—or Italian or Armenian or Greek—and instead embarrassed themselves in front of their children by trying to wrap their Mediterranean or Latin American mouths around English. Their children would retain only a handful of phrases from the mother tongue and would know the culture of the Old Country primarily as a collection of recipes and swear words and maybe from the occasional visit of a grandparent who arrived in the United States as a sort of time traveler, stumbling about the apartment or the cul-de-sac in an old fedora, like my grandfather did when he came to visit us. When they had enough money, they tried to enroll their children in tennis lessons or Little League or any other American institution that would let them get a foot in the door.

About halfway into the twentieth century, the Mexican writer Octavio Paz had wandered into a Los Angeles similar to the one my parents encountered on their arrival, the Los Angeles of the Pax Americana at its apex. In *The Labyrinth of Solitude*, his seminal treatise on Mexican identity, Paz describes the latent

Mexican feel of the city then, a faint but discernible "delight in decorations, carelessness and pomp, negligence, never quite vanishing." Of the people of Mexican origin he encountered in Los Angeles, he wrote: "They have lived in the city for many years wearing the same clothes as the other inhabitants, and they feel ashamed of their origin. . . . They act like persons who are wearing disguises, who are afraid of a stranger's look because it could strip them and leave them stark naked."

Unbeknownst to Octavio Paz, inside those withdrawn Angelenos there was a garrulous, self-confident Latin city waiting to be born. My father became a pioneer of this new city when he decreed that I would always speak to him in Spanish. At school, and in the Hollywood alleyways and side streets where I played with my friends, I did math, joked, and whined in English, but at home my father fought back against the Anglo-Saxon linguistic torrent with a steady stream of *castellano*: to this day he is always *papa*. At the same time, he would have been deeply upset if I didn't learn English, then as now the language of commerce and government. My undeniably accent-free English, with its native speaker intonations and fluency in the peculiar vowel sounds no native Spanish speaker can ever quite master, was in a sense a measure of his family's achievement. He admired American institutions, and his favorite class at Los Angeles City College was U.S. history, with its crimson-bound textbook, which he passed down to me as a kind of heirloom, telling me to pay particular attention to the chapters on the Civil War. My father was ambivalent about the United States, and in that, too, he was a pioneer: His ambivalence about WASP culture never faded, never surrendered to acceptance. He made learning English his own obsession too, taking night school classes and making himself fluent enough to write business letters, but he also went to political meetings and seethed in Spanish about *imperialism* in group discussions led by a Guatemalan leftist whose circle of would-be rebels later contemplated hijacking a plane to Cuba—it was a bit of a fad in those days. My father told me that Che had fought to free Cuba and that he was fighting for us too, for Guatemala, where our extended family lived under a blue sky and puffy tropical clouds I got to see every Christmas vacation. If we wanted to hear Che's voice, we could take our shortwave radio, string up a copper wire over our duplex apartment, and grab his words from the atmosphere. My father marked the frequency for Radio Habana Cuba on the glass face of the receiver with a piece of cellophane tape and a marker, a blue line that ran parallel to another one for TGW, Radio Nacional de Guatemala, a much weaker signal that came in only on certain summer evenings, when he and my mother would sit and listen to the sound of the Guatemala marimba orchestra force its way through layers of static into our living room. I remember that music vividly because it usually led my mother to quiet tears whenever she heard it. As for Che, to this day I can't tell you what his voice sounded like.

My father spoke to me about El Che in that earnest and gentle tone adults have when they speak to children about things like God and history. We are part of a bigger world, his voice said, full of beauty and horrors, where brave and smart men battle the forces of ignorance and darkness. Our history and our future cannot be contained within borders. This message, I believe, is essentially the same one communicated to new generations of Californians. Today all of California, Latino and non-Latino, is increasingly immersed in the collective, cross-border narrative of its eleven million inhabitants of Latin American descent. In my own household these stories have their starting point in my grandparents' villages, in places with names like Huehuetenango and Rincón Tigre (Tiger's Corner), and in a cluster of adobe buildings with plaster skins, set amid the banana plantations of the United Fruit Company.

I grew up believing it was my destiny to advance this essentially Latin American story into new, northern territories. In the Los Angeles of today, however, the narrative traffic goes in two directions. It is not just the story of the peasant whose children follow the North Star to the California oasis of orange groves, rationality, and good wages; the story also flows southward, back down to the birthplace of the passionate, the chaotic, and the spiritual. If you grow up Latino in Los Angeles, you feel the pull of the south, of its pop singers, its revolutions, and its fads. If you can, you go to the south, in body or in mind. The frightened Mexican Americans of Octavio Paz's day are a fading anachronism because people feel free to dress, think, speak, or plan their futures thinking of the south.

I can remember standing and looking to the south—literally and figuratively—one day at about the turn of the millennium in the East Los Angeles neighborhood of City Terrace. I was standing on the deck of the family home of my *comadre*, which is what you call your child's godmother. The very fact that I was using such a term, "code-switching" it into my English (as a linguist would say), was itself a step backward in what should have been a steady march forward into North American assimilation. "¡Hola, comadre, how's it going? Such a long time, *qué no?*" My *comadre*, María Cabildo, and her husband, Manuel Bernal, who was also my *compadre*, had invited a group of friends over for their annual New Year's Day tamale brunch, which we celebrated on a patio overlooking the Eastside on one of those rare days of crystalline skies winter brings us in Southern California. In the distance you could see the Art Moderne tower of the seventy-five-year-old Sears building on Olympic Boulevard sticking up from the flat urban plain, the splashes of green palm fronds amid the gray and earth-toned cityscape of naked jacarandas and dormant maple trees, and stubby apartment buildings and warehouses. We filled the conversation with our southern obsessions. Our friend Evangeline Ordaz had been to Chiapas as a human rights monitor, encountering Mexican soldiers and Mayan rebels outfitted with antique rifles; she had also met the famous guerrilla leader known as Subcomandante Marcos. María's brother Miguel talked about his work for the Mexico City investigative magazine *Proceso*; in recent days he had come under threat from the murderous Tijuana drug cartel. This was a conversation, like most others in the still small circles of the Latino Los Angeles upper middle class that began in English and drifted frequently into Spanish, a language we speak with widely varying degrees of fluency. Another visitor told us the story of a recent visit to his family's Mexican village, a place deep in the dry valleys and windswept high plains made famous in the work of the writer Juan Rulfo. Our friend had wandered into the town square to find a man tied up on an enormous cross, hanging in the air with a crown of thorns on his head and just three nails short of an actual crucifixion.

"What are you doing up there?" he asked.

"I am showing devotion to Jesus!"

"You should get down before you get a sunburn!"

We listened to his story, and for a moment we were lost in the strangeness and wonder of it—a familiar sensation because all of us have been to the places where such stories are born. Los Angeles is filled with people like us, people who have Latin American villages and peasants hovering around their lives. There are campesinos in our dreams, on our lawns cutting the grass, in the pickup trucks next to us on the freeway, in the picture frames on the walls of our living rooms. The peasants in the pictures might come from the age of the Mexican Revolution, or they might be twenty-first-century campesinos in villages connected to California by bus lines and extended family relationships. We can go down below María's family home and hear roosters crowing at sunrise from backyard chicken coops. In the newer Mexican suburbs of Watts and Compton, we can find stalks of corn growing in the front yards, a crop from the old country seemingly about to burst from its age of wire fencing to populate all the other lawns and a reminder to all that the gardener or the mechanic inside was once a campesino—and perhaps still longs to be one.

Selection 15

SONIA NAZARIO (b. 1960) grew up in Kansas and Argentina and received her bachelor's degree from Williams College and her master's degree in Latin American studies from the University of California, Berkeley. Awarded honorary doctorates by Mount St. Mary's College and Whittier College, Nazario writes about immigration, drug addiction, hunger, and the toll they take upon children. *Enrique's Journey* (2006), which relates a young boy's encounters with treacherous people aboard freight trains and the threat of robbery and rape at the hands of smugglers and police as he migrates from Central America to the United States, won a Pulitzer Prize for feature writing as well as the George Polk Award for International Reporting and the Grand Prize of the Robert F. Kennedy Journalism Award, among other honors.

"The Boy Left Behind," the first in the series of *Los Angeles Times* articles compiled in *Enrique's Journey*, chronicles an eleven-year-old boy's harrowing quest to reunite with his mother and the special suffering Central American immigrants experience as neoliberal economic violence dismembers their family. In this selection we enter the immigrant's double subjectivity of an undocumented Honduran mother, Lourdes, who must simultaneously endure the exploitation where she stands, as a disposable worker in LA's sweatshops and bars, while a stream of telephone calls she answers torture her for failing to reunite her fractured family. Interestingly, in a passage in which Lourdes mulls her departure, Nazario explores the immigrant's double world within the formal confines of U.S. daily journalism: "Lourdes knows. She understands, as only a mother can, the terror she is about to inflict, the ache Enrique will feel, and finally the emptiness." Here the narrator fuses the clipped declarative, active-voice sentences that signify journalistic objectivity with the New Journalism's interior monologue to simulate a fully realized novelistic character. The text illustrates the hardships caused by economic migration not only to migrants but also to their families left behind and particularly their helpless children. It also shows that the experience is even more dangerous for women. At the same time, it opens the reader's eyes to some of the reasons migrants refuse to return to their home country: the embarrassment of coming back empty-handed and the fear of being unable to reenter the United States illegally.

"The Boy Left Behind"

Excerpt from *Enrique's Journey*

SONIA NAZARIO

The boy does not understand.

His mother is not talking to him. She will not even look at him. Enrique has no hint of what she is going to do.

Lourdes knows. She understands, as only a mother can, the terror she is about to inflict, the ache Enrique will feel, and finally the emptiness.

What will become of him? Already he will not let anyone else feed or bathe him. He loves her deeply, as only a son can. With Lourdes he is openly affectionate. "*Dame pico, mami.* Give me a kiss, Mom," he pleads, over and over, pursing his lips. With Lourdes he is a chatterbox. "*Mira, mami.* Look, Mom," he says softly, asking her questions about everything he sees. Without her he is so shy it is crushing.

Slowly, she walks out onto the porch. Enrique clings to her pant leg. Beside her he is tiny. Lourdes loves him so much she cannot bring herself to say a word. She cannot carry his picture. It would melt her resolve. She cannot hug him. He is five years old.

They live on the outskirts of Tegucigalpa, in Honduras. She can barely afford food for him and his sister, Belky, who is seven. She's never been able to buy them a toy or a birthday cake. Lourdes, twenty-four, scrubs other people's laundry in a muddy river. She goes door to door selling tortillas, used clothes, and plantains.

She fills a wooden box with gum and crackers and cigarettes, and she finds a spot where she can squat on a dusty sidewalk next to the downtown Pizza Hut and sell the items to passersby. The sidewalk is Enrique's playground.

They have a bleak future. He and Belky are not likely to finish grade school. Lourdes cannot afford uniforms or pencils. Her husband is gone. A good job is out of the question.

Lourdes knows of only one place that offers hope. As a seven-year-old child, delivering tortillas her mother made to wealthy homes, she glimpsed this place on other people's television screens. The flickering images were a far cry from Lourdes's childhood home: a two-room shack made of wooden slats, its flimsy tin roof weighted down with rocks, the only bathroom a clump of bushes outside. On television she saw New York City's spectacular skyline, Las Vegas's shimmering lights, Disneyland's Magic Castle.

Lourdes has decided: She will leave, she will go to the United States and make money and send it home. She will be gone for one year—less, with luck—or she will bring her children to be with her. It is for them she is leaving, she tells herself, but still she feels guilty. She kneels and kisses Belky and hugs her tightly. Then she turns to her own sister. If she watches over Belky, she will get a set of gold fingernails from el Norte.

But Lourdes cannot face Enrique. He will remember only one thing that she says to him: "Don't forget to go to church this afternoon."

It is January 29, 1989. His mother steps off the porch.

She walks away.

"¿Dónde está mi mami?" Enrique cries, over and over. "Where is my mom?"

His mother never returns, and that decides Enrique's fate. As a teenager—indeed, still a child—he will set out for the United States on his own to search for her. Virtually unnoticed, he will become one of an estimated forty-eight thousand children who enter the United States from Central America and Mexico each year, illegally and without either of their parents. Roughly two-thirds of them will make it past the U.S. Immigration and Naturalization Service.

Many go north seeking work. Others flee abusive families. Most of the Central Americans go to reunite with a parent, say counselors at a detention center in Texas, where the INS houses the largest number of the unaccompanied children it catches. Of those, the counselors say, 75 percent are looking for their mothers. Some children say they need to find out whether their mothers still love them. A priest at a Texas shelter says they often bring pictures of themselves in their mother's arms.

The journey is hard for the Mexicans but harder still for Enrique and the others from Central America. They must make an illegal and dangerous trek up the length of Mexico. Counselors and immigration lawyers say only half of them get help from smugglers. The rest travel alone. They are cold, hungry, and helpless. They are hunted like animals by corrupt police, bandits, and gang members deported from the United States. A University of Houston study found that most are robbed, beaten, or raped, usually several times. Some are killed.

They set out with little or no money. Thousands, shelter workers say, make their way through Mexico clinging to the sides and tops of freight trains. Since the 1990s Mexico and the United States have tried to thwart them. To evade Mexican police and immigration authorities, the children jump onto and off of the moving train cars. Sometimes they fall and the wheels tear them apart.

They navigate by word of mouth or by the arc of the sun. Often they don't know where or when they'll get their next meal. Some go days without eating. If a train stops even briefly, they crouch by the tracks, cup their hands, and steal sips of water from shiny puddles tainted with diesel fuel. At night they huddle together on the train cars or next to the tracks. They sleep in trees, in tall grass, or in beds made of leaves.

Some are very young. Mexican rail workers have encountered seven-year-olds on their way to find their mothers. A policeman discovered a nine-year-old boy near the downtown Los Angeles tracks. "I'm looking for my mother," he said. The youngster had left Puerto Cortes in Honduras three months before. He had been guided only by his cunning and the single thing she knew about her: where she lived. He had asked everyone, "How do I get to San Francisco?"

Typically, the children are teenagers. Some were babies when their mothers left; they know them only by pictures sent home. Others, a bit older, struggle to hold onto memories: One has slept in her mother's bed; another has smelled her perfume, put on her deodorant, her clothes. One is old enough to remember his mother's face, another her laugh, her favorite shade of lipstick, how her dress felt as she stood at the stove patting tortillas.

Many, including Enrique, begin to idealize their mothers. They remember how their mothers fed and bathed them, how they walked them to kindergarten. In their absence these mothers become larger than life. Although in the

United States the women struggle to pay rent and eat, in the imagination of their children back home, they become deliverance itself, the answer to every problem. Finding them becomes the quest for the Holy Grail.

Confusion

Enrique is bewildered. Who will take care of him now that this mother is gone? Lourdes, unable to burden her family with both of her children, has split them up. Belky stayed with Lourdes's mother and sisters. For two years Enrique is entrusted to his father, Luis, from whom his mother has been separated for three years.

Enrique clings to his daddy, who dotes on him. A bricklayer, his father takes Enrique to work and lets him help mix mortar. They live with Enrique's grandmother. His father shares a bed with him and brings him apples and clothes. Every month Enrique misses his mother less, but he does not forget her. "When is she coming for me?" he asks.

Lourdes and her smuggler cross Mexico on buses. Each afternoon she closes her eyes. She imagines herself home at dusk, playing with Enrique under a eucalyptus tree in her mother's front yard. Enrique straddles a broom, pretending it's a donkey, trotting around the muddy yard. Each afternoon she presses her eyes shut and tears fall. Each afternoon she reminds herself that if she is weak, if she does not keep moving forward, her children will pay.

Lourdes crosses into the United States in one of the largest immigrant waves of the country's history. She enters at night through a rat-infested Tijuana sewage tunnel and makes her way to Los Angeles. There, in the downtown Greyhound Bus terminal, the smuggler tells Lourdes to wait until he runs a quick errand. He'll be right back. The smuggler has been paid to take her all the way to Miami.

Three days pass. Lourdes musses her filthy hair, trying to blend in with the homeless and not get singled out by police. She prays to God to put someone before her, to show her the way. Whom can she reach out to for help? Starved, she starts walking. East of downtown, Lourdes spots a small factory. On the loading deck, under a gray tin roof, women sort red and green tomatoes. She begs for work. As she puts tomatoes into the boxes, she hallucinates that she is slicing open a juicy one and sprinkling it with salt. The boss pays her fourteen dollars for two hours' work. Lourdes's brother has a friend in Los Angeles who helps Lourdes get a fake Social Security card and a job.

She moves in with a Beverly Hills couple to take care of their three-year-old daughter. Their spacious home has carpet on the floors and mahogany panels on the walls. Her employers are kind. They pay her $125 a week. She gets nights and weekends off. Maybe, Lourdes tells herself—if she stays long enough—they will help her become legal.

Every morning, as the couple leave for work, the little girl cries for her mother. Lourdes feeds her breakfast and thinks of Enrique and Belky. She asks herself: "Do my children cry like this? I'm giving this girl food instead of feeding my own children." To get the girl to eat, Lourdes pretends the spoon is an airplane. But each time the spoon lands in the girl's mouth, Lourdes is filled with sadness.

In the afternoon, after the girl comes home from prekindergarten class, they thumb through picture books and play. The girl, so close to Enrique's age, is a constant reminder of her son. Many afternoons Lourdes cannot contain her grief. She gives the girl a toy and dashes into the kitchen. There, out of sight, tears flow. After seven months she cannot take it. She quits and moves to a friend's place in Long Beach. Boxes arrive in Tegucigalpa bearing clothes, shoes, toy cars, a Robocop doll, a television. Lourdes writes: Do they like the things she is sending? She tells Enrique to behave, to study hard. She has hopes for him: graduation from high school, a white-collar job, maybe as an engineer. She pictures her son working in a crisp shirt and shiny shoes. She says she loves him.

Enrique asks about his mother. "She'll be home soon," his grandmother assures him. "Don't worry. She'll be back."

But his mother does not come. Her disappearance is incomprehensible. Enrique's bewilderment turns to confusion and then to adolescent anger.

When Enrique is seven, his father brings a woman home. To her Enrique is an economic burden. One morning she spills hot cocoa and burns him. His father throws her out. But their separation is brief.

"Mom," Enrique's father tells the grandmother, "I can't think of anyone but that woman."

Enrique's father bathes, dresses, splashes on cologne, and follows her. Enrique tags along and begs to stay with him. But his father tells him to go back to his grandmother.

His father begins a new family. Enrique sees him rarely, usually by chance. In time Enrique's love turns to contempt. "He doesn't love me. He loves the children he has with his wife," he tells Belky. "I don't have a dad."

His father notices. "He looks at me as if he wasn't my son, as if he wants to strangle me," he tells Enrique's grandmother. Most of the blame, his father decides, belongs to Enrique's mother. "She is the one who promised to come back."

For Belky their mother's disappearance is just as distressing. She lives with Aunt Rosa Amalia, one of her mother's sisters. On Mother's Day, Belky struggles through a celebration at school. That night she cries quietly, alone in her room. Then she scolds herself. She should thank her mother for leaving; without the money she sends for books and uniforms, Belky could not even attend school. She reminds herself of all the other things her mother ships south: Reebok tennis shoes, black sandals, the yellow bear and pink puppy stuffed toys on her bed. She commiserates with a friend whose mother has also left. They console each other. They know a girl whose mother died of a heart attack. At least, they say, ours are alive.

But Rosa Amalia thinks the separation has caused deep emotional problems. To her it seems that Belky is struggling with an unavoidable question: How can I be worth anything if my mother left me?

"There are days," Belky tells Aunt Rosa Amalia, "when I wake up and feel so alone." Belky is temperamental. Sometimes she stops talking to everyone. When her mood turns dark, her grandmother warns the other children in the house, "¡Pórtense bien porque la marea anda brava! You better behave, because the seas are choppy!"

Confused by his mother's absence, Enrique turns to his grandmother. Alone now, he and his father's elderly mother share a shack thirty feet square. María Marcos built it herself of wooden slats. Enrique can see daylight in the cracks. It has four rooms, three without electricity. There is no running water. Gutters carry rain off the patched tin roof into two barrels. A trickle of cloudy white sewage runs past the front gate. On a well-worn rock nearby, Enrique's grandmother washes musty used clothing she sells door to door. Next to the rock is the latrine—a concrete hole. Beside it are buckets for bathing.

The shack is in Carrizal, one of Tegucigalpa's poorest neighborhoods. Sometimes Enrique looks across the rolling hills to the neighborhood where he and his mother lived and where Belky still lives with their mother's family. They are six miles apart. They hardly ever visit.

Lourdes sends Enrique fifty dollars a month, occasionally one hundred dollars, sometimes nothing. It is enough for food but not for school clothes, fees, notebooks, or pencils, which are expensive in Honduras. There is never enough for a birthday present. But Grandmother María hugs him and wishes him a cheery *¡Feliz cumpleaños!* "Your mom can't send enough," she says, "so we both have to work."

Enrique loves to climb his grandmother's guayaba tree, but there is no more time for play now. After school Enrique sells tamales and plastic bags of fruit juice from a bucket hung in the crook of his arm. "*¡Tamarindo! ¡Piña!*" he shouts.

Sometimes Enrique takes his wares to a service station, where diesel-belching buses rumble into Carrizal. Jostling among mango and avocado vendors, he sells cups of diced fruit.

After he turns ten, he rides buses alone to an outdoor food market. He stuffs tiny bags with nutmeg, curry powder, and paprika, then seals them with hot wax. He pauses at big black gates in front of the market and calls out, "*¿Va a querer especias?* Who wants spices?" He has no vendor's license, so he keeps moving, darting between wooden carts piled with papayas. Younger children, five and six years old, dot the curbs, thrusting fistfuls of tomatoes and chiles at shoppers. Others offer to carry purchases of fruits and vegetables from stall to stall in rustic wooden wheelbarrows in exchange for tips. "*¿Te ayudo?* May I help you?" they ask. Arms taut, backs stooped, the boys heave forward, their carts bulging.

In between sales some of the young market workers sniff glue.

Grandmother María cooks plantains, spaghetti, and fresh eggs. Now and then she kills a chicken and prepares it for him. In return, when she is sick, Enrique rubs medicine on her back. He brings water to her in bed. Two or three times a week, Enrique lugs buckets filled with drinking water, one on each shoulder, from the water truck at the bottom of the hill up to his grandmother's house.

Every year on Mother's Day, he makes a heart-shaped card at school and presses it into her hand. "I love you very much, Grandma," he writes.

But she is not his mother. Enrique longs to hear Lourdes's voice. Once he tries to call her collect from a public telephone in his neighborhood. He can't get the call to go through. His only way of talking to her is at the home of his mother's cousin María Edelmira Sánchez Mejía, one of the few family members who has a telephone. His mother seldom calls. One year she does not call at all.

"I thought you had died, girl!" María Edelmira says, when she finally does call.

Better to send money, Lourdes replies, than burn it up on the phone. But there is another reason she hasn't called: her life in the United States is nothing like the television images she saw in Honduras.

Lourdes shares an apartment bedroom with three other women. She sleeps on the floor. A boyfriend from Honduras, Santos, joins her in Long Beach. Lourdes is hopeful. She's noticed that her good friend Alma saves much faster now that she has moved in with a Mexican boyfriend. The boyfriend pays for Alma's rent and bills. Alma can shop for her two girls in Honduras at nice stores such as JCPenney and Sears. She's saving to build a house in Honduras.

Santos, who once worked with Lourdes's stepfather as a bricklayer, is such a speedy worker that in Honduras his nickname was El Veloz. With Santos here, Lourdes tells herself, she will save enough to bring her children within two years. If not, she will take her savings and return to Honduras to build a little house and corner grocery store.

Lourdes unintentionally gets pregnant. She struggles through the difficult pregnancy working in a refrigerated fish factory, packing and weighing salmon and catfish all day. Her water breaks at five one summer morning. Lourdes's boyfriend, who likes to get drunk, goes to a bar to celebrate. He asks a female bar buddy to take Lourdes to the public hospital. Lourdes's temperature shoots up to 105 degrees. She becomes delirious. The bar buddy wipes sweat dripping from Lourdes's brow. "Bring my mother. Bring my mother," Lourdes moans.

Lourdes has trouble breathing. A nurse slips an oxygen mask over her face. She gives birth to a girl, Diana.

After two days Lourdes must leave the hospital. She is still sick and weak. The hospital will hold her baby one more day. Santos has never shown up at the hospital. He isn't answering their home telephone. His drinking buddy has taken Lourdes's clothes back to her apartment. Lourdes leaves the hospital wearing a blue paper disposable robe. She doesn't even have a pair of underwear. She sits in her apartment kitchen and sobs, longing for her mother, her sister, anyone familiar.

Santos returns the next morning, after a three-day drinking binge. "¿Ya vino? Has it arrived?" He passes out before Lourdes can answer. Lourdes goes, alone, to get Diana from the hospital.

Santos loses his job making airplane parts. Lourdes falls on a pallet and hurts her shoulder. She complains to her employer about the pain. Two months after Diana's birth, she is fired. She gets a job at a pizzeria and bar. Santos doesn't want her to work there. One night Santos is drunk and jealous that Lourdes has given a male coworker a ride home. He punches Lourdes in the chest, knocking her to the ground. The next morning there is coagulated blood under the skin on her breast. "I won't put up with this," Lourdes tells herself.

When Diana is one year old, Santos decides to visit Honduras. He promises to choose wise investments there and multiply the several thousand dollars the couple has scrimped to save. Instead, Santos spends the money on a long drinking binge with a fifteen-year-old girl on his arm. He doesn't call Lourdes again.

By the time Santos is gone for two months, Lourdes can no longer make car and apartment payments. She rents a garage—really a converted single carport. The owners have thrown up some walls, put in a door, and installed a toilet. There is no kitchen. It costs three hundred dollars a month.

Lourdes and Diana, now two years old, share a mattress on the concrete floor. The roof leaks, the garage floods, and slugs inch up the mattress and into bed. She can't buy milk or diapers or take her daughter to the doctor when she gets sick. Sometimes they live on emergency welfare.

Unemployed, unable to send money to her children in Honduras, Lourdes takes the one job available: work as a *fichera* at the Long Beach bar called El

Mar Azul Bar #1. It has two pool tables, a long bar with vinyl stools, and a red-and-blue neon facade. Lourdes's job is to sit at the bar, chat with patrons, and encourage them to keep buying grossly overpriced drinks for her. Her first day is filled with shame. She imagines that her brothers are sitting at the bar, judging her. What if someone she knows walks into the bar, recognizes her, and word somehow gets back to Lourdes's mother in Honduras? Lourdes sits in the darkest corner of the bar and begins to cry. "What am I doing here?" she asks herself. "Is this going to be my life?" For nine months she spends night after night patiently listening to drunken men talk about their problems, how they miss their wives and children left behind in Mexico.

A friend helps Lourdes get work cleaning oil refinery offices and houses by day and ringing up gasoline and cigarette sales at a gas station at night. Lourdes drops her daughter off at school at 7:00 a.m., cleans all day, picks Diana up at 5:00 p.m., drops her at a babysitter, then goes back to work until 2:00 a.m. She fetches Diana and collapses into bed. She has four hours to sleep.

Some of the people whose houses she cleans are kind. One woman in Redondo Beach always cooks Lourdes lunch and leaves it on the stove for her. Another woman offers, "Anything you want to eat, there is the fridge." Lourdes tells both, "God bless you."

Others seem to revel in her humiliation. One woman in posh Palos Verdes demands that she scrub her living room and kitchen floors on her knees instead of with a mop. It exacerbates her arthritis. She walks like an old lady some days. The cleaning liquids cause her skin to slough off her knees, which sometimes bleed. The woman never offers Lourdes a glass of water.

There are good months, though, when she can earn $1,000 to $1,200 cleaning offices and homes. She takes extra jobs, one at a candy factory for $2.25 an hour. Besides the cash for Enrique, every month she sends $50 each to her mother and Belky.

Those are her happiest moments, when she can wire money. Her greatest dread is when there is no work and she can't. That and random gang shootings. "La muerte nunca te avisa cuando viene," Lourdes says. "Death never announces when it is going to come." A small park near her apartment is a gang hangout. When Lourdes returns home in the middle of the night, gangsters come up and ask for money. She always hands over three dollars, sometimes five. What would happen to her children if she died?

The money Lourdes sends is no substitute for her presence. Belky, now nine, is furious about the new baby. Their mother might lose interest in her and Enrique, and the baby will make it harder to wire money and save so she can bring them north. "How can she have more children now?" Belky asks.

For Enrique each telephone call grows more strained. Because he lives across town, he is not often lucky enough to be at María Edelmira's house when his mother phones. When he is, their talk is clipped and anxious. Quietly, however, one of these conversations plants the seed of an idea. Unwittingly, Lourdes sows it herself.

"When are you coming home?" Enrique asks. She avoids an answer. Instead, she promises to send for him very soon.

It had never occurred to him: If she will not come home, then maybe he can go to her. Neither he nor his mother realizes it, but this kernel of an idea will take root. From now on, whenever Enrique speaks to her, he ends by saying, "I want to be with you."

"Come home," Lourdes's own mother begs her on the telephone. "It may only be beans, but you always have food here." Pride forbids it. How can she justify leaving her children if she returns empty-handed? Four blocks from her mother's place is a white house with purple trim. It takes up half a block behind black iron gates. The house belongs to a woman whose children went to Washington DC, and sent her the money to build it. Lourdes cannot afford such a house for her mother, much less herself.

But she develops a plan. She will become a resident and bring her children to the United States legally. Three times she hires storefront immigration counselors who promise help. She pays them a total of $3,850. But the counselors never deliver.

One is a supposed attorney near downtown Los Angeles. Another is a blind man who says he once worked at the INS. Lourdes's friends say he's helped them get work papers. A woman in Long Beach, whose house she cleans, agrees to sponsor her residency. The blind man dies of diabetes. Soon afterward Lourdes gets a letter from the INS. Petition denied.

She must try again. A chance to get her papers comes from someone Lourdes trusts. Dominga is an older woman with whom Lourdes shares an apartment. Dominga has become Lourdes's surrogate mother. She loans Lourdes money when she runs short. She gives her advice on how to save so she can bring her children north. When Lourdes comes home late, she leaves her tamales or soup on the table, under the black velvet picture of the Last Supper.

Dominga is at the Los Angeles INS office. She's there to try to help a son arrested in an immigration raid. A woman walks up to her in the hallway. My name, she tells Dominga, is Gloria Patel. I am a lawyer. I have friends inside the INS who can help your son become legal. In fact, I work for someone inside the INS. She hands Dominga her business card. IMMIGRATION CONSULTANT. LEGAL PROFESSIONAL SERVICES. It has a drawing of the Statue of Liberty. Residency costs three thousand dollars per person up front, five thousand dollars total. Find five or six interested immigrants, the woman tells Dominga, and I'll throw in your son's residency papers for free.

"I found a woman, a great attorney!" Dominga tells Lourdes. "She can make us legal in one month." At most three months. Dominga convinces other immigrants in her apartment complex to sign up. Initially, the recruits are skeptical. Some accompany Dominga to Patel's office. It is a suite in a nice building that also houses the Guatemalan consulate. The waiting room is full. Two men loudly discuss how Patel has been successful in legalizing their family members. Patel shows Dominga papers—proof, she says, that her son's legalization process is already under way.

They leave the office grateful that Patel has agreed to slash her fee to thirty-five hundred dollars and require only one thousand dollars per person as a first installment. Lourdes gives Patel what she has: eight hundred dollars.

Soon Patel demands final payments from everyone to keep going. Lourdes balks. Should she be sending this money to her children in Honduras instead? She talks to Patel on the phone. She claims to be Salvadoran but sounds Colombian.

Patel is a smooth talker. "How are you going to lose out on this amazing opportunity? Almost no one has this opportunity! And for this incredible price."

"It's that there are a lot of thieves here. And I don't earn much."

"Who said I'm going to rob you?"

Lourdes prays. *God, all these years, I have asked you for only one thing: to be with my children again.* She hands over another seven hundred dollars. Others pay the entire thirty-five hundred dollars.

Patel promises to send everyone's legalization papers in the mail. A week after mailing in the last payments, several migrants go back to her office to see how things are going. The office is shuttered. Gloria Patel is gone. Others in the building say she had rented space for one month. The papers the migrants were shown were filled-out applications, nothing more.

Lourdes berates herself for not having dated an American who asked her out long ago. She could have married him, maybe had her children here by now . . .

Lourdes wants to give her son and daughter some hope. "I'll be back next Christmas," she tells Enrique.

Enrique fantasizes about Lourdes's expected homecoming in December. In his mind she arrives at the door with a box of Nike shoes for him. "Stay," he pleads. "Live with me. Work here. When I'm older, I can help you work and make money."

Christmas arrives, and he waits by the door. She does not come. Every year she promises. Each year he is disappointed. Confusion finally grows into anger. "I need her. I miss her," he tells his sister. "I want to be with my mother. I see so many children with mothers. I want that."

One day he asks his grandmother, "How did my mom get to the United States?" Years later Enrique will remember his grandmother's reply—and how another seed was planted: "Maybe," María says, "she went on the trains."

"What are the trains like?"

"They are very, very dangerous," his grandmother says. "Many people die on the trains."

When Enrique is twelve, Lourdes tells him yet again that she will come home.

"*Sí,*" he replies. "*Va, pues.* Sure. Sure."

Enrique senses a truth: Very few mothers ever return. He tells her that he doesn't think she is coming back. To himself he says, "It's all one big lie."

The calls grow tense. "Come home," he demands. "Why do you want to be there?"

"It's all gone to help raise you."

Lourdes has nightmares about going back, even to visit, without residency documents. In the dreams she hugs her children, then realizes she has to return to the United States so they can eat well and study. The plates on the table are empty. But she has no money for a smuggler. She tries to go back on her own. The path becomes a labyrinth. She runs through zigzagging corridors. She always ends up back at the starting point. Each time she awakens in a sweat.

Another nightmare replays an incident when Belky was two years old. Lourdes has potty-trained her daughter. But Belky keeps pooping in her pants. "*Puerca!* You pig!" Lourdes scolds her daughter. Once Lourdes snaps. She kicks Belky in the bottom. The toddler falls and hits her face on the corner of a door. Her lip splits open. Lourdes can't reach out and console her daughter. Each time she awakens with Belky's screams ringing in her ears.

All along Enrique's mother has written very little; she is barely literate and embarrassed by it. Now her letters stop.

Every time Enrique sees Belky, he asks: "When is our mom coming? When will she send for us?"

Lourdes does consider hiring a smuggler to bring the children but fears the danger. The coyotes, as they are called, are often alcoholics or drug addicts. Usually, a chain of smugglers is used to make the trip. Children are passed from one stranger to another. Sometimes the smugglers abandon their charges.

Lourdes is continually reminded of the risks. One of her best friends in Long Beach pays for a smuggler to bring her sister from El Salvador. During her journey the sister calls Long Beach to give regular updates on her progress through Mexico. The calls abruptly stop.

Two months later the family hears from a man who was among the group headed north. The smugglers put twenty-four migrants into an overloaded boat in Mexico, he says. It tipped over. All but four drowned. Some bodies were swept out to sea. Others were buried along the beach, including the missing sister. He leads the family to a Mexican beach. There they unearth the sister's decomposed body. She is still wearing her high school graduation ring.

Another friend is panic-stricken when her three-year-old son is caught by Border Patrol agents as a smuggler tries to cross him into the United States. For a week Lourdes's friend doesn't know what's become of her toddler.

Lourdes learns that many smugglers ditch children at the first sight of trouble. Government-run foster homes in Mexico get migrant children whom authorities find abandoned in airports and bus stations and on the streets. Children as young as three, bewildered, desperate, populate these foster homes.

Víctor Flores, four years old, maybe five, was abandoned on a bus by a female smuggler. He carries no identification, no telephone number. He ends up at Casa Pamar, a foster home in Tapachula, Mexico, just north of the Guatemalan border. It broadcasts their pictures on Central American television so family members might rescue them.

The boy gives his name to Sara Isela Hernández Herrera, a coordinator at the home, but says he does not know how old he is or where he is from. He says his mother has gone to the United States. He holds Hernández's hand with all his might and will not leave her side. He asks for hugs. Within hours he begins calling her "Mama."

When she leaves work every afternoon, he pleads in a tiny voice for her to stay—or at least to take him with her. She gives him a jar of strawberry marmalade and strokes his hair. "I have a family," he says, sadly. "They are far away."

Francisco Gaspar, twelve, from Concepción Huixtla in Guatemala, is terrified. He sits in a hallway at a Mexican immigration holding tank in Tapachula. With a corner of his Charlie Brown T-shirt, he dabs at tears running down his chin. He is waiting to be deported. His smuggler left him behind at Tepic, in the western coastal state of Nayarit. "He didn't see that I hadn't gotten on the train," Francisco says between sobs. His short legs had kept him from scrambling aboard. Immigration agents caught him and bused him to Tapachula.

Francisco left Guatemala after his parents died. He pulls a tiny scrap of paper from a pants pocket with the telephone number of his uncle Marcos in Florida. "I was going to the United States to harvest chiles," he says. "Please help me! Please help me!"

Clutching a handmade cross of plastic beads on a string around his neck, he leaves his chair and moves frantically from one stranger to another in the hallway. His tiny chest heaves. His face contorts in agony. He is crying so hard that he struggles for breath. He asks each of the other immigrants to help him get back to his smuggler in Tepic. He touches their hands. "Please take me back to Tepic! Please! Please!"

For Lourdes the disappearance of her ex-boyfriend, Santos, hits closest to home. When Diana is four years old, her father returns to Long Beach. Soon afterward Santos is snared in an INS raid of day laborers waiting for work on a street corner and deported. Lourdes hears he has again left Honduras headed for the United States. He never arrives. Not even his mother in Honduras knows what has happened to him. Eventually, Lourdes concludes that he has died in Mexico or drowned in the Rio Grande.

"Do I want to have them with me so badly," she asks herself of her children, "that I'm willing to risk losing their lives?" Besides, she does not want Enrique to come to California. There are too many gangs, drugs, and crimes.

In any event she has not saved enough. The cheapest coyote, immigrant advocates say, charges three thousand dollars per child. Female coyotes want up to six thousand dollars. A top smuggler will bring a child by commercial flight for ten thousand dollars. She must save enough to bring both children at once. If not, the one left in Honduras will think she loves him or her less.

Enrique despairs. He will simply have to do it himself. He will go find her. He will ride the trains. "I want to come," he tells her.

Don't even joke about it, she says. It is too dangerous. Be patient.

Selection 16

Journalist and author RUBÉN MARTÍNEZ (b. 1962) was born in Los Angeles, a city featured in his writings in which he explores the topics of globalization, immigration, and Central American and Mexican politics and culture. During the first phase of his journalistic career in Los Angeles, Martínez won an Emmy Award for hosting KCET's *Life & Times* news show and later a Lannan Foundation fellowship, among his many awards. His published books include *The Other Side: Notes from the New L.A., Mexico City, and Beyond* (1993); *East Side Stories* (with Joseph Rodriguez, 1998); *Crossing Over: A Mexican Family over the Migrant Trail* (2001), in which he follows the trials and tribulations of several migrant Mexican families on their way to and across the United States; *Flesh Life: Sex in Mexico* (with Joseph Rodriguez, 2006); and *Desert America: Boom and Bust in the New Old West* (2012), dealing with neglected communities, extreme poverty, and ecological disasters in the southwestern United States. He is currently Loyola Marymount's Fletcher Jones Chair of Literature and Writing.

In "My Father's House" Martínez interrogates what "place" means to a native Angeleno who confronts gentrification in the Silver Lake neighborhood where he grew up. Silver Lake, once a multiethnic immigrant working-class enclave enlivened by bohemian expatriate artists, intellectuals, and gay and lesbian neighbors, is now a haven for hipsters: "Ultimately, of course, the arrival of the hipsters (and their elders, the ones with the real money) drove out the immigrant working class altogether, leaving only a faint aura in old signage preserved by the newcomers for authenticity's sake." But in contrast to "Beach Blanket Baja," which takes us back to East LA's recent incarnation as a working-class barrio hemmed in by a Fordist society's segregating barriers, Martínez speaks for a subsequent generation of LA Latina/os as they again struggle to hold onto a patrimony. The rats that invade his father's house, a metonym of urban indigenous genealogy, do not represent the non-city wilderness of LA's twentieth-century writers but the gnawing presence of environmental chaos spawned by neoliberal capitalism's incessantly destructive search for profit.

My Father's House

RUBÉN MARTÍNEZ

I returned to my hometown of Los Angeles after the better part of a decade away, lured by a job, by thoughts of impending fatherhood. My wife, Angela, pregnant with twins, and I start to look for a house just as the real estate bubble reached its mad height, tearing a grand canyon through the social fabric and opening up the greatest disparity in wealth since the robber barons. Even with the offer of a massive no-interest loan from my Jesuit benefactors to help with financing, we couldn't find a place to live. We were always outbid. On 1,000-square-foot houses going for $850K even though they were within sight and scent and earshot of the Golden State Freeway. (The consolation being all the latest upgrades: the drought-resistant, native plants–only gardens, the stainless steel appliances, the his-and-hers bathroom sinks.)

We were lucky to have my family's patrimony, a house in the Silver Lake district of LA, a bohemian enclave that had for decades brought together a multiethnic and socioeconomically mixed crew that included artists and activists, a strong gay and lesbian contingent, spiritual visionaries, and hucksters. But the bubble set about dismantling the scene, which was in full display back in the early 1980s at the annual Sunset Junction Street Fair, where cholos and leather daddies and aging hippies partied together, turning it into a playground for young money with aspirations for a life in relative proximity to taco trucks and 99-cent stores. Ultimately, of course, the arrival of the hipsters (and their elders, the ones with the real money) drove out the immigrant working class altogether, leaving only a faint aura in old signage preserved by the newcomers for authenticity's sake.

My grandparents bought their house, a curious blend of Deco, Mediterranean, and western rustic features nearly sixty years ago with money they'd saved from years playing Mexican folk standards for *paisanos* hungry for home and gringos thirsty for tequila. With that same stake, they started up a small Mexican restaurant just a couple of blocks away that they baptized La Ronda, which means a "round," as in "to make the rounds," a versatile Spanish bohemianism tinged with melancholy, referring to late-night pilgrimages soaked in alcohol and tears, with a torch song soundtrack sung by mariachi icons like José Alfredo Jiménez. Years of grinding labor at La Ronda (Grandfather cooked, Grandmother took the orders, Pop washed the dishes) secured a truly American middle-class existence, although my grandparents spoke only halting English and didn't know who Elvis Presley was when he stopped by to order the enchilada lunch special.

Despite its success, my family gave up the business in the winter of 1966, during which my father and grandfather had a violent drunken argument. Pop has often recounted how he, who'd mostly played the model respectful Mexican son, told the old man to fuck off after he humiliated my grandmother at a holiday gathering. Just the kind of tragic kind of turn a *ronda* often takes, which ultimately led to Grandfather's massive coronary and lifelong guilt for my father.

After my family sold the restaurant, the place became Le Bar, a classic old-school Mexican transvestite club. Big hair and busts and booties and quivering lips syncing to Madonna and Cher. I had my share of *rondas* there, a strange mix of desire and familial nostalgia. Le Bar remained long enough for me to think it would always be there for queer or curious Latin men and queer or curious white Latinophiles to cheer the big revue shows on weekend nights. It was never "discovered" by middle-class bohos looking for the next proletarian cool, although in retrospect I suppose I myself might have been a harbinger of the gentrification to come.

In the early 2000s a wine shop opened next door (around the time Alexander Payne sold a lot of cabernet along with the pathos in *Sideways*), then an haute Vietnamese place, and then a boutique specializing in panties, just panties. Soon enough Le Bar was figuratively bulldozed and became the Cha Cha lounge, a place of sudden "buzz" and celebrity appearances (including

Jake Gyllenhaal, when *Brokeback Mountain* was still in theaters). During the Mexican years there had been little overt ethnic decor; the brown bodies sufficed. But the Cha Cha's gringo owners turned it into a Disneyfied *Tres Caballeros* effusion. Now Mexican puppets dangled from the ceiling. On the walls hung velvet paintings of 1970s vintage, spangled sombreros, Day of the Dead skulls. Bartenders mixed drinks under an approximation of a beach *cabaña*, palm fronds and all. A Jimmy Buffet *ronda*.

Shortly after we moved into my grandparents' old Silver Lake house, I took Angela to show her the ghosts. I played history detective, snooping for some evidence that my grandparents and the transvestites had once been here, cooked food, danced, flirted, even fucked. Between the back of the toilet and the wall, in a corner of the ceiling, trapped beneath several layers of paint: a trace of DNA. It was early enough that Angela and I were the only customers; the "scene" happened late in the evening when bouncers picked out the lucky scene-sters for admission. Bizarrely juxtaposed to the Mexican memorabilia was a big Willie Nelson poster on the wall near the front door. A vintage turntable spun Neil Young's voice: "Mother Nature on the run in the 1970s."

The bartender-deejay lifted the tone arm from the album and tossed Neil's terribly scratched voice into the void. In the sudden silence I noticed the table upon which my hands were folded. Beneath several coats of lacquer, there was a life-sized, airbrushed face, hair curled into large, frosted waves, batwing eyebrows, thick eyeliner, mascara, blush, the lips lustrous and puckered. Below her the name *Paquita* in flowing cursive. I remembered her. She was part of the Le Bar revue. You know, "back in the day." I was stunned by this. I got up and looked at the other tables. They each had a Mexican transvestite immortalized like a prehistoric bug in amber.

From our perch in the house above the hipster scene of the Cha Cha, Angela and I obsessed on MLS listings for months. Recognizing our desperation, my father offered to sell it to us. Predictably, this would eventually set off a family *ronda*.

I was about to buy my father's house. What was the line from Scripture? *In my father's house there are many mansions.*

Which, if you believe in a benevolent God, is a comforting thought about His boundless love for all His children, especially those seeking a home for their lost souls. And which, in the context of father-son relationships steeped in the narrative of real estate during the boom-and-bust cycle of the first decade of the twenty-first century, is tailor-made for (Mexican) American melodrama.

On cue the mansions of my father's house, which had been his father's before him, were filling with rats. Literally.

It began when we unwittingly presented the rodents with a generous supply of a very nutritious food source: dog kibble. Not just any kibble; at the new dog boutique down the street, we bought haute canine cuisine, the kind soaked in salmon oil for that extra kick of Omega-3s. We had two dogs: Bear, the noble, aging Akita, and Lenny, the young, rambunctious Lab. They were both big and ate a lot. We placed their bowls just outside the back door, and the boys often left a few nuggets after feeding.

We started to see rat droppings in the mornings, like pudgy grains of wild rice, next to the suspiciously empty bowls. So now we made sure to clean up after doggy dinner. But it was too late. The rats knew there was food and it was just a matter of getting to it. Now they traipsed through an old cat door into the kitchen, where we stored the huge forty-eight-pound bags. The rats easily gnawed into the bags and took their fill.

Then we placed the kibble in a plastic tub with a lid. The rats gnawed through the plastic. So I boarded up the old cat door.

But there were so many other ways to get into the old house! There were gaps under the red tile on the roof, around pipes and drains where old caulking had crumbled. There was a trapdoor at the bottom of the fireplace that could easily be nudged open and of course the chimney where the rats could come down like little gray Santas. There were exhaust flues for the bathroom fan, for the clothes dryer and the dishwasher. The ducting for the heating and air conditioning units routed to every room.

Houses got old, and they filled with holes—just like people. You could see the age of the house most clearly in the garage, which sat beneath the living room; it was the house's architectural triumph, with a dramatic arched ceiling and a Batchelder fireplace mantel with a German forest motif, above which hovered my grandmother's huge yellowing print of the Virgen de Guadalupe. The ceiling of the garage was of rough unpainted plaster, perforated in a couple of dozen places by ducting and piping and the hammers of generations of Mexican plumbers making their way to a leaking kitchen drain or toilet or shower. There was even a hole in the plaster next to the thick black steel pipe main drain, which sank into the concrete floor of the garage on its way to the sewer in the street, producing the most nightmarish image of all: a wave of rats surging up from the very bowels of the city, the underworld, from the subsoil that the foundations of our American houses and the rites of real estate rise from.

The situation was more and more like Polanski's *Rosemary's Baby*. Young couple, expecting their first kid (in our case, twins), move into the old house, into the middle class, and into all the Faustian bargains that you buy into along the way. This was the American and my father's dream flipped upside down. The house not as sanctuary but as source of violence—the American violence of property infecting you, bleeding you, owning you.

My father himself had sown a hint of the truth long ago. Pop the lithographer, bent over the light table for years at the print shop on Highland Avenue in Hollywood. (Crucially, this was a steady union gig with a salary that inflated the harder he worked—time and a half after eight hours, double time after twelve hours and on weekends—and he worked his ass off. This is what kept us in Silver Lake as the neighborhood gradually shifted from middle-to-lower to middle- to-upper.) His job was stripping negatives and performing the color separation (the physical tasks of print production in the pre-digital days) for thousands of movie posters, including, in 1979, *The Amityville Horror*, which he brought home and hung on a wall in the TV room. The ad featured the facade of a shingled New England house, a fiery light issuing through two attic windows separated by a brick chimney—the face of hell. In bold text at the center of the poster: FOR GOD'S SAKE, GET OUT!

How many holes did it take to fill my family's house?

We brought the babies home from Cedars-Sinai, hospital to the stars. (An entire wing of the maternity ward was cordoned off during our stay for Tori Spelling and her team of doulas.) We were sleepless in Silver Lake and still at war with the rats. We bought a big aluminum garbage can to protect the dog food, which worked very well, for a few days. But the rats had now discovered many other food sources. Like the avocados in the fruit baskets on the kitchen counter. This caused a major freak-out because the twins' baby bottles were just a few inches away from the violated fruit. We imagine the rats standing on hind legs, sniffing, licking, gnawing. Now at night we draped a towel over the bottles.

From the kitchen they ventured into the living room. Droppings appeared along the baseboards behind the curtains. Strange little piles of insulation and ducting materials started showing up in the corners. One morning I found rat shit in one of the high chairs. Now it was war. I made the trip to Home Depot, where I spent a lot of money on all kinds of traps—the politically correct, the medieval. None of them worked.

I made daily patrols in the garage. Through the holes had fallen a rain of droppings. And the hole by the main drain got bigger every day. I set a trap there, but they stepped around it. One time I came upon a dead baby rat. It was a hairless, vulnerable thing, and still I had a tremendous urge to stomp on it with my Timberlands. They were multiplying down there, the metropole sending wave after wave of colonists upstairs.

They got ever more brazen, the fuckers. One night Angela and my mother-in-law, Wilma, were watching TV from the couch in the living room, and a big one skittered along the hardwood floor by their feet. Then came the night of the mano a mano, the moment of truth. A friend happened to be visiting, Roberto, a Central American activist and writer, an eternally angry young man who could also be disarmingly sweet. We got into one of our typical arguments—

Rubén, the fuzzy, warm social democrat, versus Roberto, whose idea of fun was the dictatorship of the proletariat. In the midst of making one of his finger-jabbing points, Roberto yelled out, "A rat!" We leapt up from the Danish modern table I had bought at the antique store in Houston. Angela and her mother made a quick exit, leaving the men to battle with the beast. Roberto reconned the room with a broom in his hand, while I . . . I stood on a chair and queasily swept curtains open.

Deprived of all safe havens, the rat wound up underneath the TV couch. Roberto stood to one side as I lifted one end of it up. With a mighty arcing swing, Roberto brought the broom down for a direct hit. And again. And again . . . perhaps a dozen times. I imagined the LAPD on Rodney King.

We looked down.

It was not the big cat-size monster I'd been seeing—or imagining. Maybe it wasn't even a rat; maybe it was just a mouse. A scrawny little thing, eyes scrunched tight against the blows that killed it.

But it was not over. There were many more scrawny gray things roaming the house. Then came the night they took the house away from us. We were in bed and heard a scurrying along the carpet—rat claws on Berber make a very particular kind of sound. They were in the twins' room, underneath the cribs. We brought the girls into our bed, and now the rats came after us into our room. I heard one skitter along the windowsill next to the bed. Then I thought I heard one under the bed. I grabbed my big blue MAGLITE flashlight, ready to clobber, but when the rat suddenly appeared inches from my face on the bedsheet, I jumped off the bed and squealed just like you're supposed to.

Chaos. The babies were screaming, Angela was screaming, Rubén was screaming. Eventually, we isolated it in the closet and got a few minutes of sleep before sunrise, when I finally confronted the rat. Being a Silver Lake lefty, I couldn't bludgeon the thing to death. After about an hour I gently coaxed it out a French door. We called the exterminators the next day. We gave them lots of money. They said the only way to control the rats was to cover up the holes, and that is what they set about doing.

After that the rats were trapped in the bowels of the house and became very hungry, since we were meticulous about not leaving food out for them. They were so desperate they went for the peanut butter on the traps. In the quiet of the night, we would hear the loud snap, the death throes.

My father decided it would be a mistake to sell to us, after all. (Capital gains taxes. My father is a Democrat, but he hates taxes like a Republican.)

We lived in my father's house for several more months, the stench of decomposing rats wafting up occasionally from the floorboards.

During the two years that we lived at the Silver Lake house, my parents visited every few months, making the trip from their Sedona, Arizona, retirement Shangri-La (which they would flee when nativist cowboys like "America's Toughest Sheriff" Joe Arpaio started gunning for wetbacks). Within minutes of their arrival, my father would get to work. Loose doorknob on the front door. Leaky faucet in the bathroom. Drying and cracking grout in the kitchen. If there were no more crises inside the house, he'd go out to the backyard and pull weeds until he sweated through his shirt. More than once, gringos in the neighborhood asked if he was available to clean their yards, assuming he was a *mojado* gardener.

The house is falling apart, Rube, he'd say.

Which to me sounded like, *You're letting the house fall apart, you good-for-nothing bohemian!*

And so father and son shouted, echoing my father and his father in this very house a generation ago. The argument had not changed since I was a young man and my father was the age that I am today. My father held that the house, the actual physical structure of it, was at the very center of the family's existence. Caring for the house was caring for the family.

The son countered that the building was less important than the quality of the relationships that filled it. Better that a doorknob fell off than a failure of intimacy. These are, of course, caricatures of the more nuanced positions my father and I actually occupied. And, of course, there was a basic truth in each.

In my father's house there was often both love and order, upward mobility coinciding with a fulfilling family life and a constellation of relationships that connected us to families in houses nearby. I often asked my parents what those years of my childhood were like for them, the adults; the tumult of civil rights and hippies and assassinations and senseless murder and carpet bombing in Vietnam. They always answered that they didn't really sense that anything extraordinary was happening because they were so focused on the babies that needed a diaper or a visit to the doctor, the room that needed a new coat of paint—life so very full of its minutiae. It is a favorite word of my father's. He pronounces it *minu-tay*.

There was a golden moment in the early 1970s, when my parents were in their mid-thirties and I, their eldest, was just starting middle school. We lived in an old house on St. George Street in Silver Lake (later to be known as Franklin Hills), which intersected a mile away with Waverly Drive, a street name that baby boomers always immediately recognize as linked to the Manson murders of 1969 and Joan Didion's famous appraisal of the area as a "serial killer kind of neighborhood" in *The White Album*.

My parents—so focused on the minu-tay!—were not particularly perturbed by the bloodbath at the LaBianca house, certainly did not consider moving, would have disagreed with Didion's verdict. If there had been any consideration of the matter at all, it probably would have been related to real estate values in the neighborhood.

The house on St. George, even older than my grandparents' place. Oleander leaves gently scraped the window screens in the breeze that always arrived a couple of hours before the dawn. Here my mother was central to the narrative. She came to the United States as part of a small but conspicuous exodus from El Salvador, a cohort of single women of modest (but not poor) means sent by their families to gain a toehold in the United States. In the 1950s the easiest way to do that was to marry an American—doctor, lawyer, certainly a professional, someone who wore a tie and carried a briefcase to work. The kind the Salvadoran elders had seen in tattered copies of *Good Housekeeping* and throughout Hollywood.

My mother and several of her cohort succeeded in just the way that had been imagined for them, in many ways beyond the greatest expectations back home. When I was in my early teens, she returned to school, making her AA degree at Los Angeles City College, then a BA and eventually an MA in psychology at Antioch University. She held managerial positions at senior centers in East Los Angeles and Culver City, started up a private therapy practice. She left El Salvador with a love of poetry (all Salvadorans are poets, for real), and she attended workshops, put together chapbooks, and published in zines. My mother guided us into the language of Neruda and of humanistic psychology, threw in a dash of New Age in the 1980s. She tried pot once or twice and swears she hallucinated the face of Abraham Lincoln in the clouds. She danced to cha-cha-cha, merengue, *cumbia*, and rock and roll.

Most of my mother's Salvadoran friends opened similar paths. (To this day we talk of immigrants becoming American, denying the agency, the imagination they bring, how much they change us.) They married Americans, most of them white, and with them started "mixed" families. Of course the term didn't exist then.

The cohort stayed close, settling largely in the middle-class enclaves of Northeast LA. Our closest family friend was Argentina Alvarenga, a distant cousin of my mother, who married American-as-can-be Wayne Eisenhower, World War II vet and distant cousin of the president, Republican of course, and with a personalized license plate on his Chrysler that read, simply, IKE. Argentina, "Argie" for short, was the keeper of the social calendar, and the Eisenhowers' house was the hub of the social scene. It was two doors down from my grandparents' place, a midcentury mutt house, rustic here and modern there. There was a bonus room downstairs with a wet bar and a fireplace. The terraced backyard was filled with tropical plants, and at the bottom level was a full-sized swimming pool with a little tiki-style hut for a dressing room.

At Wayne and Argie's the Salvadorans and Americans gathered, without the hyphen. The languages and foods and musics came together. Beyond history raging on the streets on TV. We were "hybrid" long before the social theorists conceived the idea, before the United Colors of Benneton, before Obama.

The Golden Moment was a Thanksgiving at the Eisenhowers', circa 1972. The potluck spread included a big turkey, of course, and also Salvadoran-style tamales and Swedish meatballs and ambrosia and lasagna and a big iceberg lettuce salad dripping with oily dressing, empanadas with pineapple filling, and the soundtrack veered from *cumbia* to rock to easy listening, from Los Hermanos Flores to Creedence Clearwater Revival to Ray Coniff. Ultimately, the scene really was of the women's making, their immigrant energy, their ease with and love of difference. The American men had no choice but to follow the crazy Latinas. The Salvadoran women led their stiff-hipped gringo husbands onto the dance floor.

We crossed practically every social border that would divide the country in the "culture wars" to come. Nationality, language, class, race, gender, even sexual orientation. We lived in Silver Lake, after all, long a gay mecca. (No longer—the largely breeder hipsters are rapidly erasing the history of several queer generations.) My parents owned a duplex a block away from my grandparents' place and rented to a longtime lesbian couple. An openly gay Salvadoran man was the life of the party at the Eisenhowers' parties.

Soon enough it was over. Many of the cohort's couples had divorced, kids had rebelled and self-destructed, alcoholism and tobacco had claimed the lives of many of the elders. Later aids ravaged more than one generation. Still, the Golden Moment lasted the better part of my childhood and included the world beyond my mother's peculiar social space. Silver Lake was a decidedly mixed neighborhood in every sense. Working- and middle-class. When I was growing up, there were still remnants of the "Okies" who flooded Southern California during the Depression and remained poor long after it. Brown and Jewish and several shades of white and Chinese and Japanese (Issei, Nisei, Sansei), gay and straight, the believers and the communists. Yes, there was gay bashing, and the LAPD made sure to rough up the Mexican kids to let them know where the borders were (north of Sunset was mostly white and middle-class, south was more brown and working-class). I got spit on by a white hippie one time walking home from school, was stopped by the cops with my backpack suspiciously full of . . . books. But for the most part I was at home in a world of difference.

In the end even my father's neuroses about "keeping up" or "improving" the structures of our lives contributed profoundly to the Golden Moment. The house on St. George Street had plenty of aesthetic elegance, but it didn't have a den, and that's where the overtime from the print shop salary went one summer, when the house crawled with construction workers (shirtless white men with tans and chest hair, back before the building trades had been assigned to brown laborers with little or no chest hair). Over the years Pop realized that we also needed a patio deck and a basketball hoop and even a swimming pool and a hi-fi stereo with both turntable and 8-track player for an endless summer soundtrack. But the centerpiece of it all was the den, and at the heart of the den was the television and the Beta video deck, to play the movies that Pop had rendered the posters for. The most important "stuff" in the house, in the end, wasn't material at all but a matter of light and color and sound, of words and music and narrative echoing nightly in the den during screenings of everything from B movies to cinema-as-art to the wonderful social realist sitcoms of the 1970s and of course the evening news—the headlines about death squads in El Salvador, Cold War nukes, recession, the Hillside Strangler.

Real estate was rat shit. Pop did overemphasize the material side of life like any good mid-twentieth-century American. And the houses where we lived were fantastic places to grow up. My father might not have articulated the project of the larger, symbolic house—he was too deep inside it to see himself acting within its own set of structures. But it was a safe space from which to apprehend the movement of history, even as we were a part of it.

The problem was where the rat shit was leading the neighborhood, the inevitable impact of speculation, the force with which it would tear Silver Lake apart and erase the memory of the Golden Moment.

Our daughters spent their first two years in the Silver Lake house, becoming the fourth generation of family on my father's side to live in it. (That is an eternity in LA.) It took time, but my father and I reconciled after the very dark *ronda* in the wake of his decision not to sell to us. Eventually Angela and I bought our own house in the neighborhood of Mt. Washington, east of the Los Angeles River (to the horror of my father, who has always underscored the part of his biography where his parents moved west across the river, that is, out of the barrio). It is an old middle-class neighborhood next to the largely immigrant and working-class district of Highland Park. (I live, as has been my wont throughout my adult life, on the border.) The *New York Times* keeps trying to compare Highland Park to Brooklyn and thus fan the flames of gentrification. The house is at the bottom of the "mountain" (which peaks at just under a thousand feet), next to a modest slice of open space—an honest-to-goodness California canyon of black walnut trees and white sage and nopal cactus and coyotes howling in the evenings. It isn't quite Joni's Laurel Canyon, but it's close enough for me.

My parents moved back from Sedona and into the Silver Lake house, and they live there now, my mother hanging on through chemo for cancer of the marrow and my father holding onto the house—which now doubles as hospice—for dear life. During my mother's long hospitalization, he purchased two pieces of decorative tile that he had a Salvadoran handyman named Nelson affix to a wall of the pink stucco exterior (a questionable "improvement" from years ago) that is plainly visible from the street. One piece was colonial tacky, picturing caravels riding the high seas. Above this one was placed the other, which my father had custom made. In Castilian script it reads: CASA DE MARTINEZ. My father. Captain of the ship that is my birthright.

Source Acknowledgments

"With the Amicable People of Ensenada de Palmas" by Ignacio María Nápoli, S.J. Excerpt from *Breve relación de la nueva entrada al sur, en la copiosa gentilidad de la nación de los coras . . . , por el padre* (1721). In *Crónicas jesuíticas de la antigua California*, edited by Ignacio del Río (Mexico City: Universidad Autónoma de México, 2000). Courtesy of Universidad Autónoma de México.

"The Public Outcry. Noteworthy Pamphlet" by Francisco P. Ramírez. *El Clamor Público* 4, no. 38 (Los Angeles: Francisco P. Ramírez, 1855–59), RB 225168, Huntington Library, San Marino CA. Digital access courtesy of the University of Southern California Digital Archive. Translation by Robert Rudder.

"The Repercussions of a Lynching" by Ricardo Flores Magón. First appeared in *Regeneración*, November 12, 1910. Translation courtesy of the author.

"To Womankind, a Manifesto" by Blanca de Moncaleano. First appeared in *Fraternidad*, September 7, 1915.

Excerpt from "The Memoirs of Alfredo Cobos" is previously unpublished. Courtesy of Victor Valle.

Excerpts from the *Journals of Anaïs Nin*, vol. 5: *1947–1955*. Copyright © 1974 by Anaïs Nin. Reprinted by permission of Houghton Mifflin Harcourt Publishing Company. All rights reserved. Excerpts from the *Journals of Anaïs Nin*, vol. 6: *1955–1966*. Copyright © 1966, 1976 by Anaïs Nin. Reprinted by permission of Houghton Mifflin Harcourt Publishing Company. All rights reserved. Excerpts from the *Journal of Anaïs Nin*, vol. 7: *1966–1974*. Copyright © 1980 by Rupert

Notes

1. Bryson, "Los Angeles Literature," 169–72.
2. As quoted in Villa, *Barrio-Logos*, 31.
3. Gamboa, "Phantoms in Urban Exile," 11.
4. Villa, *Barrio-Logos*, 235.
5. Hayden, *Power of Place*, 86.
6. Renee Stepler and Mark Hugo Lopez write that "more than half (53%) of the nation's Hispanics lived in 15 metropolitan areas in 2014. There were 11 metropolitan areas where at least 1 million Hispanics resided." They continue, "Among the top 15 metropolitan areas, nine are located within two states—California (four) and Texas (five)." http://www.pewhispanic.org/2016/09/08/5-ranking-the-latino-population-in-metropolitan-areas/.
7. Sassen, "City," 5.
8. Kanellos, *Hispanic Immigrant Literature*, 21–22.
9. Kanellos, *Hispanic Immigrant Literature*, 22.
10. Benjamin, *Origins of German Tragic Drama*, 44.
11. Brenner, "Introduction," 15.
12. Fraser, *Toward an Urban Cultural Studies*, 14.
13. Fraser, *Toward an Urban Cultural Studies*, 21.
14. Carrigan and Webb, *Forgotten Dead*, 5.
15. Pérez, *Decolonial Imaginary*, 67; Kanellos, "Early Feminist Call to Action," 588.
16. Bosquet, "Lizard People's Catacomb City Hunted."
17. Kanellos, *Hispanic Immigrant Literature*, 37.
18. Kanellos, *Hispanic Immigrant Literature*, 40.
19. Frank O. Sotomayor's article "The Pulitzer Long Shot: How Our 1983 Latino Stories for L.A. Times Won Journalism's Top Prize" (jourviz.com/long-shot/index .html) offers a rare glimpse into how a team of Mexican American journalists overcame an editorial culture's institutional prejudices to win a Pulitzer Prize.
20. Goldberg, "Racism without Racism," 1713–14.
21. Davis, "Hauntology, Spectres and Phantoms," 378–79.

22. Lounsberry, *Art of Fact*, xvi; Steinberg and Root, "Interview with Michael Steinberg," 147.

23. Miller, "How the Media Biopoliticized Neoliberalism," 23.

24. Foucault, *Foucault Effect*, 102.

25. Marx, "Literature and Governmentality," 67.

26. Marx, "Literature and Governmentality," 67.

27. Miller, "How the Media Biopoliticized Neoliberalism," 26.

28. Sarfatti Larson, *Blackwell Companion to the Sociology of Culture*, 322.

29. Walker, *Chronicles of California*, 151.

30. Walker, *Chronicles of California*, 151.

31. Walker, *Chronicles of California*, 152.

32. Walker, *Chronicles of California*, 127.

33. Fine, *Los Angeles in Fiction*, 2.

34. Fine, *Los Angeles in Fiction*, 209–22, 16–17.

35. Mohr, *"Poetry Loves Poetry,"* xiv.

36. Mohr, *"Poetry Loves Poetry,"* i.

37. Mohr, *"Poetry Loves Poetry,"* i.

38. Mohr, *"Poetry Loves Poetry,"* xiv.

39. Babitz, *Los Angeles Stories*, xi.

40. Fine, *Imagining Los Angeles*, 257.

41. Vangelisti, *L.A. Exile*, 8.

42. Interview conducted on March 12, 2015.

43. Vangelisti, *L.A. Exile*, 8.

44. Vangelisti, *L.A. Exile*, 15.

45. Ulin, *Another City*, xiv.

46. Ulin, *Another City*, xv.

47. Ulin, *Another City*, xvi.

48. Ulin, *Writing Los Angeles*, xvi.

49. Ulin, *Writing Los Angeles*, xvi.

50. Leal, "Octavio Paz and the Chicano," 16.

51. Chabram-Dernersesian, "En-countering the Other Discourse," 266.

52. Bartra, *La jaula de la melancolía*, 48.

53. Paz, *Labyrinth of Solitude*, 16.

54. Chabram-Dernersesian, "En-countering the Other Discourse," 272.

55. Rolfe, *Literary LA*, 13, 57.

56. Timberg and Gioia, *Misread City*, xiii.

57. Timberg and Gioia, *Misread City*, xv.

58. Timberg and Gioia, *Misread City*, xiv.

59. Timberg and Gioia, *Misread City*, 6–7.

60. Pelzer, "Cambridge Companion to the Literature of Los Angeles" (review), 331.

61. Bryson, *Cambridge Companion to the Literature of Los Angeles*, 173.

62. Mohr, *Hold-Outs*, 94–95.

63. Mohr, *Hold-Outs*, 119.

64. Mohr, *Hold-Outs*, 41.

65. Laurence Goldstein's *Poetry Los Angeles: Reading The Essential Poems of the City* made critical advances relative to the most recent canonic entries in his 2014 essay "Californios, and the Fertile Blood of Poetry" when he broached borderlands theory in his discussion of Latina/o poets writing about the city and their invention of "hybrid of binational" identities (223). He also demonstrated how Tijuana's spatial metaphors in English-language literature, illustrated by his discussion of Curtis Zahn's eponymous 1992 poem, implicitly marked the depraved criminality Mexicans allegedly brought to the city (202). Yet projecting "Californio" identities on Chicana/o poetry carelessly implicated the poets he selected in a colonizing project many have rejected and suffered as descendants of New Spain's native and mestiza/o majorities (192–93). And characterizing their poetry as simply a literature of *ressentiment* projects a hopeless impotency upon the Latina/o intellectuals whose denunciations of class and racial inequality have helped make social justice in LA a continuing possibility (209).

Published the following year, Suzanne Lummis's 2015 anthology, *Wide Awake: Poets of Los Angeles and Beyond*, and Sophie Rachmuhl's critical history, *A Higher Form of Politics: The Rise of a Poetry Scene, 1950–1990*, implicitly recognize, via their selections of a recent generation of Latina/o poets, the relation between the inventive possibilities of LA's cultural hybridity and globalization. In Lummis this dawning awareness of LA's standing as a global city coincides with a rejection of the canon's city-without-memory motif, which is stereotyped as the place of simulacra where failed actors wind up on Hollywood's "Boulevard of Broken Dreams" (xvii–xvii). Still, these works, and predecessors such as *Stand Up Poetry: An Expanded Anthology* (2002) and *The Sons and Daughters of Los: Culture and Community in L.A.* (2003), revealed a superficial engagement with U.S. Latina/o and Latin American literary criticism. Goldstein illustrated that tendency when he cited only one work of Latino literary criticism, Rafael Perez-Torres's *Movements in Chicano Poetry* (1995), to reflect upon the coloniality of Latina/o poetry and how it diverges from slavery's legacy in African American poetry yet failed to acknowledge the Latina/o, Latin American, and feminist criticism, including Anzaldúa's *Borderlands / La Frontera: The New Mestiza*, that would have bolstered his argument (193). Instead, Goldstein stressed that early contradictory moment in which Anzaldúa essentialized "White dominant society" as the source of all Chicano oppression but did not apply her truly generative theorizations of race, gender, sexuality, and postcolonial hybridity to Aleida Rodríguez's subversive post-national poem "My Mother's Art" (220–23). The lopsided bi-literacy of these works also made their absences felt when they ignored the nineteenth-century Spanish-language poetry published in Los Angeles (*Hispanic Poetry*) and the ease with which these canonic texts injected references to eighteenth- and nineteenth-century English-language literature but not from the vast archive of Hispanic literary criticism.

66. Anzaldúa, "Border Arte," 180.
67. Díaz, *Dismantle*, 2.
68. Mignolo, "Role of the Humanities," 1242.
69. California Faculty Association, *Equity Interrupted*, 7–8.
70. Mignolo, "Epistemic Disobedience," 161.
71. Ulloa, "Nearly $50 Million in the California State Budget" and "California Lawmakers Attempt to Increase Oversight and Restrictions"; Almahrek and Lau, "County Supervisors Create a New Office"; Ulloa, "California Lawmakers Prepare to Take a Stand."
72. Harkinson, "California Mobilizes for War against Trump."

"DECOLONIZING LATINA/O NONFICTION"

1. The Texas Higher Education Coordinating Board lists Raymund A. Paredes as Texas commissioner of higher education (http://www.thecb.state.tx.us/index.cfm?objectid=FBE1507F-C5D0-FC95-369EF7AC883B5F24). The biography linked to from its web page states that "Dr. Paredes spent most of his academic career at UCLA where for 30 years he taught as an English professor and served for ten years as vice chancellor for Academic Development. In addition, he served as special assistant to the president of the University of California System in outreach efforts to improve access to higher education for students from educationally disadvantaged communities."
2. Paredes, "Los Angeles," 240–41.
3. Paredes, "Special Feature," 82; and "Early Mexican-American," 1088.
4. Hernandez, *Postnationalism*, 70.
5. Ernesto Galarza, intellectual architect of the United Farm Workers movement and author of the classic autobiography *Barrio Boy*, questioned the wisdom of building a Chicano studies academic project based on an ethnic construct when he said: "I don't think it leads very far, because if you look at these terms—you'll find people who are called Chicanos in San Jose; they're called Chicanos in Imperial Valley; they're called Chicanos in San Francisco. But if you know those people, the occupational differences are more important, to me, anyway. It may be because I have a certain bias against ethnic identity. I don't think

people should be handled that way . . . should be catalogued . . . because it's not a permanent characteristic other than to those who believe in very strong racial, ethnic characteristics—and I don't" ("Burning Light," n.p.).

6. It has been translated in different ways: *The Shipwrecked Men*; *Castaways: The Narrative of Alvar Núñez Cabeza de Vaca*; *Cabeza de Vaca's Adventures in the Unknown Interior of America*; *The Narrative of Cabeza De Vaca*. Although the book is sometimes known as *La relación of Álvar Núñez Cabeza de Vaca*, it is widely known as *Naufragios*.

7. Morton, *Ecology*, 48; Cohen and Glover, *Colonial*, 9.

8. Lockhart, *Nahuas*, 381–82.

9. Boone, "House," 28; Mignolo, "Afterword," 293–94.

10. Carrasco and Sagarena, "Religious," 231–32.

11. Marcos, "Embodied," 371, 376–77.

12. Mignolo, *Darker*, xiii.

13. Saldívar, *Dialectics*, 4.

14. Kanellos, *Hispanic Immigrant Literature*, 36, 37.

15. Kanellos, *Hispanic Immigrant Literature*, 13.

16. There are important studies on Spanish-language journalism in the United States by Ramón D. Chacón, Juan Gonzales, and Richard Griswold del Castillo, among others; on testimonial writing, such as Rosaura Sánchez's *Telling Identities: The Californio Testimonios* (1995), a discourse analysis of group identity formation in thirty 1870s testimonies from the original Spanish-speaking settlers of Alta California; and on political writing, such as Juan Gómez-Quiñones's *Las ideas políticas de Ricardo Flores Magón* (1977) and Paul Bryan Gray's *A Clamor for Equality: Emergence and Exile of Californio Activist Francisco P. Ramírez* (2012). Yet because these works ignore or de-emphasize the writings they examine as aesthetic forms or performances and over-determine their meaning as informational content, much more work still needs to be done on U.S. Latino nonfiction, particularly when written in Spanish.

17. Kanellos, *Hispanic Immigrant Literature*, xxii, 11.

18. Kanellos, *Hispanic Immigrant Literature*, 18.

19. Murphet, *Literature*, 123.

20. Murphet, *Literature*, 131.

21. Valle and Torres, *Latino Metropolis*, 104–7. Murphet's privileging of poetry continues in his appreciation of the 1989 poetry anthology *Invocation LA*. He recognized the award-winning collection, in which "the streets of African Americans, Chicanos and Asians were finally emblazoned in the city's imaginary" (107). But the implicit assertion of chronological primacy his praise expressed overlooked one of its key predecessors, *201 / Two Hundred and One: Homenaje a la ciudad*

de Los Ángeles / Latino Experience in Literature and Art. The 1982 multi-genre anthology, which collected the works of Chicana/o, Mexican, Chilean, and Colombian writers, included the Latin American–styled nonfiction *testimonio* of Bert Corona that appears in this anthology and a selection that troubled the foundations of Chicano nationalism and the literary criticism that had reified it. The anthology included Marisela Norte's prose poem "Each Street / Each Story," which simultaneously acknowledged the ways the Mexican immigration was transforming the Eastside and deliciously mocked the pathetic male gaze of Whittier Boulevard's bar and dance hall street signage (57). The recognition of an urban, pan-Latino working-class experience in its title, together with works that deployed ironic understatement to stress the city's postcolonial and transnational industrial urbanity, also drew a deliberate contrast to the pastoral tendencies and identity politics of the 1960s era poetry. The slender volume's introduction also explicitly identified the city's nineteenth-century *crónica* as a forerunner of its twentieth-century Latina/o literature and thus the first LA literary anthology to acknowledge such a lineage.

3. "THE REPERCUSSIONS OF A LYNCHING"

1. "Los chicanos participaron en la revolución mexicana a través de la actividad del PLM, mientras al mismo tiempo tomaban parte en el movimiento radical de Estados Unidos" ("La repercusión de un linchamiento," 14).
2. "Las dos razas pobladoras de este hermoso continente" ("La repercusión de un linchamiento," 138).
3. *Translator's note*: The Spanish word "linchamiento" has been translated as "lynching." However, in English this word has two meanings: simply murdering someone or murdering someone by hanging them. Although the second meaning is perhaps more common in English, as seen in the *crónica*, the victim was burned alive.

4. TO WOMANKIND, A MANIFESTO

1. Pérez, *Decolonial Imaginary*, 69.
2. Kanellos, "Early Feminist Call to Action," 587.
3. Kanellos, "Early Feminist Call to Action," 589.
4. Kanellos, "Early Feminist Call to Action," 592.

6. EXCERPTS FROM *THE JOURNALS OF ANAÏS NIN*

1. Rachmuhl, *Higher Form of Politics*, 82, 230.
2. Green and Karolides, *Encyclopedia of Censorship*, 96–97.

7. BERT CORONA'S "STRUGGLE"

1. Villa, *Barrio-Logos*, 110.
2. Pulido, *Black, Brown*, 221.

10. LIGHT AT THE END OF TUNNEL VISION

1. Benavidez, *Gronk*, 38.
2. Rodriguez, "Light at the End of Tunnel Vision," 140.
3. Gamboa, *Urban Exile*, 99.
4. Gerardo Velázquez appears in the photograph *Gerardo Velázquez, synthesized music composer*, 1991 (from the series *Chicano Male Unbonded*). Ray Navarro appears in the photograph *Belted Consent*, 1984. These two Los Angeles–based Chicano artists died of AIDS-related complications.
5. Gamboa, "In the City of Angels," 121–30.
6. Goldman, "Brown in Black and White."
7. María de Los Angeles Padron, "Cafe en blanco y negro, por Gamboa," *La Opinión*, May 20, 1982.
8. Hollander, "Report from Los Angeles," 57–61.
9. Steinberg, "Images Capture Human Drama."
10. Phoenix Art Museum, *Contemporary Identities*, 26–29.

Bibliography

Almahrek, Adam, and Maya Lau. "County Supervisors Create a New Office That Would Help Immigrants Receive Assistance." *Los Angeles Times*, January 10, 2017. http://www.latimes.com/local/lanow/la-me-county-immigration-office-20170110-story.html.

Anzaldúa, Gloria E. "Border Arte: Nepantla, el lugar de la frontera." In *The Gloria Anzaldúa Reader*, edited by AnaLouise Keating. Durham NC: Duke University Press, 2009.

———. "Chicana Artists: Exploring nepantla, el lugar de la frontera." *Nacla: Reporting on the Americas since 1967*. January 10, 2016.

Babitz, Eve. Introduction. In *Los Angeles Stories: Great Writers on the City*, edited by John Miller. San Francisco: Chronicle Books, 1991.

Baca, Jimmy Santiago. *A Place to Stand: The Making of a Poet*. New York: Grove Press, 2001.

Bartra, Roger. *La jaula de la melancolía: Identidad y metamorfosis del Mexicano*. New York: Random House Mondadori, 2013.

Benavidez, Max. *Gronk*. Los Angeles: UCLA Chicano Studies Research Center Press, 2007. Print.

Benjamin, Walter. *The Origins of German Tragic Drama*. Translated by John Osborne. London: Verso, 1998.

Bielsa, Esperança. *The Latin American Urban Crónica: Between Literature and Mass Culture*. Lanham MD: Lexington, 2006.

Boone, Elizabeth Hill. "The House of the Eagle." *Cave, City, Eagle's Nest: An Interpretive Journey through the Mapa de Cuauhtinchan No. 2*. Edited by David Carrasco and Scott Sessions. Albuquerque: University of New Mexico Press, 2007.

Bosquet, Jean. "Lizard People's Catacomb City Hunted: Engineer Sinks Shaft under Fort Moore Hill to Find Maze of Tunnels and Priceless Treasures of Legendary Inhabitants." Pt. 2. *Los Angeles Times*, January 29, 1934.

Brenner, Neil. "Introduction: Urban Theory without an Outside." In *IMPLOSIONS/EXPLOSIONS: Toward a Study of Planetary Urbanization*. Berlin: JOVIS, 2013.

Bryson, J. Scott. "Surf, Sage Brush, and Cement Rivers: Reimagining Nature in Los Angeles." In *The Cambridge Companion to the Literature of Los Angeles*, edited by Kevin R. McNamara, 167–75. New York: Cambridge University Press, 2010.

California Faculty Association. "Equity Interrupted: How California Is Cheating Its Future." CalFac.org, 2017. http://www.calfac.org/equity-interrupted.

Carrasco, David, and Roberto Lint Sagarena. "The Religious Vision of Gloria Anzaldúa: Borderlands / La Frontera as a Shamanic Space." In *Mexican American Religions: Spirituality, Activism, and Culture*, edited by Gaston Espinosa, 223–41. Durham NC: Duke University Press, 2008.

Carrigan, William D., and Clive Webb. *Forgotten Dead: Mob Violence against Mexicans in the United States, 1848–1928*. New York: Oxford University Press, 2013.

Chabram-Dernersesian, Angie. "En-countering the Other Discourse of Chicano-Mexicano Difference." *Cultural Studies* 13, no. 2 (1999): 263–89.

Chacón, Ramón D. "The Chicano Immigrant Press in Los Angeles: The Case of 'El Heraldo de México,' 1916–20." *Journalism History* 4, no. 2 (Summer 1977): 48–50, 62–64.

Clinton, Michelle T., Sesshu Foster, and Naomi Quiñones. *Invocation L.A.: Urban Multicultural Poetry*. Los Angeles: West End Press, 1989.

Cohen, Matt, and Jeffrey Glover. *Colonial Mediascapes*. Lincoln: University of Nebraska Press. 2014.

Colón, Jesús. *A Puerto Rican in New York, and Other Sketches*. New York: Mainstream, 1961.

Corona, Ignacio, and Beth E. Jörgensen. Introduction to *The Contemporary Mexican Chronicle: Theoretical Perspectives on the Liminal Genre*, edited by Ignacio Corona and Beth E. Jörgensen. Albany: State University of New York Press, 2002.

Davis, Colin. "Hauntology, Spectres and Phantoms." *French Studies* 59, no. 3 (July 2005): 373–79.

Davis, Mike. *Magical Urbanism: Latinos Reinvent the U.S. City*. London: Verso, 2001.

Derrida, Jacques. *Positions*. Translated by Alan Bass. Chicago: University of Chicago Press, 1981.

Díaz, Junot. Introduction to *Dismantle: An Anthology of Writing from the VONA/Voices Writing Workshop*, edited by Marissa Johnson-Valenzuela. Philadelphia: Thread Makes Blanket Press, 2014.

Eire, Carlos. *Waiting for Snow in Havana: Confessions of a Cuban Boy*. New York: Free Press, 2003.

Fine, David M. *The City: The Immigrant and American Fiction, 1880–1920*. Metuchen NJ: Scarecrow Press, 1977.

———. *Imagining Los Angeles: A City in Fiction*. Albuquerque: University of New Mexico Press, 2000.

———. *Los Angeles in Fiction: A Collection of Original Essays*. Albuquerque: University of New Mexico Press, 1984.

Fonseca, Diego, and Aileen El-Kadi. *Sam no es mi tío: Veinticuatro crónicas migrantes y un sueño americano*. Doral FL: Santillana USA, 2012.

Foucault, Michel. "Governmentality." In *The Foucault Effect: Studies in Governmentality, with Two Lectures by and an Interview with Michel Foucault*, edited by Graham Burcell, Colin Gordon, and Peter Miller. Chicago: University of Chicago Press, 1991.

Fraser, Benjamin. *Toward an Urban Cultural Studies: Henri Lefebvre and the Humanities*. New York: Palgrave Macmillan, 2015.

Frías, Carlos. *Take Me with You: A Memoir*. New York: Atria Books, 2008.

Galarza, Ernesto. *Barrio Boy*. Notre Dame: University of Notre Dame Press, 1971.

———. "The Burning Light: Action and Organizing in the Mexican Community in California." *Interviews by Gabrielle Morris and Timothy Beard, 1977, 1978 and 1981*. Transcript. Regional Oral History Office, Bancroft Library, University of California, 1982. https://libraries.ucsd.edu/farmworkermovement/essays/essays/Ernesto%20 galarza.pdf.

Gamboa, Harry, Jr. "In the City of Angels, Chameleons, and Phantoms: Asco, a Case Study of Chicano Art in Urban Tones (or Asco Was a Four-Member Word)." *Chicano Art: Resistance and Affirmation*, 121–30. Los Angeles: Wight Art Gallery, University of California, 1991.

———. "Phantoms in Urban Exile." In *I Am Aztlan: The Personal Essay in Chicano Studies*, edited by Chon A. Noriega and Wendy Belcher. Los Angeles: UCLA Chicano Studies Research Center Press, 2004.

———. *Urban Exile: Collected Writings of Harry Gamboa Jr*. Edited by Chon A. Noriega. Minneapolis: University of Minnesota Press, 1998.

Goldberg, David Theo. "Racism without Racism." *PMLA* 123, no. 5 (October 2008): 1712–16.

Goldman, Shifra. "Brown in Black and White." *Artweek* (June 1982).

Goldstein, Laurence. *Poetry Los Angeles: Reading the Essential Poems of the City*. Ann Arbor: University of Michigan Press, 2014.

Gómez-Quiñones, Juan. *Las ideas políticas de Ricardo Flores Magón*. Translated by Roberto Gómez Ciriza. Mexico City: Era, 1977.

Gonzales, Juan. "Forgotten Pages: Spanish-Language Newspapers in the Southwest." *Journalism History* 4, no. 2 (Summer 1977): 50–52.

González, Ray, ed. *Muy macho: Latino Men Confront Their Manhood*.New York: Anchor Books, 1996.

Grande, Reyna. *The Distance between Us: A Memoir*. New York: Atria Books, 2012.

Gray, Paul Bryan. *A Clamor for Equality: Emergence and Exile of Californio Activist Francisco P. Ramírez*. Lubbock: Texas Tech University Press, 2012.

Green, Jonathon, and Nicholas J. Karolides. *Encyclopedia of Censorship*. Rev. ed. New York: Facts on File, 2005.

Griswold del Castillo, Richard. "The Mexican Revolution and the Spanish-Language Press in the Borderlands." *Journalism History* 4, no. 2 (Summer 1977): 42–47.

Guillermoprieto, Alma. *Looking for History: Dispatches from Latin America*. New York: Pantheon, 2001.

Hamilton, Denise. *Los Angeles Noir 2: The Classics*. New York: Akashic Books, 2010.

Hanna, Phil Townsend. *Libros californianos*. Los Angeles: J. Zeitlin, Primavera Press, 1931.

Harkinson, Josh. "California Mobilizes for War against Trump: From Immigration and Climate Change to Pot and Guns, the President-Elect Faces a Big Blue Firewall." *Mother Jones*, January 13, 2017. http://www.motherjones.com/politics/2017/01 /california-trump-immigration-climate-healthcare-marijuana-guns-tech.

Harnisch, Larry. "Getting Up to Date on a 19th Century L.A. Activist." *Los Angeles Times*, January 8, 2013; web, January 14, 2013.

Hayden, Dolores. *The Power of Place: Urban Landscapes as Public History*. Cambridge MA: MIT Press, 1997.

Hernandez, Ellie D. *Postnationalism in Chicana/o Literature and Culture*. Austin: University of Texas Press, 2009.

Hollander, Kurt. "Report from Los Angeles: Community Access." *Art in America* (June 1992): 57–61.

James, David. E. *The Sons and Daughters of Los: Culture and Community in L.A*. Philadelphia: Temple University Press, 2003.

Kanellos, Nicolás. "An Early Feminist Call to Action: 'Manifesto a la Mujer,' by Blanca Moncaleano." *Latino Studies* 11, no. 4 (December 2013): 587–97.

———. *Hispanic Immigrant Literature: El sueño del retorno*. Austin: University of Texas Press, 2011.

———. *Hispanic Periodicals in the United States: A Brief History and Comprehensive Bibliography*. Houston: Arte Público Press, 2000.

———. "A Socio-Historic Study of Hispanic Newspapers in the United States." In *Recovering the U.S. Hispanic Literary Heritage*, edited by Ramón Gutiérrez and Genaro Padilla, 2:107–28. Houston: Arte Público Press, 1993.

Leal, Luis. "Octavio Paz and the Chicano." *Latin American Literary Review* 5, no. 10 (Spring 1977): 115–23.

Lockhart, James. *The Nahuas after the Conquest: A Social and Cultural History of the Indians of Central Mexico, Sixteenth through Eighteenth Centuries*. Stanford: Stanford University Press, 1992.

Lounsberry, Barbara. *The Art of Fact: Contemporary Artists of Nonfiction*. Westport CT: Greenwood Press, 1990.

Lummis, Suzanne. *Wide Awake: Poets of Los Angeles and Beyond*. Venice CA: Beyond Baroque Books / Pacific Coast Poetry Series, 2015.

Mahieux, Viviane. "The Chronicle." In *Oxford Bibliographies in Latin American Studies*, edited by Ben Vinson. New York: Oxford University Press, 2012.

———. *Urban Chroniclers in Modern Latin America: The Shared Intimacy of Everyday Life*. Austin: University of Texas Press, 2011.

Marcos, Sylvia. "Embodied Religious Thought: Gender Categories in Mesoamerica." *Religion* 28 (1998): 371–82.

Martí, José. *En los Estados Unidos: Periodismo de 1881–1892*. Madrid: Allca XX, 2003.

Marx, John. "Literature and Governmentality." *Literature Compass* 8, no. 1 (2011): 66–79.

McPhee, John. *The Control of Nature*. New York: Farrar, Straus and Giroux, 1989.

McWilliams, Carey. *North from Mexico: The Spanish-Speaking People of the United States*. Philadelphia: Lippincott, 1949.

Mena, Jesús, J. L. Navarro, Victor Manuel Valle, and Helena María Viramontes, eds. *201 / Two Hundred and One: Homenaje a la ciudad de Los Ángeles / Latino Experience in Literature and Art*. Los Angeles: Los Angeles Latino Writers Association, 1982.

———. "Testimonio de Bert Corona: Struggle Is the Ultimate Teacher." *201 / Two Hundred and One: Homenaje a la ciudad de Los Ángeles / Latino Experience in Literature and Art*, 27–36. Los Angeles: Los Angeles Latino Writers Association, 1982.

Mignolo, Walter D. "Afterword: Writing and Recorded Knowledge in Colonial and Postcolonial Situations." In *Writing without Words: Alternative Literacies in Mesoamerica and the Andes*, edited by Elizabeth Hill Boone and Walter D. Mignolo, 291–313. Durham NC: Duke University Press, 1994.

———. *The Darker Side of the Renaissance: Literacy, Territoriality, and Colonization*. Ann Arbor: University of Michigan Press. 1995.

———. "Epistemic Disobedience, Independent Thought, and Decolonial Freedom." *Theory, Culture & Society* 26, nos. 7–8 (2009): 159–81.

———. "The Role of the Humanities in the Corporate University." PMLA 115, no. 5 (October 2000): 1238–45.

Miller, Toby. "How the Media Biopoliticized Neoliberalism; or, Foucault Meets Marx." *Revista Galáxia* 20 (2010): 22–31.

Mohr, Bill. *Hold-Outs: The Los Angeles Poetry Renaissance, 1948–1992*. Iowa City: University of Iowa Press, 2011.

———. *"Poetry Loves Poetry": An Anthology of Los Angeles Poets*. Santa Monica CA: Momentum Press, 1985.

Moraga, Cherríe. *Loving in the War Years: Lo que nunca pasó por sus labios*. Boston: South End Press, 1983.

Morales, Armando. *Ando Sangrando (I Am Bleeding): A Study of Mexican American–Police Conflict*. La Puente CA: Perspectiva Publications, 1972.

Morton, Timothy. *Ecology without Nature: Rethinking Environmental Aesthetics*. Cambridge: Harvard University Press, 2007.

Murphet, Julian. *Literature and Race in Los Angeles*. Cambridge: Cambridge University Press, 2001.

Nazario, Sonia. *Enrique's Journey*. New York: Random House, 2006.

———. *Enrique's Journey: The True Story of a Boy Determined to Reunite with His Mother*. New York: Delacorte Press, 2013.

Nin, Anaïs. *The Journals of Anaïs Nin, 1947–1955*. Edited by Gunther Stuhlmann. New York: Quartet Books, 1974.

———. *The Journals of Anaïs Nin, 1955–1966*. Edited by Gunther Stuhlmann. New York: Quartet Books, 1966.

———. *The Journals of Anaïs Nin, 1966–1974*. Edited by Gunther Stuhlmann. New York: Quartet Books, 1980.

Olivas, Daniel, ed. *Latinos in Lotusland: An Anthology of Contemporary Southern California Literature*. Tempe AZ: Bilingual Press / Editorial Bilingüe, 2008.

Padron, María de Los Angeles. "Cafe en blanco y negro, por Gamboa." *La Opinión*, May 20, 1982.

Paredes, Raymund A. "Early Mexican-American Literature." *Western American Literature* 20, no. 2 (1987): 1079–1118.

———. "Los Angeles from the Barrio: Oscar Zeta Acosta's *The Revolt of the Cockroach People*." In *Los Angeles in Fiction: A Collection of Essays*, edited by David Fine. Albuquerque: University of New Mexico Press, 1995.

———. "Special Feature: The Evolution of Chicano Literature." *MELUS* 5, no. 2, Interfaces (Summer 1978): 71–110.

Paz, Octavio, and Antonio Saborit. *Crónica trunca de días excepcionales*. Mexico City: Universidad Nacional Autónoma de México, 2007.

———. *The Labyrinth of Solitude*. Translated by Lysander Kemp. New York: Grove Press, 1985.

Pelzer, Jaquelin. "The Cambridge Companion to the Literature of Los Angeles." Review. *Western American Literature* 46, no. 3 (Fall 2011): 331–33.

Pérez, Emma. *The Decolonial Imaginary: Writing Chicanas into History*. Bloomington: University of Indiana Press, 1999.

Pew Hispanic Center. "U.S.-Born Hispanics Increasingly Drive Population Developments." Fact sheet, January 1, 2002. www.pewhispanic.org/2002/01/01/u-s-born -hispanics-increasingly-drive-population-developments/.

Phoenix Art Museum. *Contemporary Identities*. Phoenix: Phoenix Art Museum, 1992.

Pulido, Laura. *Black, Brown, Yellow, and Left: Radical Activism in Los Angeles*. Los Angeles: University of California Press, 2006.

Rachmuhl, Sophie. *A Higher Form of Politics: The Rise of a Poetry Scene, Los Angeles, 1950–1990*. Los Angeles: Otis Books / Seismicity Editions, 2015.

Ramírez, Francisco P. "Folleto notable." *USC Digital Archive*. March 3, 2007.

Rechy, John. *About My Life and the Kept Woman: A Memoir*. New York: Grove Press, 2008.

Río, Ignacio del. *Crónicas jesuíticas de la antigua California*. Mexico City: Universidad Nacional Autónoma de México, Coordinación de Humanidades, Programa Editorial, 2000.

Rodríguez, Luis J. *Poems across the Pavement*. Chicago: Tía Chucha Press, 1989.

Rodriguez, Richard T. Review of *Urban Exile: Collected Writings of Harry Gamboa, Jr.*, edited by Chon A. Noriega. *Theatre Journal* 52, no. 1 (March 2000): 140–41.

Rodríguez, Richard. *Hunger of Memory: The Education of Richard Rodríguez—An Autobiography*. New York: Bantam Books, 2004.

Rolfe, Lionel. *Literary LA*. Los Angeles: California Classic Books, 2002. First published 1981 by Chronicle Books.

Ruíz, Reynaldo. *Hispanic Poetry in Los Angeles, 1850–1900: La poesía Angelina*. Lewiston ME: Edwin Mellen, 2000.

Saldívar, José David. *The Dialectics of Our America: Genealogy, Cultural Critique, and Literary History*. Durham NC: Duke University Press, 1991.

Sánchez, Rosaura. *Telling Identities: The Californio Testimonios*. Minneapolis: University of Minnesota Press, 1995.

Santiago, Esmeralda. *When I Was Puerto Rican*. New York: Vintage Books, 1994.

Sarfatti Larson, Magali. "Professions as Disciplinary Cultures." *The Blackwell Companion to the Sociology of Culture*. New York: Blackwell, 2005.

Sassen, Saskia. "The City: Its Return as a Lens for Social Theory." *City, Culture and Society* 1 (2010): 3–11.

Smith, Sidonie, and Julia Watson. *Reading Autobiography: A Guide for Interpreting Life Narratives*. Minneapolis: University of Minnesota Press, 2010.

Sotomayor, Frank O. "The Pulitzer Long Shot: How Our 1983 Latino Stories for L.A. Times Won Journalism's Top Prize." *JourViz* (2017). jourviz.com/long-shot/index .html.

Steinberg, David. "Images Capture Human Drama." *Albuquerque Journal*, February 28, 1992.

Steinberg, Michael, and Robert Root. "Interview with Michael Steinberg." *Fourth Genre: Explorations in Nonfiction* 12, no. 2 (Fall 2010): 147–59.

Stepler, Renee, and Mark Hugo Lopez. "Ranking the Latino Population in Metropolitan Areas." Sec. 5 of "U.S. Latino Population Growth and Dispersion Has Slowed since Onset of the Great Recession." Report, Pew Research Center, Hispanic Trends, September 8, 2016. www.pewhispanic.org/2016/09/08/5-ranking-the-latino -population-in-metropolitan-areas/.

Tablada, José J., and Palacios E. Hernández. *La babilonia de hierro, crónicas neoyorkinas*. Xalapa, Mexico: Universidad Veracruzana, 2000.

Thomas, Piri. *Down These Mean Streets*. New York, Knopf, 1967.

Timberg, Scott, and Dana Gioia, eds. *The Misread City: New Literary Los Angeles*. Los Angeles: Red Hen Press, 2003.

Townsend, Phil Hanna. *Libros californianos: or Five Feet of California Books*. Los Angeles: J. Zeitlin, Primavera Press, 1931.

Ulin, David L. *Another City: Writing from Los Angeles*. San Francisco: City Lights, 2001.

———. *Writing Los Angeles: A Literary Anthology*. New York: Library of America, 2002.

Ulloa, Jazmine. "California Lawmakers Prepare to Take a Stand on Immigration against the Federal Government." *Los Angeles Times*, December 5, 2016. http://www.latimes .com/politics/essential/la-pol-ca-essential-politics-updates-california-lawmakers -prepare-to-take-a-1480982506-htmlstory.html.

———. "Nearly $50 Million in the California State Budget Will Go to Expanded Legal Services for Immigrants." *Los Angeles Times*, June 15, 2017. www.latimes.com /politics/essential/la-pol-ca-essential-politics-updates-nearly-50-million-in-the -california-1497576640-htmlstory.html.

Urrea, Luis Alberto. *The Devil's Highway: A True Story*. New York: Little, Brown, 2004.

Valle, Rosamel del. *Crónicas de New York*. Providencia, Chile: RiL Editores, 2002.

Valle, Victor, and Rodolfo Torres. *Latino Metropolis*. Minneapolis: University of Minnesota Press, 2000.

Vangelisti, Paul, with Evan Calbi. *L.A. Exile: A Guide to Los Angeles Writing, 1932–1998*. New York: Marsilio Publishers, 1999.

Villa, Raúl Homero. *Barrio-Logos: Space and Place in Urban Chicano Culture*. Austin: University of Texas Press, 2000.

Walker, Franklin D. *A Literary History of Southern California*. Berkeley: University of California Press, 1950.

Webb, Charles Harper. *Stand Up Poetry: An Expanded Anthology*. Iowa City: University of Iowa Press, 2002.

www.ingramcontent.com/pod-product-compliance
Lightning Source LLC
Chambersburg PA
CBHW031953060726
47497CB00016B/2007